UNFORGETTABLE BRI
(1988/89 EDITION)

OTHER BOOKS BY ANGELA LANSBURY
Enquire Within Upon Travel and Holidays (Barrie & Jenkins)
See Britain at Work (Exley Publications), UK: Two Continents, New York
The A to Z of Shopping by Post (Exley Publications)
Etiquette for every Occasion (Batsford)

Unforgettable British Weekends

A guide to unusual and celebration holidays

1988/89 EDITION

Angela Lansbury

Settle Press (UK)
Hippocrene Books (USA)

While every reasonable care has been taken by the author and publisher in presenting the information in this book, no responsibility can be taken by them for any inaccuracies.

© Angela Lansbury 1988

All rights reserved. No part of this publication may be reproduced or transmitted in any form or by any means without written permission.

First published by Settle Press, 32 Savile Row, London W1X 1AG

ISBN (Hardback) 0907070 361
ISBN (paperback) 0907070 37X

Published in U.S.A. by Hippocrene Books Inc.
171 Madison Avenue, New York

ISBN 0-87052-438-0

Printed by Villiers Publications Ltd
26a Shepherds Hill, London N6 5AH

Dedication
To my nine-year old son Anthony, keen hotel inspector

Acknowledgements
My thanks to the English Tourist Board, Wales Centre, Scottish Tourist Board, London Tourist, and all Britain's local tourist boards, particularly Tyne & Wear, and the press offices of hotel groups such as Quality International, THF, Embassy Hotels, Crest and others.

Photograph of the author by Trevor Sharot.

CONTENTS

PART I

THE ROMANTIC, THE EXOTIC, THE INDULGENT

1. Nostalgia and Second Honeymoons — 13
2. Romance — 20
3. Best Beds and Baths — 27
4. Privilege and Luxury — 37
5. Gourmet Treats — 46

PART II

BIZARRE AND UNUSUAL BREAKS

6. The Plot Thickens: Murder Weekends and Dracula House-parties — 53
7. Odder Places for Eating and Sleeping — 61
8. Haunted Hotels — 68
9. Medieval Costume Banquets — 74

PART III

THE TASTE OF TRADITION

10. Olde-Worlde Hotels — 81
11. A Classic English Weekend around Arundel — 92
12. Imprints of Royalty — 97

PART IV

BREAKS FOR SPECIAL INTERESTS AND ACTIVITIES

13. Sports and Activities — 103
14. Water Appeal: Spa Baths and beautiful pools — 118
15. Theme Parks and Special Interests — 128

PART V
WEEKENDS AROUND THE REGIONS
16.	Scotland	138
17.	Wales	147
18.	North East to Catherine Cookson country	157
19.	England's Lake District	161
20.	Stratford 'Shakespearience' and Oxford and Cambridge	167
21.	The Prince Regent's Brighton – Britain's first seaside resort	174
22.	The Far South West – Cornwall	180
23.	Offshore Fairy Isles	188

PART VI
BARGAINS AND BUDGET BREAKS AND OTHER TIPS
24.	City Breaks	203
25.	Bed and Breakfast, Caravanning, Farms, Friaries	213
26.	How to Read a Hotel Brochure and Test the Service	222
27.	Useful Information	228
	(i) Booklist	228
	(ii) Some Highlights of the British Calendar	230
	(iii) Addresses: Hotel Groups and Tour Operators, and Tourist Boards	235

INTRODUCTION

The British invented the weekend. In 'Unforgettable British Weekends' you will find the ingredients of enjoyable and memorable weekend outings and holidays – the oldest, best or most bizarre of their kind, pretty locations, peculiar buildings, theme weekends, unusual events, stories associated with the famous and infamous, deliciously different food, and hotels offering the best beds and most exotic bathrooms.

The breaks proffered in these pages range from the luxurious to the down-to-earth, with a sprinkling of the amusingly offbeat. Here are unashamed extravagances and unashamed bargains. You will find the intriguingly obscure and the gloriously renowned. There are drolleries and eccentricities, and the sound assurances of traditional England.

Note: Hotel and holiday details
If you are booking for hotels or other accommodation, you should of course check in advance direct with the hotel etc. to confirm prices and where necessary services. The prices given in this book should be read as approximate, as hotel charges and holiday packages are subject to change from one season to another.

Opening times of places such as stately homes and gardens are also subject to alteration.

The information in this book is presented in a way which should make it easy for a reader to know what particular hotel or holiday he or she wants to follow up and also how to follow it up. Addresses and telephone numbers of hotels and tourist services and places to visit are usually given along with the description of them, that is, where the item on the hotel etc. occurs in the main text of the book.

Many hotels belong to larger hotel groups. In these cases, the central marketing office of the group is able to deal with enquiries and reservations and brochures regarding all hotels in the group. The addresses of these hotel groups are given at the end of the book under the chapter 'Useful Information'.

Also included in these addresses are holiday and travel companies which operate the special breaks mentioned in the book.

Tourist Boards
More information about any aspect of holidays in Britain can be obtained from the Tourist Boards. There are five national Tourist Boards for the British Isles, for England, Wales, Scotland, Northern Ireland, and the Irish Republic (Eire). There are also regional and local tourist boards for every part of the country.

The British Tourist Authority (BTA) performs this same service overseas for all the United Kingdom. It is the official overall body for British tourism.

Tourist Boards will provide information on accommodation, events, attractions, towns and countryside, places, museums, entertainments, facilities, etc.

The British Travel Centre in Regent Street in London combines BTA with other tourist services such as British Rail, Room Centre, and American Express, to provide a comprehensive booking service as well as an information service.

Addresses of all the national Tourist Boards are given at the end of this book under 'Useful Information'. For the convenience of readers, addresses of the London centres of the Tourist Boards of mainland Britain are repeated here (overleaf). All are open to callers in person except the English Tourist Board office.

Tourist Boards – addresses of London offices:
British Travel Centre, 12 Regent Street, Piccadilly Circus, London SW1Y 4PQ. Tel: 01-730 3400.
English Tourist Board, Thames Tower, Black's Road, Hammersmith, London W6 9El. Tel: 01-846 9000. (Written and telephone enquiries only.)
Wales Centre (Wales Tourist Board), 34 Piccadilly, London W1. Tel: 01-409 0969.
Scottish Tourist Board, 19 Cockspur Street, (by Trafalgar Square), London SW1Y 5BL. Tel: 01-930 8661.
Also for the London region, there is:
London Tourist Board Information Centre, Victoria Station Forecourt, London SW1. Tel: 01-730 3488.

PART I

The Romantic, the Exotic, the Indulgent

CHAPTER 1
Nostalgia and Second Honeymoons

For nostalgia – and for that second honeymoon of a lifetime – Burgh Island Hotel is the prize place, with its Thirties and Art Deco and Agatha Christie associations. Or you can return to the height of English eminence and stability in the Edwardian era by going to Chilston Park Hotel, where you will be in surroundings of a splendid country house full of antiques, with maids in long skirts and footmen in the genuine attire of that time.

NOSTALGIA AND ART DECO: Burgh Island
This 'great escape' is to Agatha Christie's Burgh Island (south Devon, near Plymouth).

Who could turn down the chance to visit the island hotel where Agatha Christie wrote her book *Evil Under the Sun*, stay in an art deco hideaway, and meet Bea Porter, one of the three sisters who were involved in the famous Biba clothes store near Harrods in London? But how do you get to an offshore island fifteen miles south east of Plymouth?

'Come down by car and lunch in our fourteenth century Pilchard Inn,' suggested Bea's husband Tony Porter, when I telephoned. 'Turner stayed in it and painted the island, so his biography says. Park on the mainland, phone us from the red public call box, and we'll send our Sea Tractor to fetch you.

'It's worth the trip. Noel Coward arrived for three days but spent three weeks. Kirk Douglas came here. So did the Beatles. And The Dave Clark Five made a film here. The Prince of Wales, who later became King Edward VIII, visited the hotel, we presume with Mrs Simpson, though the discreet official records only say that he was with Lord Mountbatten.'

Driving slowly over the brow of a hill we saw Burgh Island across the golden sands – a green mound with a white hotel halfway up and frothing blue sea beyond trying to circle it from both sides. This was the view which persuaded Bea and Tony, the owners, to sell everything, their house, Jaguar, and yacht, to raise the half a million pounds needed to buy the island and turn the old building back into a hotel as it had been in the 1930s, which they re-opened in 1986. It had once housed a casino and been referred to as 'Monte Carlo'.

At lunchtime we parked and phoned for transport which arrived after some delay.

'Sorry, our vehicle got stuck in the sand, so I've come to collect you with the jeep,' said Tony Porter.

We jolted across the sands, mounted a concrete ramp, and the jeep lurched uphill past the Pilchard Inn, around a sharp corner and through trees to the hotel. Inside the entrance, on the left was a doorway open to reveal a small writing desk.

'We're not a hotel,' said Tony, 'there's no reception desk, no phone in the bedrooms. We're a sanctuary. In winter we just open for long weekends, Thursday to Tuesday, which we call the Great Escape.'

We were shown up in the art deco lift to our apartment or suite, where we had a bedroom and lounge – kitchen fully equipped with a cover on the sink – ideal for preparing your own food for vegetarian, kosher, or other diets. My eyes yo-yoed between the fan shaped art deco armchair, and sea views in three directions.

The house was built in 1929 by Archibald Nettlefold, the millionaire who was a founder of GKN. He was the 'N', and also owned the Comedy Theatre which staged Agatha Christie's plays in London. This accounts for her presence here, where she wrote at least two books. Agatha had sat writing in an octagonal gazebo of which the base remains.

She described this hotel as the Jolly Roger Hotel on

Smuggler's Island, and her book *Evil Under the Sun* (now a Fontana paperback) starts with a map of the island. Characters include Poirot the detective enjoying a relaxing holiday until he has to investigate the murder of Arlena. Her demise leaves Stuart a widower, throwing suspicion on Rosamund Darnley who is in love with Stuart. Or should we suspect Miss Brewster?

Episodes of an Agatha Christie Miss Marples TV series were filmed on Burgh Island in September 1986. The first Murder Weekend to be planned for the island has been held.

In real life a tunnel is supposed to lead from the back of the island to the pub, and the story goes that there's still treasure in it. Unfortunately the treasure island's tunnel is now blocked, forming a natural locked 'safe'. So we walked back down the path to the haunted inn, where history records that unlucky smuggler Tom Crocker was shot outside the door by a customs officer.

To remove the remaining chill, a log fire burns in the grate upstairs in the inn. Food is served below, with bench tables outdoors. We drank local cider, eating a traditional Devon 'ploughman's lunch', a large bread roll with English cheddar cheese and pickles. Bearded Jimbo, the tractor operator, pulls pints of real ale in the pub when he's not driving. The pub enjoys a thriving business serving day trippers who walk across the sands at low tide for a pub lunch or drink. They sit surveying their children digging sandcastles and climbing over slippery seaweedy rocks.

The tide reveals the sands for six hours, then rises between three and seven feet high, twice a day, with alarming, dangerous, undercurrents. The time of Plymouth's high tide is listed in *The Times* and also in local newspapers, or any ship, lifeguard, customs officer, radio or TV station will know. A notice warns that the lifeboat was called out several times last year.

We returned to the deserted hotel nonchalantly passing the sign saying that the hotel was open to us residents only. Wandering into the circular Palm Court lounge and bar at the centre of the building we found time had stood still, transporting us back into the 1930s. A ghost reputedly haunts the house, pushing you from behind.

Agatha Christie's sun shone, but there was no evidence of the evil. The glass ceiling and glass doors created a heavenly light airy feeling. Water tinkled in the goldfish pond inside the semicircular staircase to the upper level. Mirror top tables, and octagonal mirror glass mats, reflected palms and drinks, a feast for the eyes. The bar menu offered drinks mostly named after Agatha Christie's characters and books, including Burgh Island Sling, Poirot's Poison, Death in the Afternoon, and Arlena's Revenge.

In the afternoon we could order a traditional English cream tea with scones and jam. The cream is delicious Jersey cream from local cows. You get unlimited amounts, because Tony was one of five children and remembers the constant injunction not to take too much cream. Coffee also arrives in unlimited supply – one price for a cafetière holding six cups, which is more than you can drink.

On the bar I saw a bottle cover shaped like a man wearing a bow tie. When I lifted it a music box played. If anyone haunts this place it must be Noel Coward sitting in a silk dressing gown.

The back of the hotel incorporates the Captain's cabin and part of an old ship, the Ganges, built in Bombay, rescued from Plymouth. Tony Porter – for all his easygoing air – is a canny marketing man, and arranged a reunion of 16,000 sailors who had trained or served on the Ganges.

Steep steps lead down the red cliffs to the peaceful green waters of the mermaid pool in the tiny cove. It is hard to imagine that this was where Roy and his Mayfair Four used to play lively music in the open air on a platform back in 1929, floodlit at night, in the hotel of the fashionable fast set, as you can see from a picture in the Palm Court.

A brisk uphill walk leads through thorn briers to the cove where Arlena's body was found in *Evil Under The Sun*. From the clifftop it is impossible to get down to Elfin Cove, which Agatha Christie called Pixie Cove in her book. However, when the sea is calm you can go around the island on a surf ski, which is flat like a surf board. You sit on it in your swimming costume.

On the clifftop, continuing clockwise, you pass other coves, and a hilltop ruined chapel supposedly haunted by a monk, until you return to overlook the hotel. In the distance across the sands are the gleaming cliffs of England's southern coast, recalling the wartime song, 'blue skies over the white cliffs of Dover'.

Late afternoon as the tide came in we took the noisy bone-shaking tractor to the mainland just for the ride. On a long weekend you could visit Plymouth. But for the first twenty four hours we did not want to go anywhere else.

Leaving this haven of peace we drove back to London. Burgh Island's signpost points back to 'England', for good reason. Burgh Island is 28 acres devoted to the past. And as L. P. Hartley wrote in *The Go-between*, the past is a foreign country.

Two day break prices vary according to numbers sharing accommodation, from about £25 to £40 per person per night including dinner and continental breakfast. If the hotel is full other good hotels and restaurants (including a Routiers) are nearby, or you could visit the Pilchard pub for lunch as a side trip from Plymouth.

Details from: *Burgh Island, Bigbury-on-Sea, South Devon, TQ7 4AU, tel: Bigbury (0548) 810514.*

EDWARDIAN EXPERIENCE WEEKEND: **Chilston Park**

To experience an Edwardian weekend go to Chilston Park Country House, near Maidstone south of London. It is a country house hotel in a huge park with a disconcertingly long driveway leaving you wondering whether you will end up in a field of cows. Get full directions, and their brochure map.

The novel idea of maids in Edwardian costume unpacking my suitcase lured me down. But when I saw the house full of priceless antiques I decided against revealing my non-millionheiress clothes.

The mansion is a grade 1 listed building owned by the Millers who publish Miller's Antiques Guide. Seven foot high flower arrangements stand in the entrance hall. Beyond the columns is the wood panelled stairwell, with carved faces of the kings of England over the fireplace. You can sit in the sedan chair in the hall to make a phone call.

A wooden staircase leads up to the gallery and bedrooms. Intriguing antiques are on dressers and shelves in every room. Apart from the oriental bedroom and the one with the amazing ceiling there was the rug with an animal head which a guest asked to be removed. Two suites are attic rooms. The most stunning bedroom has an antique carved headboard and an A-shaped beamed ceiling. Antique plates hang on the crossbeams. The bigger four-poster is in the Regency room. I stayed in the four-poster Hogarth bedroom and enjoyed sitting in bed surveying my view of a room full of antiques framed by an arched curtain. The bedroom fire can be lit if you request it.

There are 250 candles on the ground floor and at night the dining room seems to be lit by dozens of candles reflected in the mirrors. But you don't have to be formal. They like life to be fun. The library where private parties dine has a clutter of books, old medicine bottles and a coachman's jacket hanging on the door.

The converted Stable Restaurant opens several nights a week from April to New Year's Eve. Meals average £25 for two including wine. After we enquired whether there were any kosher wines they started stocking some. In the old stable block you can have wild eccentric parties served by young ladies in jodhpurs. The tables are in the old horse boxes and if the girls can't reach the end of the table they walk down the centre!

Chilston Park's drawing room where residents can have afternoon tea, pre-dinner drinks, and after-dinner coffee, has white pillars, a horsehair alabaster ceiling, books, fans, and enough curios to keep you busy for hours.

Beyond are the music room and snooker room, with antique and modern games. 'How to Host A Murder' is played on demand. It is like 'Cluedo', but you act the parts and go to the library and other rooms. The layout of Chilston is quadrangular, like the board game. And there are Murder Weekends. They also offer sporting activities including clay pigeon shooting, hot air ballooning and riding.

Young Russell Clamp, deputy Steward and butler, encourages an offbeat atmosphere. He wears a black tail coat which he opens to reveal a collection of badges inside. A customer pinned a badge on him, others added more, and now people send him badges from all over the world. He can't offend anyone so he wears them all. His father was former owner of Borthwick Hall hotel in Scotland.

The last thing I did was photograph the staff on the doorstep in their authentic uniforms of striped gilt waistcoats, and coats

Nostalgia and Second Honeymoons 19

with gold braid, worn over shirts whose detachable wing collars and cuffs are attached by studs. Even the buttons on the footmen's shoes were arranged by consultants on period costume.

Double bedrooms are around £80–£140 per night. Two night champagne break or any two nights is £110 per person including several meals. Better Life Holidays, specialising in vegetarian holidays (see gourmet chapter 5) offers to arrange for Americans to be picked up at Heathrow in a Rolls Royce and transferred to Chilston.

Chilston Park Country House, Sandway, Maidstone, Kent, ME17 2BE, tel: 0622 859803.

OTHER HOTELS

The Prestige consortium of independent hotels features several luxury hotels with a history.

The colour brochure of the luxury Prestige hotels shows you pictures of all their hotels. In addition to the Ritz in London, and several country mansions, they have a hotel on a Scottish island, and two hotels in English Castles. Creeper-covered Castle Hotel at Taunton has four-posters. So does the Thornbury Castle near Bristol. L'Horizon at St Brelade's Bay, Jersey, had fresh flowers in the telephone boxes when I visited it. I have described Pennyhill Park in Chapter 5 (gourmet food). The Royal Crescent, Bath, has suites with spa baths fed by spring water.

Viscount Astor's former home, Cliveden at Taplow now owned by the National Trust and run by Blakeney, is in the Prestige Hotels brochure. If you are prone to shock, sit down before you ask the price.

Prestige Hotel, 412–422 Strand, London WC2R 0PT, tel: 01-439 2365. In North America tel: New York (212) 535 9530 or nationwide toll free (800) 223 5581.

More hotels can be booked by using the Keith Prowse agency brochure featuring Posh and Pampered weekends. Derek Johansen's large format hotel guidebook has colour photographs of hotels, with brief descriptions.

CHAPTER 2
Romance

To celebrate Valentine's day, or entertain that special person, why not spend a romantic weekend away? Choose hotels and restaurants with exotic oriental or Caribbean settings, beautiful views of lakes or estuaries, clifftop hotels overlooking surging seas, the peaceful surroundings of waterfalls, countryside castellated mansions, or hotels associated with famous and notorious lovers.

ROMANTIC WEEKENDS IN LONDON
Cadogan Hotel (London)
Weekend packages with champagne breakfasts are offered by numerous hotels including the Cadogan, former London home of actress Lillie Langtry, where she entertained her lover, the future King Edward VII. Lillie's portrait can be seen in the cocktail bar. Oscar Wilde used to visit Lillie's home, in fact he was arrested in what is now one of the bedrooms at the Cadogan Hotel. Like Oscar Wilde, waiters sport fresh carnations in their jacket buttonholes.
Cadogan Thistle Hotel, 75 Sloane Street, London SW1X 9SG, tel: 01-235 7141.

Mountbatten Hotel (Central London)
Near Tottenham Court Road Station, Covent Garden and Charing Cross Road's bookshops is the oriental restaurant of the Mountbatten Hotel. The red and white temple roof is the exotic setting for the restaurant at the Mountbatten Hotel, which takes as its theme Earl Mountbatten of Burma. The restaurant menu includes à la carte cuisine minceur, tiny portions of interestingly shaped food on huge plates, and an Indian set lunch.

The Mountbatten's tea lounge serves elevenses – 'tiffin'. It's a haven at afternoon tea time, too. After enjoying the razzamatazz of nearby Covent Garden with its street entertainers, relax, taking tea in the Mountbatten lounge, next to the harp. While a weekend here with meals would run up a large bill, if you are short of time and want to impress a good friend a pot of coffee in truly elegant surroundings will cost less than £5.

If you're passing on your way to one of the nearby theatres, pop in to see the display of souvenirs from Mountbatten's life in the hall, have a cocktail in the bar and look at the cartoons and newscuttings about the late Earl's early days.

Residents stay in bedrooms decorated with exotic oriental paintings depicting dusky ladies in colourful sarees entertaining their lovers under palm trees watched by large-eyed animals. The en suite bathrooms are marble.

The Mountbatten Hotel organises special weekends for out-of-towners. You can combine a weekend here with a luxury train trip sipping bubbly on the Bournemouth Belle. It travels down to Mountbatten's stately home, Broadlands, where the Princess of Wales spent the first night of her honeymoon.

Mountbatten Hotel, Seven Dials, Covent Garden, London, WC2H 9HD, tel: 01-836 4300.

OUTSIDE LONDON

Sheraton Skyline Hotel (Heathrow Airport, west of London)

Leave central London, if you prefer to, for the tropical surroundings of the Caribbean style swimming pool at Heathrow's Sheraton Skyline Hotel. Steel bands play in a tropical garden of trees and potted plants. You can sit sipping a Caribbean cocktail in the evenings illuminated by the romantic glow of flickering lamps around the indoor pool. Or enjoy a themed Sunday lunch. Some bedrooms overlook the exotic swimming pool which also has underwater bar seats.

Sheraton Skyline Hotel, Bath Road, Hayes, Middlesex, UB3 5BP, tel: 01-759 2535.

Chewton Glen Hotel (The New Forest, Hampshire)

If you're flying into London's Heathrow airport a chauffeur-driven Jaguar can meet you to take you down to Chewton Glen

Hotel, or you could land your helicopter on the lawn. Chewton Glen is on the south coast between Bournemouth and the Isle of Wight, and bedroom suites are named after characters in books by Captain Marryat, who wrote *The Children of the New Forest* when he stayed here in 1846. Broadlands, the Beaulieu Motor Museum, and Stonehenge, are all within reach.

Furnishings are of exceptional quality. The three lounges are in fashionable pastel colours, and there is an outdoor pool. Canopy beds are in two bedrooms, and one has a four-poster. Most bathrooms have two basins with gold taps, some have double sunken baths, others jacuzzis in single baths.
Chewton Glen Hotel, New Milton, Hampshire BH25 6QS, tel: 04252 5341.

Copthorne Hotel (Gatwick Airport)
A courtesy bus goes from Gatwick airport to beamed Copthorne Hotel. In front of the hotel is a small lake with swans. I was told that the swans cannot fly off the lake because they have one wing clipped. After a drink in the bar, I speculated upon whether they go round in circles and come back like boomerangs, poor things!

In the hotel entrance hall stands a large-faced antique clock. The description next to it explains that an ancient tax on timepieces discouraged people from owning clocks. This led to public houses having public clocks with large dials so that everyone could see the time. Many other features of the old beamed building remain, such as a raised area which was originally a barn built on stilts to keep rats and insects out of the grain. The old building has been extended so that the pretty restaurants are in different styles, a mixture of olde worlde and modern ones including one featuring a stained glass ceiling and modern bamboo furniture.
The Copthorne London Gatwick Hotel, Crawley, Sussex, tel: 0342 714971.

Pennyhill Park (Bagshot, near Windsor)
Pennyhill Park west of London near Windsor has a wedding party package which includes sending the bridal couple off by helicopter to a sister hotel nearer Gatwick. When I celebrated an anniversary at sumptuous Pennyhill Park, as we arrived staff were sweeping the car park!

Pennyhill Park Hotel, College Ride, Bagshot, Surrey GU19 5ET, tel: (0276) 71774.

AROUND THE REGIONS

Last Drop Village (Bolton, near Manchester)

A large, lively centre is the Last Drop Village at Bolton. The complex was built using derelict farm buildings, as you can see from 'before and after' photographs in the bar. A sedan chair containing a telephone separates the bar from the dining room in the former stables where tables are constructed from big cartwheels.

Across the cobbled street is another restaurant and a jolly bar where honky-tonk singsongs are played on the piano. Around the village are some small shops, and a tea room. Craft fairs and other events are held on weekend afternoons. Mrs Thatcher and various famous people have paid visits.

The hotel bedrooms, including a beamed four-poster bedroom with drapes, stretch along both sides of the street. A leisure centre with a spa bath is in another building. Entertainment is available on the complex itself at all prices, ranging from a beer in the bar, to a meal in the more expensive restaurant, staying in an exclusive sumptuous suite with its own separate entrance. From Bolton you can take an excursion to the award-winning Wigan Pier.

Last Drop Village, Bromley Cross, Bolton, Greater Manchester, tel: 0204 591131.

Miller Howe (Windermere, Lake District)

The Lake District is the most beautiful area of England for scenery, vying with the Trossachs area of Scotland around Loch Lomond. Overlooking Lake Windermere, past a fountain of cuddly cupids, are the arched dining room windows of the Miller Howe Hotel. The second dining room has trompe l'œil murals. Bedrooms are comfortably furnished with books, magazines and records, and there's a four-poster. More details about the food and the Lake District are elsewhere in Chapter 23 of this book.

Miller Howe, Rayrigg Road, Windermere, Cumbria, LA23 1EY, tel: 09662 2536.

Bontddu Hall Country House Hotel, (near Barmouth, West Wales)

Waterfalls are a feature of west Wales. In addition to the Fairy Glen and Swallow Falls at Bettws-y-Coed, along the coast you will see other signposts by carparks at the entrances of paths leading to the falls. Maps and tourist literature give exact locations if you want to plan ahead. Picturesque Portmeirion village and hotel are described in Chapter 17 on Wales.

On the west coast is the very pretty small town of Barmouth, where stone cottages edge the river, and the High Street gives a view of the sea at one end, and a church on the hillside behind the town.

Nearby is Bontddu Hall Country House Hotel. As you drive towards it the riverside road gives numerous wonderful views of the Mawddach estuary. Bontddu Hall perched on the hill above the road has a restaurant and lounges overlooking the idyllic scenery, and a sun terrace with tables, an outdoor landscaped garden for putting, and a modern extension with more bedrooms all enjoying the same spectacular view.

The house is one of those Victorian buildings which looks as though it could have been a castle, featuring arched gothic windows and high pointed gables. Inside the house is equally fantastic. In the entrance hall is a Welsh dresser displaying a collection of blue plates. A grandfather clock and a china King Charles Spaniel are by the log fire, and the reception desk is beyond columns linked by arches. One of the bedrooms has similar dark marble columns contrasting with the white icing effect of the bases, capitals and arches. Other bedrooms have four-poster beds.

The lounges have high ceilings, marble fireplaces and oak panelling. A romantic olde worlde bar with a wooden ceiling was converted from the former gentleman's billiard room. You can sit in the bench seated alcoves admiring the bar's stained glass frieze and wood carving. All this is immediately apparent to the onlooker. The hotel brochure, or the owners, young Michael and Margaretta Ball, will additionally tell you that the hotel was built in 1873 as a country mansion for the sister of the statesman

Joseph Chamberlain.
Bontddu Hall Hotel, Bontddu, Nr Barmouth, Gwynedd, Wales, LL40 25U tel: 0341 49661.

Renishaw Hall (Near Sheffield, Yorkshire).
Renishaw Hall, a large castellated private home, was the house of the literary Sitwell family for 350 years, the most famous of them being Edith Sitwell. The house is now owned by Edith's nephew Reresby Sitwell. He has rooms with four-poster beds available to the public, bookable through an agency, *Heritage Placements Ltd. 4 Wellington House, Greenberry Street, London NW8 7AB, tel: 01-586 3665*, which offers a choice of several similarly grand locations.
Renishaw Hall, nr. Sheffield, Yorkshire, S31 9WB, tel: 0246 432042.

Brocket Hall (Welwyn, Hertfordshire)
Heritage Placements can also book groups into Brocket Hall, which is so delightfully unusual that although individuals cannot stay here, I am including it in case you ever have occasion to want an unusual venue for entertaining a business or social group. Brocket Hall was the home of Lady Caroline Lamb, wife of Prime Minster Melbourne, where for a surprise on her husband's birthday she jumped out of a soup tureen, naked, and danced on the table!

The 65 ft dining table was the second longest in the country after the one at Windsor Castle, and is in the Grand Salon where Lady Caroline Lamb introduced the waltz to England – which was at first considered quite shocking as people danced together and touched each other! She was also notorious for her passionate affair with Byron. The house has been the home of two prime ministers, the other one being Lord Palmerston, and Queen Victoria stayed here. It is currently the home of the Rt. Hon. Lord and Lady Brocket, and a member of the Prestige group of hotels.

There are about 46 double bedrooms, the whole of the hall being reserved exclusively for each group, so it is only economic if 20 or more people are booking together. The Prince Regent's oriental bedroom has a bed with a red pagoda style headboard and hand painted silk wallpaper dating back to the 1700's. Lord Melbourne's room has an en suite bathroom with marble walls,

two basins, a bidet, and a bath in an alcove with drapes at both ends.
Brocket Hall, Welwyn, Hertfordshire, AL8 7XG, tel: 0707 335241.

HOTEL GROUPS

The Best Western Hotels Getaway Breaks brochure has symbols indicating which hotels offer romantic weekend breaks. The breaks vary from four-posters, flowers, fruit, and Jacuzzis to a champagne breakfast in bed. Very often the four-poster is the best bedroom in a friendly three or four star hotel.
Best Western Hotels, Vine House, 143 London Road, Kingston upon Thames, Surrey KT2 6NA, tel: 01-541 0033.

THF (Trusthouse Forte) has a list of four-poster hideaways. Couples Weekends are offered. For a supplementary payment you receive a superior room, champagne and flowers.
Trusthouse Forte Hotels, 24-30 New St, Aylesbury, Bucks HP20 2NW, tel: 01-567 3444.

De Luxe hotels where every room is luxuriously decorated, with adjoining elegant bathrooms, are shown in the Prestige hotels booklet.
Prestige Hotels, 418-422 Strand, London WC2R 0PT, tel: 01-439 2365.

The Holiday Inn brochure offers Twos Company romantic weekends.

CHAPTER 3
Best Beds and Baths for Clean Weekends

Four-posters, half-testers, canopy beds, circular beds, and waterbeds – British hotels offer a range of delightful bedrooms, and en suite bathrooms, hidden bathrooms, love seat baths, corner baths, spa baths, even Queen Victoria's bath, to make dirty weekends into clean weekends.

Many of these luxury hotels also merit a mention in other chapters which focus on other aspects of memorable weekends. But they are grouped here because they have specific features in their bedrooms or in their bathroom facilities which are desirable and which you may wish to request.

Four-poster beds can be Elizabethan carved oak, reproduction Regency style, modern pine, or brass with 'lace' – not authentic but pretty. Honeymoon couples may get champagne and pay less – sometimes more – for the privilege, so always enquire. Reductions are often made for honeymooners.

Draped four-posters provide privacy and keep out the draughts. In medieval times the bed's roof stopped the insects falling on you from the thatched roof, and the high bed kept you above the dogs and their jumping fleas.

Half-testers, looking like an economy version of the four-poster, had drapes over the pillow, and were designed to hide the mistress's face from the curious glances of the maid who brought in the lord's breakfast in the morning.

Most four-posters are double beds, although twin four-posters are not unknown. They used to be available in at least two hotels, one of which was the Belfry, near Birmingham.

Increasing numbers of European package tour hotels are installing twin beds which enable the hoteliers to let double rooms to two single companions. At busy times of year when only twin-bedded rooms are available you can push two single beds together to make a kingsize double – assuming the bedside table doesn't separate them. Fortunately Britain is the last bastion of the double bed in Europe. Couples should ask for a double bed, not just a double room, and check the size of the bed.

A development in recent years is the fashion for waterbeds. When buying a waterbed in America, I was told that there are four grades of waterbed, the more expensive, the more internal baffles and less movement. Top grade is almost rigid like a well-pumped up airbed. If anyone tells you that you cannot make love in a waterbed, but have to temporarily move onto the floor, don't believe them. It is just a rumour. You can verify the truth for yourself, in a hotel with a waterbed.

Regarding baths, although Californian 'hot tub' parties are popular, some Americans and others prefer individual private whirlpool baths in their hotel room, rather than sitting with strangers in the communal whirlpool.

Whirlpools attached to bedrooms cost about £5 per person per night at Crest hotels around Britain. A double bedroom with a private jacuzzi for an extra £10 per night for two should satisfy those who think sharing a jacuzzi with strangers is unhealthy. In your own jacuzzi you can start with clean water and fresh bubble bath.

Obviously rates vary according to the room chosen and the time of year. In some cases where there are particularly high prices or low price bargain breaks I have quoted them to give you an idea (but remember that the prices I give are approximate).

LONDON

The Savoy (London, near Trafalgar Square)
To be truly pampered at a top hotel and treated to life's little luxuries you could pick a hotel from the Savoy group. Handmade horsehair mattresses are made by three men in a Drury Lane factory especially for the Savoy group of hotels and the hotels' clients who can have a bed made to any size and shipped off as far away as America or Canada. The Savoy group includes

The Savoy, The Berkeley which opened in 1972, and Claridges, where callers who ask to speak to the King are asked, 'Which King?'.

The Savoy was opened by D'Oyly Carte after his success at the Savoy theatre with operettas by Gilbert & Sullivan, whom he had introduced to each other. D'Oyly Carte installed Ritz and Escoffier in his Savoy hotel. Johann Strauss played waltzes in the restaurant, and Pavlova danced. Nowadays the Savoy's American bar has photos of celebrities, and set lunches are from about £17. If you want a souvenir, and don't want to buy a whole bed, the Savoy coffee which was supplied to Eisenhower during the Second World War can be bought from the Savoy Gift Shop in the foyer at about £1.70 a tin, or by post.

In your Savoy Hotel bedroom the sheets are linen. A night at 'The Savoy in Style' including English Breakfast, flowers, chocolates, champagne on arrival, dinner and dancing in The Savoy Restaurant or pre-theatre dinner in The Savoy Grill costs about £190 for two on the first night, and about £130 for each additional night (with English Breakfast). Optional extras are personally monogrammed Savoy bathrobes, and theatre seats. The 'Two's Company' package includes one night's accommodation, champagne, flowers, chocolates, your own butler, dinner in your suite, breakfast and a set of Savoy table linen, total £450 for two, additional nights without meals at £300 per night.

The Savoy, The Strand, London WC2R 0EU, tel: 01-836 4343.

The Berkeley (London, near Harrods)

If you think larger hotels like the Savoy are a bit overwhelming, the Berkeley in Belgravia near Knightsbridge is designed more like a private house, and one of the restaurants is very modern. If you stay the night or dine at the Berkeley, try to see the fairytale Berkeley Ballroom, whose mirror ceiling reflects the chandeliers. Some bedroom suites have two bathrooms, and all have full length baths, providing comfort for tall guests.

Single bedrooms are about £165, doubles averaging from £200, suites from about £320 per night, without breakfast. A Savoy Group desk is at London's Heathrow Terminal 3 Arrivals, tel: 01-759 1305. Americans can book packages combining British Caledonian flights, staying at the Savoy hotels, and visiting National Trust properties, through Horizon Travel Inc, 1210 Nacogdoches Road, San Antonio, Texas, call collect 512 824 7900 or outside Texas toll free 1-800 842 8887. *The Berkeley, Wilton Place, Knightsbridge, London SW1X 7RL, tel: 01-235 6000.*

Norfolk Hotel (London, near South Kensington Museums)
Jacuzzi attachments enable whirlpools to be fixed to any shaped bath including the traditional cigar shape bath which is big enough for only one person. Couples who like to jacuzzi bath together might be disappointed that London's beautifully decorated Norfolk Capital Hotel has opted for this - though it would suit the single and the shy, or two romantic contortionists. However, the advantage is the hotel has no shortage of Jacuzzis - one in every bathroom. A small number of bedrooms have en suite shower-rooms only, so Jacuzzi enthusiasts should insist on a bathroom.
Norfolk Hotel, Harrington Road, London SW7, tel: 01-589 7000. 01-589 7000.

Marlborough Crest Hotel (London, near The British Museum)
For sheer luxury try the Marlborough Crest Hotel which has a large corner bath in a suite. You can sit up to your neck clothed in bubbles, alone or with your beloved - delightful. The elegant bathroom has everything you could want, including speakers relaying the news or TV programmes. An advantage of the private pool is being able to bathe in the nude, so you do not need to remember your bathing costume. You can also whirlpool in your hotel bedroom at midnight, while some public whirlpools shut at hours like 8 pm.

You could entertain in the Marlborough Crest suite's lounge where antiquarian books reside in the bookcase. Exploring your suite is half the fun. It took me ten minutes just to sort out the telephone extensions, including one which you carry around with you. You pay more at the London Marlborough Crest and other hotels where only the grandest suite has a large corner bath with whirlpool and you're paying for the private sitting room as well.

Marlborough Crest Hotel, Bloomsbury Street, London WC1B 3QD, tel: 01-636 5601.

Portobello Hotel (London, Notting Hill)
A hotel with a circular bed is the Portobello in London. The bedroom's L-shape alcove has an Edwardian bath with a brass shower fitting surrounding you with numerous shower jets, and a wave machine. The cost is about £121 per night.
Portobello Hotel, 22 Stanley Gardens, London W11 2NG, tel: 01-727 2777.

OUTSIDE LONDON

Old Palace Lodge (Dunstable, Bedfordshire)
Smart hotels in central London are pricey. Taking a short drive from London north into Bedfordshire for a weekend you could stay in Dunstable at The Old Palace Lodge in the town centre. It offers double bedrooms with elaborately carved dark medieval style four-posters and charming bedcovers depicting men and women in medieval headdress. I was told that the bedcover material came from Harrods. Bedrooms have pretty en suite bathrooms with bidets. Some of the rooms overlook the thatched public house next door. All year weekend breaks are about £33 per person per night for Friday and Saturday, dinner, bed and breakfast, with a choice of lunch instead of dinner on Saturday if preferred.
Old Palace Lodge Hotel, Church Street, Dunstable, Bedfordshire, tel: 0582 62201.

Flitwick Manor (Flitwick, Bedfordshire)
The St Pancras to Bedford railway line takes you to Flitwick Manor, also in Bedfordshire, a tranquil country house hotel with log fires and assorted antiques such as a child's rocking cradle lining the corridors. The bedrooms are luxuriously equipped with books, games and colourful drapes. In addition to the normal four-poster and half-tester beds, one 'four-poster' has no posts, just curtains attached to the ceiling, presumably stapled onto runners, around a star-shaped pleated oblong

canopy. This appeals to me as I have always thought that the drapes are more important than the posts.

The best bathroom has two single baths beside each other, but set back half overlapping like loveseats. They are in the centre of the bathroom which also has a sauna. Sometimes the couple who have this room invite in friends to use the sauna as Helene Moore, who often delivers drinks, explained.

Her husband, Somerset Moore, the rotund and jolly owner-chef, speaks about food on Chiltern radio and keeps live seafood in tanks outside the kitchen. The Moores create a very happy atmosphere. Don't expect change out of £100 for the sauna room.
Flitwick Manor, Flitwick, Bedfordshire, tel: 0525 712242.

Inn on the Lake Hotel (Godalming, Surrey)
South of London, The Inn on the Lake at Godalming near Guildford has some newly decorated bedrooms with thick pile carpets and glossy magazines, and beautiful bathrooms with coloured suites, spa baths, and plants. The owner won the innkeeper of the year award in 1986-7 from Guinness and the British Institute of Innkeepers.
Inn on the Lake Hotel, Godalming, Surrey, tel: 04868 5575.

REGIONS

Stone Green Hall (Ashford, Kent)
Not much rivals the four-poster bath at Stone Green Hall. They have fewer than half a dozen bedrooms. Another has a shower and bidet. Prices for rooms with en suite bathrooms are about £70 per night for two including breakfast.
Stone Green Hall, Mersham, Ashford, Kent, TN25, tel: 0233 72418.

Highcliff Hotel (Bournemouth, Dorset)
Highcliff Hotel has one pair of satin sheets. They bought from an exotic mail order catalogue satin sheets which are brought out for special occasions. The sheets have to be dry cleaned. The hotel can do 'naughty but nice' weekends on demand, using the

satin sheets and giving you chocolates, cream cakes and champagne. The hotel has a sauna and if you want to use it you must remember to book your sauna session.
Highcliff Hotel, St Michael's Road, West Cliff, Bournemouth, Dorset, BH2 5DU, tel: 0202 27702.

Huntsham Court Hotel (Huntsham, Devon)
Down in Devon a country house party atmosphere is created at Huntsham Court, a Victorian manor house where you listen to classical records as you sit by log fires. Bedrooms have open fireplaces, and so have some bathrooms. The main suite is the Beethoven suite with a four-poster and a double bathroom with king and queen size baths in the middle of the room and huge windows overlooking the lawn and woods.

You eat as guests of the owner around one long table. In the bar no money changes hands. You help yourself and there is a book for each room which you sign. Placecards call you by bedroom names such as Mr and Mrs Mozart, Verdi, Bach, Chopin, Schumann, or Schubert, and you may choose to identify yourself if you wish! Picnic hampers are provided, and bicycles to explore the countryside around Taunton. You can book through Heritage Placements Ltd, 4 Wellington House, Greenberry Street, London NW8 7AB, tel: 01-586 3665.
Huntsham Court Country House Hotel, Huntsham, Devon EX16 7NA, tel: 03986 210.

Trelydan Hall (Welshpool, Mid Wales)
In Wales charming Tudor Trelydan Hall has the sort of sumptuous four-posters and half-tester bedrooms which make you rush around calling, 'Come and look at this!' The romantic Welsh Oak Suite has massive bulbous posts attached to the ceiling beams supporting thick drapes, and a beamed bathroom with pictures, plants and candelabra light fittings. Most bathrooms have bidets.

In the Green Tudor suite a mirror above the headboard of the half-tester bed reflects the old furniture and diamond shape beams on the white plaster walls. The red drawing room suite has an enormously high bed with ruched red drapes behind the pillows as well as drawing all the way round them, plus a fireplace, armchairs, and a kitchen–diner. Another bedroom is

Victorian with a lace canopy above the pillows, roses crowding the wallpaper, and co-ordinating flowered bedding and curtains, and pictures with mottoes 'God is our refuge and strength', 'Who daily loadeth us with benefits'. Champagne and fresh flowers can be placed in the rooms if required. Optional dinner is served by candle-light.
Trelydan Hall, Welshpool, Powys, Wales, tel: 0938 2773.

Palé Hall (Bala, North Wales)
Palé Hall is a countryside mansion in north Wales where Queen Victoria stayed for three weeks, visiting Henry Robertson, son of a liberal Member of Parliament, and Victoria knighted Henry junior.

You can see Queen Victoria's bath across the end of the bathroom which also has a bidet and two basins, plus an antique half-tester bed in the adjoining bedroom. Queen Victoria's walk by the riverside can be taken, and residents can be shown around the water-driven turbine which provides electricity for the house. In fact free electricity was used to run eighteen electric fires for twenty years when the house was left empty!

In the lounge hall you can have tea around the fireplace. A grand piano is at the foot of the grand staircase, and a stained glass dome lights the hall. Leading from the hall are other impressive rooms. The bar is constructed from two white marble fireplaces.

This may sound a little awesomely austere for younger people. However, there is one stunning red and white bedroom suite which would make a modern sixteen year old bride ecstatic. Adjoining the lacey four-poster bedroom is a small circular lounge with views of the woods, and vibrant red plush chairs, and round tables with white ornaments on red cloths draped over long white ones. The bathroom has red and white tiles, and even a red hair drier fixed on the wall. In addition to the red and white Beaumaris suite, The Dolbadarn has a corner bath and shower; the Carnarvon a jacuzzi.

Music concerts are held once a month through the winter. Winterbreaks cost about £80 per couple for one night, dinner, bed and breakfast, £150 for two nights. Room 5 with the circular spa bath, and champagne and fruit on arrival, costs about £110 per couple for a one night stay, including dinner, bed and

breakfast, reducing to £100 per night for two nights or more.
Palé Hall, Llandderfel, nr Bala, Gwynedd, North Wales, tel: 067 83 285.

String of Horses (Near Carlisle)
The String of Horses is a beamed pub at a countryside crossroads south of Carlisle. It won an award as pub of the year a while ago. Pretty bedrooms are small and cosy, several having four-poster beds, circular baths, and the colourful Bonsack bathroom suites you see for sale in Harrods. Assorted designs include key patterns and gold taps. Downstairs are the indoor spa bath, sauna, and outdoor swimming pool.
String of Horses Inn and Restaurant, Heads Nook, Faugh, near Carlisle, Cumbria CA4 9EG, tel: 022870 297.

Dalston Hall (near Carlisle)
Dalston Hall's sunken bath with the overhead mirror, en suite with a four-poster bedroom reached by a spiral staircase, is described in detail under Olde Worlde Hotels (Chapter 10). Tel: 0228 710271.

Ramside Hall Hotel (Durham)
A castle-style hotel near Durham is Ramside Hall Hotel which has a castellated exterior and beamed bedrooms. Five suites have whirlpool corner baths which everyone will want to try, and one offers a circular bed which everyone will want to see, so don't take too many friends on your weekend away. Ramside Hall Hotel charges about £40 per person for one night including dinner and breakfast, about £65 per person for a two night break.
Ramside Hall Hotel, Carrville, Durham, tel: 0385 65282.

Lumley Castle (Chester-le-Street, County Durham)
In the north at Lumley Castle Hotel is what looks like the tallest four-poster bed in the world, six foot wide and about sixteen feet high. Three more four-posters are in other rooms, including the haunted room with creaking floors, but thick fitted white carpets. It is the perfect combination of modern comfort amidst flagstones, pillars and battlements.
One room has no visible bathroom door. When you finally

open the central wardrobe door you find that the central section of the wardrobe is a corridor! The back of the wardrobe and the wall are both cut out to reveal a bathroom beyond. It is full size and L-shape with the basin hidden to your left, the toilet hidden down the corridor to the right, the corner bath ahead of you. Wonderful! All 'gold fittings' – are they brass? – 1901 massive taps, even 'gold' plugs. The supports for basin and toilet are white, embossed with gold patterns.

Another four-poster bedroom, number 46, has a freestanding bath in a curtained alcove in the main room with a phone next to the bath, and a fireplace with wood panelling. (More on Lumley Castle in Chapters 8 and 9 on Haunted Hotels and Medieval Banquets.)
Lumley Castle Hotel, Chester-le-Street, Co Durham DH3 4NX, tel: 0385 891111.

Wheel Inn (Perth, Scotland)
If you prefer waving up and down in bed, there are three waterbeds at the Wheel Inn, one of which is kingsize. Because it takes so long to heat up the water it is kept at a constant temperature – lovely and warm. Winter breaks are about half normal prices, only £40 per person for two nights bed, breakfast and evening meal.
The Wheel Inn, Angus Road, Scone, Perth, Scotland, tel: 0738 51518.

Fitzpatrick Castle (Killiney, Co Dublin)
South of Dublin is the Fitzpatrick Castle, a crenellated family hotel which has several four-posters, including one in a turret suite, all with en suite bathroom. The hotel has an indoor swimming pool.
Fitzpatrick Castle Hotel, Killiney, County Dublin, Eire, tel: 0001 851533.

Many grand castle hotels in Eire can be booked through Time Off Ltd, whose brochure is available from travel agents.

CHAPTER 4
Privilege and Luxury

Exclusive tours by jet, balloon, limousine or luxury train can be arranged, staying at stately homes, meeting a Marquess, or playing polo. If you want to be really eccentric, Take-A-Guide can deal with that too.

Take-A-Guide
Take-A-Guide supplies an entertaining driver–guide who offers you complete flexibility, tailoring a tour exactly to your needs. For example, the current most popular tour is simply to book accommodation at Cliveden. You can be picked up at the airport and taken directly to Cliveden where the butler and footman meet you and then go on an escorted weekend tour in a Mercedes limousine. London half-day tours cost about £69 per car, not per person, in a medium car seating one to three, up to £104 for a limousine seating one to six. Windsor, Shakespeare country and other tours are offered.

However, should you require something more special, you might like to hear what Mr Pearson who runs Take-A-Guide has arranged for three previous clients. There were jet tours, balloon tours, and eccentric impulse-of-the-day tours, any of which you could copy.

Mr Pearson explains that one client arrived by jet at Heathrow for his second wedding anniversary with his wife. He wanted to fly to Scotland to a castle in a private jet with a guide. Mr Pearson sent them aloft accompanied by the guide wearing her London Tourist Board badge, the pilot banking left and right as they were given a guided tour by air across Britain to a fishing lodge in Scotland. On a return visit the client did a circular tour of Castles in Wales by air taking aerial photos of Caernarvon Castle, hearing about how the first Prince of Wales was created at Caernarvon.

Another client required a guided balloon tour. Observing

England from the air by balloon you can see the markings left by the field systems and cultivation of Saxon and medieval times. The ridges and furrows made by medieval farming stand out clearly. Flying over Stonehenge, Woodhenge, Avebury and Silbury Hill, you can wonder at Britain's prehistory. In a balloon, Roman, medieval, and prehistoric features can be seen beneath the surface of today's fields: the hidden imprints of our ancestors revealed from the air.

Mr Pearson went on to tell me of a recent 'eccentric impulse tour' which he arranged. A medium wanted a tour with nothing booked in advance, just planned day by day, as she received inspiration as to where she should spend the following night. For the first night she wanted to stay in a thatched cottage with pink roses round the door. Mr Pearson thought of a suitable thatched hotel and phoned to ask the astonished manager what colour his roses were, as the booking depended upon it.

Fortunately the hotel had pink roses, not red ones. I don't know what the lady was paying, but I suspect that an enterprising tour arranger or hotel manager could have nipped down to the local garden centre, bought a nice pink trailing rose bush and planted it right by the front door and added the cost to the bill.

Next morning the lady arose, pink but satisfied, and at 7.15 am she phoned to say that night two she'd decided she had to be within 100 yards of the sea, on the west coast of England, looking towards America. 'I had a fraught morning fixing her accommodation and transport across the country to St Ives . . . and so it went on,' Mr Pearson recalled.

'I was afraid there would not be enough time to move her to the next destination. But night three she simply wanted to sleep next to horses and that was easy. You can have bed and breakfast for yourself and your horse at a hotel in Tetbury, Gloucester, and there's another place with horses at High Bullen, Dartmoor.' (There's also Plumber Manor, Sturminster Newton, Dorset, tel: 0258 72507, a Jacobean mansion with bedrooms in a converted barn and stabling for your horse – so you can join the local hunt.)

For night four she wanted to be within walking distance of a spectacular ruin. 'I knew a ruin the size of Buckingham Palace, Whitley Abbey near Abberley, Worcester, and she stayed at the

Elms Hotel in Abberley, within walking distance. When the BTA in New York get unusual requests like that they are quite relieved to be able to pass the customer onto me!'

After that Mr Pearson says it is pretty easy for him to organise a ghost-hunting tour, a beautiful bedroom in Bailiffscourt honeymoon suite near Chichester, a room with a circular bath at Maison Tolbooth, or accommodation nobody would find fault with at the immaculate Four Seasons in Oxford. Contact:
Fred Pearson, Take-A-Guide Ltd, (TAG), 85 Lower Sloane Street, London SW1, tel: 01-221 5475/730 9144.

The Take-a-Guide office in New York is:
Take-A-Guide, 63, East 79th Street, New York, NY 10021 USA, tel: tollfree 800 223 6450.

The Val Cooper Portfolio

Val Cooper runs a small private company arranging exclusive tours for individuals, organisations and travel groups, going to private country homes not open to the public where you are entertained to coffee, lunch, tea or dinner as personal guests of the owners. You can visit Althorp, home of the Earl and Countess Spencer, Ragley Hall, home of the Marquess and Marchioness of Hertford, and Sutton Park home of Mrs Sheffield, and dine as their privileged guest.

Naturally Dukes and Duchesses, Earls and Countesses, go on holiday, have a busy schedule attending meetings, and work, and want to eat with their own families, so they are not always available to join you for dinner. But often they will preside at a group cocktail party before the dinner held in their home.

Blue badge guides, members of the Guild of Guide lecturers, limousines, and itineraries are supplied. Contact:
Val Cooper Travel Ltd, 29 Dollis Park, London N3 1HJ, tel: 01-346 4268.

Ragley Hall (Alcester, Warwickshire)

Tour operators can arrange private conducted tours at Ragley Hall with sherry or champagne, champagne receptions, vintage wines and ports. There's also dinner, bed and breakfast for up to three couples. So you can sleep in a marquess's bed, but bring your own partner.

Luncheons and dinners for groups of 2-30 are held in private or state dining rooms and for 30-150 people in the Great Hall. The menus include asparagus, avocado or salmon mousse, main courses such as Lamb Shrewsbury (fillets of lamb served with red wine sauce, redcurrant jelly and rosemary), or roast venison, and Meringue Mont Blanc (meringues filled with sherry flavoured chestnut puree and cream), coffee and petit fours.

The Great Hall looks like a pink Wedgwood plate, a pink background decorated with white plasterwork columns, arches, urns, and busts, dating from 1750. You can hire it for concerts, exhibitions and balls.

If all you want to do is visit Ragley Hall when you are in Stratford, it is open to visitors in summer (closed certain Mondays and Fridays). See the house, the garden designed by Capability Brown, adventure wood and country trail, maze, children's amusements, sailing, lake and cricket pitch. For further information contact:
The Marquess of Hertford, Ragley Hall, Alcester, Warwickshire, tel: 0789 762455.

Meeting Members of Parliament
If you work in politics, public affairs, or journalism, or are a visiting VIP, arrangements can be made for your holiday to include an introduction to a Member of Parliament. This happens in the Houses of Parliament at a group meeting to promote a cause that the MP supports. The travel organiser includes it in the itinerary for groups, or occasionally individuals, by contacting his or her local MP, or one he or she knows well.

If you have an opportunity to go to a meeting don't miss it. The Houses of Parliament, besides having interesting external architecture, are beautifully decorated inside with gigantic gilded murals depicting Elizabeth I and other historical figures.

Playing Polo
You can learn to play the game of kings, at Windsor, by kind permission of The Guards Polo Club, staying for five days, Monday to Friday, at a Queen Anne mansion, the Royal Berkshire Hotel. If you stay on for Saturday night you can enter the Members Club House of the Guards Polo Club on Sunday afternoon. Weekends and short courses can also be arranged.

The school is directed by Olympic show-jumper Peter Grace who founded The Rangitiki Polo team which has played in the USA at the Polo School in Florida and they play regularly at the polo school in England.
The General Manager, The Royal Berkshire Hotel, London Road, Ascot, Berkshire, SL5 0PP, tel: 0990 23322.

Scottish Train Land Cruises

Tours go from St Pancras in London to Scotland for a weekend or week, to Oban, Iona, and Fort William or Inverness, Kyle of Lochalsh, and even over the sea to Skye. The price is from £140 to about £200 which covers the rail fare, dining car meals, overnight accommodation in sleeping compartments or hotels and coach tours including a visit to Dufftown whisky distillery. One tour offers an optional golf stop. Window seats can be guaranteed and you can join the train en route at stations such as Leicester, Derby and Sheffield, or York, if London is not convenient.
Pullman Rail, 104 Birmingham Road, Lichfield, Staffs WS14 9BW, tel: 0543 254076, or
British Rail, Euston Travel Centre, Euston Station, London NW1 2HS, tel: 01-388 0519.

There are only a certain number of these tours each year, but at other times it is possible to put together your own round tour of Scotland, using ordinary overnight sleepers, stopping at a whisky distillery. For groups Pullman trains can be hired for any occasion from a hotel launch to a wedding reception, serving champagne on the train.

Exclusive train journeys for only 28 guests at a time take place on the luxury Royal Scotsman travelling through Scotland. A guide accompanies the tour which stops at private houses, castles and gardens, some of which are not normally open to the public.

The train is in plum and spilt milk colours and the antique dining car is thought to be the oldest dining car in operation in the world. The saloon car was once divided into three sections for ladies and children, gentlemen, and servants and luggage. Now it is in two sections, one for dining, one for reading, writing and playing cards. Guests are expected to dress elegantly, perhaps in tuxedo or kilt for dinner. State cabins decorated with mahogany woodwork have a shower, basin and toilet en suite, and bathrobes.

The observation car at the back of the train offers panoramic views of the enchanting Scottish scenery: Loch Lomond, the waterfalls of Glen Falloch, the peat bog and tree stumps on Rannoch Moor, Ben Nevis, Britain's highest mountain, Glenfinnan viaduct, the golfer's dream St Andrews Old Course, and lakeside Loch Shiel monument – a column with a statue on top where Bonnie Prince Charlie raised his standard in 1745 (Queen Victoria never saw a finer spot).

You rattle confidently over Dundee's Tay Bridge, known for the 1879 disaster when the bridge collapsed taking the train with it, immortalised in McGonagall's dreadful poetry.

Inverawe Smokehouse shows salmon and trout being smoked and you try a sample, while riverside Strathisla distillery, home of Chivas Regal whisky, with its hat shape architecture, provides the inevitable whisky tasting and purchases.

There are castles galore, Stirling Castle, Brodie Castle, Falkland Palace where you see the chapel royal with its wooden ceiling, Glamis Castle, childhood home of HM the Queen Mother, and Cawdor Castle, scene of Duncan's murder in Macbeth, with its amusing commentary and car stickers reading 'Three out of four ghosts prefer Cawdor Castle'. You pass Culloden where Bonnie Prince Charlie was defeated in 1746.

You visit Castle Leod which is home of the Earl and Countess of Cromartie, head of the Mackenzie clan, Achnacarry, home of Sir Donald and Lady Cameron of Lochiel; and visit Ardchattan Priory owned by Colonel Campbell-Preston.

Most people take the six day tour, covering most of these sights, but three day tours north or west are possible. Tours are run from April to November.

If the standard itinerary does not suit you, the Royal Scotsman train can be chartered and the sightseeing programme varied.

The price is from £1090 to £1320 per person for the three day tour, and £2130–£2490 for the six day tour including meals and wine. Details from:

Abercrombie & Kent Ltd, Sloane Square House, Holbein Place, London SW1, tel: 01-730 9600.

Grand Tour of Scotland by Car

A Grand Tour of Scotland by Car can cover six grand castles, all still occupied by owners, dukes, earls, a marquess and a thane. Blair Castle is a beautiful white building in grounds with massive trees. Mary Queen of Scots hunted here. There are attractive 'don't drop litter' signs depicting snails. Take notice because the Duke still has his own private army.

Other castles are Glamis which was the birthplace of Princess Margaret; and Hopetoun which has a deerpark, nature trail, and black St Kilda sheep with four horns. There's Cawdor Castle, mentioned above, Scone where Scottish kings were crowned, and Inverary Castle.

Inverary Castle is the home of The Duke of Argyll, Marquess of Kintyre, Marquess of Lorne, Earl of Campbell, Viscount of Lochow, Lord of Inverary and a few other places, who is also the chief of the Campbell Clan. The Campbells worldwide raised a third of the £1,200,000 needed to rebuild the ancestral home when it was gutted by fire in 1975. So if you are one of the 10,000 Campbells in the USA, or the 3,000 in Australia, and you'd like to shake hands with the Duke, he will be delighted to meet you if you write in advance, providing he is at home on the day you plan to visit.

SELECT HOTELS

Whilst you can book hotels direct within the UK, several organisations will make bookings for you. Abercrombie & Kent can book you into Pride of Britain hotels such as Greywalls Hotel, Muirfield, Lothian, Scotland, where King Edward VII stayed overlooking the Muirfield golfcourse; Riber Hall with its Jacobean four-poster beds in clock-ticking stillness on the hills above Matlock, Derbyshire; and the gourmet Michael's Nook on a hillside in the English Lake District, with its cascades of curtains.

The Venice Simplon Orient-Express Hotels include the oak-panelled Welcombe Hotel at Stratford-upon-Avon, where Theodore Roosevelt stayed in 1910.
   In the USA book through *VSOE Hotel, tel: New York*

212 839 0222, nationwide tel: 800 237 1236, or BTH Inc, New York tel: 212 684 1820, or nationwide tel: 800 221 1074.

The Welcombe Hotel in Stratford is represented by *UTELL International*, UK tel: 01-741 1588; USA New York tel: 212 397 1560, USA nationwide tel: 800 223 9868.

Celebrated Country House Hotels
Celebrated Country House Hotels, a member of Britain's Prestige Hotels consortium, has a Classic Country Breaks Brochure.

Billesley Manor, where Shakespeare used the library about four miles from Stratford, offers croquet and an indoor heated swimming pool, and four-poster beds. Weekend breaks are from about £100 per person for two nights sharing twin accommodation, including dinner and breakfast.
Billesley Manor, near Stratford-upon-Avon and Alcester, Warwickshire B49 6NF, tel: 0789 763737.

Oakley Court, near Windsor, is on the banks of the Thames. Visit Windsor theatre with its steep tiers and boxes. The Classic weekend break costs about £100.
Oakley Court Hotel, Windsor Road, nr Windsor, Berkshire, SL4 5UR, tel: 0628 74141.

The Elms hotel, mentioned by Take-A-Guide, has the largest herb garden in England, and from here you can visit the Cheltenham Races and the Malvern Music Festival. The Classic weekend break cost is from around £100.
The Elms, nr Abberley, near Worcester, WR6 6AT, tel: 029921 666.

For more details, contact:
Celebrated Country Hotels Ltd, Windsor Road, nr Windsor, Berkshire SL4 5UR, tel: 0628 37230. USA rep Scott Calder International 800 223 5581.

The Selected British Hotels brochure includes several hotels mentioned in detail in this book, including Pale Hall near Bala in Wales, Sunlaws House Hotel at Kelso in Scotland, and The Feathers at Ludlow. Other well-known hotels in their brochure include The Marlborough at Ipswich.

One London hotel offered is The Goring – the first hotel in the world to have a bathroom for every bedroom. It now has marble bathrooms and is near Buckingham Palace.

The other is Dorset Square Hotel, a town house hotel which also has marble bathrooms and is on the corner of Dorset Square just near Madame Tussauds. The basement restaurant features a mural showing Dorset Square when it was the first Lords Cricket Ground, and the first balloon flight in England taking off from the Dorset Square cricket ground in 1802. *Dorset Square Hotel, 39/40 Dorset Square, London NW1 6QN, tel: 01-723 7874.*

These Selected British Hotels can be booked in the USA through *Josephine Barr, 519 Park Drive, Kenilworth, Illinois 60043, USA, tel: 1-312 251 4110 or tollfree outside Illinois 1-800 323 5463.*

More details from the Scottish Tourist Board, or British Tourist Authority.

CHAPTER 5
Gourmet Treats

The Great British Breakfast has always been world-famous and good British food has recently been enjoying a revival. What distinguishes the traditional British bacon breakfast is both the quantity and the quality of hot freshly cooked food. It includes regional variations, such as freshly caught mackerel off the coast of Devon and Cornwall, black pudding in the North of England, and true Scottish porridge.

Britain equally offers gourmet temptations with lunches, teas, and dinners. Following is a brief selection of some outstanding British hospitality hotels and restaurants.

BEST GOURMET BREAKFAST

Miller Howe Hotel (Windermere, Lake District)
On Sunday morning as you descend the staircase of Miller Howe Hotel you see glasses of orange juice on the table at the foot of the stairs. Champagne is offered to turn your orange juice into Bucks Fizz, and after a few sips, you carry your glass into the dining room, feeling distinctly decadent. The twelve course Victorian breakfast is served on Wedgwood plates.

Miller Howe also provides the best packed lunch. I received smoked salmon, fan shape avocado, pâté, desserts and chocolates, plus fruit and a drink.

Dinner in Miller Howe is served at an exact time. Tables in the main dining room overlook Lake Windermere, beyond a fountain which is illuminated at night. The second dining room has trompe l'œil murals of pastoral scenes. Vegetables at the main courses are arranged around the large plate like numerals on a clockface, little pyramids of contrasting colours, green, purple, white, containing unusual ingredients – purée of beetroot, ginger, raspberry vinegar. Prices are expensive, but the hotel's bargain breaks are unforgettable.

Miller Howe Hotel, Rayrigg Road, Cumbria LA23 1EY, tel: 096 62 2536.

EXOTIC LUNCHES IN LONDON

Mountbatten Hotel (Central London)
A nouvelle cuisine lunch in the exotic surroundings of a Burmese temple, with red and white roof, is served at the Mountbatten Hotel, described in Chapter 12 on royalty. The set lunch enables you to budget.

If you just want a pot of coffee or tea in grand style, this can be sipped in elegance in the drawing room, a refuge after shopping in Foyles bookshop.

Mountbatten Hotel, Seven Dials, Covent Garden, London WC2H 9HD, tel: 01-836 4300.

Norfolk Hotel (London)
The Norfolk Capital group's Norfolk Hotel serves a deliciously exotic lunch in smart modern surroundings. The dining room wallpaper looks like marble, and is specially painted. I recall penny thin slices of South African yellow star shaped fruit among the exotic fruit salad dessert, which also included green kiwi fruit and red strawberries.

See their bathrooms described in Chapter 3. The hotel is within sight of South Kensington tube station, near the Victoria and Albert Museum, and Science Museum, and not far from Harrods.

Norfolk Hotel, Harrington Road, London SW7 3ER, tel: 01-589 8191.

Speciality Soufflé Restaurant (London)
I searched through a book called 'London Menus' which reproduces menus to find a restaurant serving truffles for an anniversary dinner. The Soufflé Restaurant specialises in soufflés, and the starter I selected was artichoke soufflé with truffles.

The artichoke arrived on a tray. The needle sharp points had been sliced off the vegetable. But the artichoke's remaining triangular green leaves were surrounded by the triangle of red 'points' of a carefully folded red napkin. It was presented on a bed of flowers and leaves. The centre of the artichoke contained a green artichoke soufflé. At the base was the artichoke heart, already cut, with a small piece of black truffle.

The main course was Boeuf Wellington: it ought to be Beef Wellington as it is an English dish. We could not finish the two soft fillet steaks per person, in pâté and puff pastry. Asking for a Doggie Bag was no problem. The waiter wrapped the remaining steaks ceremoniously in silver foil on a side table so I could see there was no substitution, and presented me with a small carrier bag on a tray.

The Soufflé Restaurant, Intercontinental Hotel, 1 Hamilton Place, Hyde Park Corner, London W1V 0QY, tel: 01-409 3131.

TEA TIME

For tea in grand manor in London, there's the Ritz.

Traditional afternoon tea-dances are held in London at the *Waldorf Hotel, Aldwych, London WC2B 4DD, tel: 01-836 2400.*

Maids of Honour Teashop (Kew, Surrey)

The Maids of Honour tea shop serves the famous Maids of Honour cakes, rather like a custard cream in a puff pastry case. As it is near Kew Gardens, at weekends and peak holiday periods you may have to queue, so go early.

Maids of Honour Teashop, Kew Road, Kew, Surrey, tel: 01-940 2752.

PERFECT DESSERTS

In the good old days before the compulsory service charge, when the waiter brought the dessert trolley he knew he was about to receive his tip. So he generously plied the customers with slender slices from every gateau and a spoonful from every basin, plus a large moat of cream, despite the vehemently insincere protests.

Nowadays the mean management places puddings in individual ramekins and dispirited staff say the dishes cannot be divided. Worse still, they charge for two desserts, losing the goodwill that the hotel chains spend thousands of pounds a year trying to capture.

Large London hotels have Sunday buffet lunches offering traditional roast meats and enabling you to take coffee spoon size helpings of desserts, tasting them all.

Sally Lunn Restaurant (St Albans, Herts)
The Sally Lunn at St Albans, candle-lit and olde-worlde, has menus which say, 'If you should desire a second helping or would like to try another dish, simply ask. It will be our pleasure to replenish your plate at no extra cost.'
Sally Lunn Restaurant, 17 St Michael Street, St Albans, Herts, tel: 0727 54405.

Pennyhill Park Hotel (Near Windsor, Surrey)
Pennyhill Park offers a different solution, the dessert assorti. Like a mixed hors d'oeuvres, it has tiny tastes of the desserts arranged in a pattern on the plate. Another plus point at this elegant hotel is the way that the main courses arrive kept hot under metal domes which are removed before you with a flourish. After dinner the favoured guest finds a chocolate in the bedroom, not a whole boxful to make you sick and guilty, just enough to make you feel self-indulged and satisfied.

Pennyhill is a Prestige hotel and has a weekend break at approximately £95 per person for two nights accommodation with breakfast each morning, dinner each evening, and early morning tea with newspapers.
Pennyhill Park Hotel, College Ride, Bagshot, Surrey, GU19 5ET, tel: 0276 71774.

Studley Priory – Chocolate and Winetasting (Oxford)
A Chocoholic weekend is held at Studley Priory, usually hosted by Helge Rubinstein, author of The Chocolate Book. Naturally your Saturday evening meal concludes with a range of chocolate desserts and a selection of chocolate truffles. During the day there are demonstrations of making, wrapping and presenting chocolates.

Unfortunately many more people choose the wine-tasting breaks, and if this trend continues the wine-tasting weekends will take over the dates previously allotted to chocolate. So chocolate lovers, put your money on the chocolate weekends, or the wine-bibbers will beat the chocoholics.

Prices are about £150-160 per person depending on size of room, including meals, wine, talks, and an excursion to a house built by Sir Christopher Wren. Wine breaks, Christmas breaks with mince pies, winter and Easter breaks are available.
Studley Priory Hotel, Horton-cum-Studley, Oxford OX9 1AZ, tel: 086 735 203 or 254.

Three Ways Hotel Pudding Club (Gloucestershire)
An Inter-Hotel, the Three Ways, has a Pudding Club every weekend. They serve your favourite English puddings, like Spotted Dick, no doubt full of currants.
Three Ways Hotel, Mickleton, Chipping Campden, Gloucestershire, GL55 6SB, tel: 0386 438429.

SOME ETHNIC AND CELTIC TABLES

Blooms Jewish Food (North London)
The famous Blooms of the East End is still there although many Jews moved to north-west London when they became prosperous. Thus there is now a popular branch of Blooms in north-west London at Golders Green.

Kosher foods means no pork, thus no lard, no shellfish (don't ask for prawns), and not mixing milk with meat during a meal. So don't ask for milk with your coffee after the salt beef. Viennas are red coloured sausages, rubbery texture, delicious taste. Fried gefillte fish, literally stuffed fish, is a tasty fried fish ball like the ones you get on cocktail sticks at weddings. Potato latkes are grated potato cakes, fried, sometimes round patties or triangular ones.

Finish your meal with Lokshen pudding made from vermicelli and sultanas, cooked till it forms a solid mass with a crisp topping. Maybe they add vanilla, maybe lemon juice, maybe brown sugar, maybe butter. Now you know why the clientele look so happy, and so fat.

Bloom's, 130 Golders Green Road, London NW11 8HB, tel: 01-455 3033.

Golders Green is always buzzing. The cars are double parked. Jewish restaurants, delis and shops are open on Sundays, Christmas day, and Boxing day, but closed for Jewish holidays. However the Indian takeaways, restaurants and supermarkets are open on Jewish holidays, plus weekends and evenings. The boisterous banter of the waiters in Jewish restaurants is a contrast to the delightfully deferential Indians who help you on with your coat and hold open the door for you.

Kaifeng Kosher Chinese Restaurant (North London)
This unlikely combination makes sense when you realise that one of the owners is Israeli, and another is his Chinese friend who ran a Chinese restaurant in Israel. The restaurant's name Kaifeng comes from the Kaifeng Jewish community in China, about 1,000 people in the 10th century, dwindling to 250 after World War II. Their names were Chinese, such as Chin, Tso and Yen.

The long narrow restaurant is attractively decorated with red Chinese lanterns and what looks like a Chinese house down one side, possibly disguising the kitchen. Jewish and Chinese waitresses wear slit-sided tight Chinese dresses. We ordered Drunken fish, sole drowned in Kosher rice wine (about £5) for one of our starters. The entire meal for four including kosher wine cost about £95. If you have the yen for kosher Chinese food it is open Sunday lunch and evenings Sunday to Thursday.
The Kaifeng Kosher Chinese Restaurant, 51 Church Road, Hendon, London NW4, tel: 01-203 1168.

Vegetarian
Kent-based Better Life Holidays organise vegetarian holidays for families where one or more wishes to eat vegetarian food. They arrange stopovers for Americans en route to Israel, seeing London and Canterbury, spending a night or two at Chilston Manor, vegetarian hotels in Kent and elsewhere, a Scottish hotel offering organic food and decor adapted for allergy sufferers, or whatever is required.
Better Life Holidays, Ross Partridge Leisure Division, Chancery House, 1 Effingham Street, Ramsgate, Kent CT11 9AT, tel: 0843 589855.

Haggis at the Stakis Treetops Hotel (Aberdeen, East Scotland)

The traditional Scottish dish is haggis made from unidentifiable ingredients – probably oats mixed with sheep's innards which most refined people in England regard with horror. The haggis I've most enjoyed eating was stuffed inside chicken; I ate it at the Stakis Treetops hotel in Aberdeen three nights running. My first course was melon, served as a melon bowl with a serrated top, containing alcoholic melon juice, decorated with speared fruit and one of those paper parasols usually found on cocktails.
Stakis Treetops Hotel, Springfield Road, Aberdeen, Grampian, Scotland, tel: 0224 313377.

The Bear Hotel (Mid Wales)

The most amusing pub lunch in Wales is at The Bear. Close the indoor shutters either side of windows. Behind the shutters are ancient paintings depicting what the traveller of olden days sought, Reviving Food, Repose, and Relaxation. The illustrations show the bed, the board, and the ladies provided. The rooms upstairs are pleasantly decorated, but bring your own lady.

They serve Welsh Laverbread, made from seaweed covered with oatmeal and made into a dark green cake fried with bacon for a lunch snack, also Penclawd cockles and mussels, and locally caught salmon, Welsh lamb cooked in local honey and wild thyme, Welsh farmhouse goat's and ewe's cheese, and Caerphilly cheese. Open all day for tea and coffee, and alcohol during pub hours – traditional beers on tap direct from barrels.
The Bear, Crickhowell, Powys, Wales, tel: 0873 810408.

The English Tourist Board produced a book called Let's Stop for Tea so they can tell you everything about where to go for tea. The Scottish Tourist Board has a Taste of Scotland scheme. Participating hotels and restaurants must have a Scottish dish on every menu. Similarly there is a Taste of Wales scheme.

PART II

Bizarre and unusual breaks

CHAPTER 6
The Plot Thickens: Murder Weekends and Dracula House Parties

The British are known for their eccentricity and as evidence there is on offer a multiplicity of bizarre breaks. You can be a guest at a house party set up for murder, or spend a weekend mingling with Dracula and his frightful accessories, described in this chapter. Other British oddities, including bizarre accommodation such as a static train hotel with a four-poster bedroom and restaurant in a stationary railway carriage, are described in the next chapter.

EXPERIENCING A MURDER WEEKEND

I went to a Southport hotel, one of many British venues, to sample a Murder Weekend where visitors act the part of house party guests, and try to solve a murder mystery. I arrived early one Friday evening and sneaked down to see a room laid out ready for a banquet.

Later, arriving at the appointed hour for the 'surprise dinner for the Huntley Ruby Wedding' I was greeted at the door by the lady organising the evening who asked me, 'Have you come far to Southport?'

'Yes, I travelled up from London,' I said, adding smugly, 'I'm the only one who arrived early enough for a sauna.'

'And how do you know my mother-in-law, Lady Huntley?' she continued.

I was momentarily disconcerted, not expecting to be plunged straight into a character role without warning.

'Er – my mother met her in the South of France,' I said. I had not fabricated a complicated story, despite the letter which had arrived two weeks previously telling me to wear red on night one, a fancy dress on the theme of British Heritage on night two, and be a character at a surprise Ruby Wedding party for Lord and Lady Huntley.

Reading the table plan I saw that the 'Huntleys' were seated at other tables. I found myself sitting next to a young man named Derek. On the other side of him was a murder weekend addict, who told us that on his previous murder weekend dinner he had chatted up a young lady sitting next to him but she was killed off before he had a chance to date her!

After dinner there was a quiz. Then disco music started. A couple of older people went to bed early but I waited, because a murder was sure to take place the first evening. Fortunately I wasn't particularly enamoured of Derek, because a few minutes later there was a loud bang and Derek fell off the chair beside me – shot dead!

Two 'Ambulance Men' carried the body out on a stretcher and an 'Inspector' arrived. He called everyone Sir, or Madam, even a couple of 12 and 14 year old boys who had asked their parents to bring them on the weekend. The Inspector asked me what Derek had said to me, then the boys questioned me. They took the sleuthing terribly seriously, making mensa-style notes, and all the guests started questioning each other. The boys did not believe my real name, Angela Lansbury, nor that I was a writer and had just published a book on Etiquette (true). It sounded too unlikely!

Next morning was supposed to be free time but they regretted 'that due to the unexpected death' of Mr G we would be required in the Incident Room at 10 am. (This left me just a very brief time to see Southport's sandy beach, promenade, and elegant shopping arcades.)

At breakfast I found the only spare seat was opposite the 'Police Inspector' who like the other actors remained 'in character' throughout the weekend, and I was forced to make polite conversation as if he were a real policeman. I did my best and said truthfully: 'I was so taken aback last night that I stared at the victim instead of looking round to try and find the gunman.' It is interesting to discover what might actually happen in a real murder situation.

Throughout the day on the walls of the Incident Room more and more pieces of evidence appeared – newspaper cuttings, Huntley family letters, and photographs. We also played house party games, chasing round after clues hidden in various parts of the hotel.

During the hotel lunch, again the Huntley family were distributed around the room. Various family arguments took place suddenly at table between Huntley husbands and wives, or in the corridor between Huntley parents and children making accusations against each other.

After lunch the Inspector called us to the drawing room where tea was served. Another guest remarked to me how awkward it was when you tried to hold a conversation with someone who suddenly started playing a character part. I could not reply because gracious 'Lady Huntley' sat down next to me and started sipping tea. A pregnant member of the Huntley family had a row with her husband in one corner. She started gasping, presumably having a baby – we weren't quite sure. She was carried off. Later we were told she had died! Another murder. (The four-star hotel had a couple of other conferences, and all this coming and going of dead bodies caused quite a gathering of puzzled crowds in the hall.)

I shared the lift down on Saturday night's fancy dress party with a young married couple dressed as bride and groom, Lady Di – and Prince Charles with a huge pair of ears!

A Belgian wore a bowler hat and pinstripe suit. An American tourist dressed as a monk. And another 'monk' wore a Reagan face on the back of his head, attracting comments that he was 'two-faced'. The American monk improvised an amusing grace before the dinner, 'I'm not used to partaking of such grand meals but I thank the Lord and ask him to help us solve this mystery – and all the other mysteries in our lives. Amen.'

After dinner we had a lively quiz game with inter-table rivalry, then, inevitably, another member of the Huntley family dropped dead. The dead body was carried off, followed by the assorted members of the fancy dress party who went through the hotel hall again. Several puzzled members of another Saturday night dinner came out to see what was going on!

I listened to a man making advances to one of the actresses, who told him to get lost. I grinned at them and took notes, assuming this was part of the plot. Later I realised it wasn't!

Sunday morning I woke to find a letter under the door telling me to fill in my guesses as to who had committed the murder, and to assemble after breakfast to hear the Inspector's verdict. During breakfast we argued about which of the Huntleys was the murderer – except those sitting at tables where the Huntleys were eating. I filled in my form.

At the final meeting the Inspector told us that we had all behaved callously throughout the weekend, laughing when murders had taken place in our midst, consistently told him lies throughout the weekend – which caused a lot more laughter, amongst everyone except the bereaved family who stayed in character, comforting each other. The Inspector said that whilst we had been at dinner the night before, all our bedrooms had been searched!

Perfectly straight-faced, he accused a charming elderly American couple of not being married to each other, but having met at Euston station. He claimed that the Birmingham group of friends had all swapped wives on night one, and that the men had slept with each other on night two!

He then went on to analyse how each of the Huntley family had reason to commit murder. Hilarity turned to silence as he described how different members of the family had lost children and parents in the Falklands or Auschwitz. We were silent and tense as the denouement came.

The murderer was accused and, as I had anticipated, the weekend ended with a final drama as the real murderer was set upon by another hysterical member of the Huntley family. A last dramatic exit was made before the actors returned to applause.

Those who had guessed who committed the murder, giving reasons, were also applauded. I was absurdly proud to receive a certificate!

The actors, like the guests, were a mixture of ages and backgrounds, mostly extroverts, some connected with amateur dramatics or teaching. Several guests travelled with sisters, family or friends. Most people make the fancy dress but train travellers can hire bulky costumes like crinolines at the destination. I caught the train back to Euston from Southport reliving the events with two other girls – one a computer operations teacher, another a nurse. If you're alone as I was it's great fun – and you get to know lots of new people. The nurse said, 'at least you think you know them!'

Booking details
Price: the cost is £110–140 including dinner and bed and breakfast Friday and Saturday, and Saturday lunch, morning coffee and afternoon tea. Each bedroom has a bath or shower and coffee maker. We had virtually all day entertainment and small prizes such as sticks of rock in competitions. The only extras were wine and alcoholic drinks. Similar weekends are held by Quality Inns at Chester, Scarborough, Harrogate and Windermere. The plot, which is devised by Joy Swift (who acts one of the parts), with the help of the other actors, changes every few weeks. She has also organised murder weekends in Brighton and the USA.

Brochure address:
Quality International, Piccadilly House, 33 Regent Street, London SW1Y 4NB, tel: 01-439 4955. Toll-free reservations: 0 800 44 44 44.

Joy Swift stages more Murder weekends at: *The North British Hotel, Edinburgh, tel: 031-556 2414; the Crest Hotel, South Mimms, tel: 0707 43311; Marsham Court Hotel, Bournemouth, tel: 0202 22111;* and *Renvyle House Hotel, Connemara, tel: 95 43434.*

Two appropriate and interesting settings are *The Manor House Hotel, Devon, tel: 0647 40355* where the 1930s version of Hound of the Baskerville's was filmed; and *Burgh Island, Bigbury-on-Sea, tel: 0548 810514,* the Agatha Christie location which is described in the first chapter.

Henllys Hall, Beaumaris, Anglesey, Gwynedd, North Wales, tel: 0248 810412, has held many offbeat weekends including Welsh love-ins in four-poster beds and Agatha Christie weekends.

ENCOUNTERS WITH DRACULA

Bedroom mirrors were half obscured by sheets of white paper with red crosses drawn upon them when apprehensive guests arrived in Scarborough, Yorkshire (where Bram Stoker wrote Dracula) to sample the first 'Dracula Weekend'. It was held at the Crown Quality Hotel in June 1986.

A small wooden crucifix, garlic, and a wooden 'stake' the size of a pencil (its point encased in red 'blood') waited on guests' pillows. A letter from the general manager, John Tiscornia, warned that 'the management is worried about your safety. So for your protection please keep them with you at all times.'

Downstairs in the bar guests got a bloody cocktail, and met genial Robert Leake, Honorary Secretary of the Dracula Society, who just happens to be seven foot tall!

'Are there many parts for a seven foot actor?' I enquired. 'No, but there aren't many people auditioning for them, either,' he replied. A disembodied voice on the Tannoy announced, 'You may think you have just drunk an innocent cocktail . . .'

Guests included a member of the Dracula Society (who also belonged to the Sherlock Holmes Society), a lady who had won the holiday as a prize in a Debenhams department store, other paying guests, plus several journalists representing radio, television, *Woman's Realm* magazine, *Northern Echo* (me) and *Today* newspapers.

As late as Friday afternoon Wendy Tindall, Sales Manager, Marian Edge, Quality International Hotels PR, and Robert Leake, had gone into Whitby's joke shop where Wendy spotted false fingers which she decided to put in the ghoulash served for dinner.

Black bats swayed in the dining room. Plastic fangs rested on every butter plate. And two squeaking black rats were concealed under folded table napkins. But I didn't hear mine squeak – I shrieked so loudly.

During dinner silent Dracula movies were screened on the video. Suddenly the lights dimmed, strobes flashed on the balcony above, and Dracula appeared in a flash of lighting. Some people screamed, while everybody else gaped, then fumbled for cameras and fixed on the flashguns – too late!

After dinner we watched a documentary film about Dracula,

shot on location in Romania, narrated by Dracula actor Christopher Lee.

As well as fangs and cloaks for pure fun, Wendy Tindall wanted a mixture of literary interest, provided by Robert Leake, whose society is rather serious about the history of Dracula. Listeners giggled as Robert read a factual account of author Bram Stoker's life, and his association with actor Sir Henry Irving. Robert and Wendy had spent a lot of time researching, starting with the Whitby Dracula Trail leaflet.

On the Saturday morning coach trip to Whitby, where Leake's society has encouraged the placing of plaques to Dracula, participants heard a recording of Bram Stoker's Count Dracula story revealing that the author was a master of suspense.

At Whitby's Dracula Museum, which opened in Easter 1986, manager Arthur Fry said, 'I'm Dracula's keeper, but it's no good taking a photo of me. I don't come out on film.'

A crab lunch was served at the haunted Smuggler's Inn, oldest inn in Whitby, because Stoker had a nightmare about Dracula after eating dressed crab.

Visitors bought books on Dracula at Caedmon's bookshop, chocolate orange fudge at Justin fudge and toffee maker, and climbed the steps up to romantic ruined Whitby Abbey.

Back in Scarborough, Hilary's Sewing Workshop hired out a dozen fancy dress costumes at under £10 each plus £5 deposit. And Hilary sold mouth imitation mouth blood capsules (you bite them and drip 'blood') at only 5p each.

The Saturday evening meal was served on coffin shaped tables, designed with the aid of the Theatre in the Round's production manager, Geoff Keys. (The Crown Hotel has arranged theatre packages for Scarborough's celebrated theatre, which is run by the famous dramatist Alan Ayckbourn). Black balloons swayed over the tables and everybody jumped whenever one of them hit a candle and went pop.

Guests wearing 'The clothes you would like to be buried in' appeared as Frankenstein (Robert Leake), a nun (Wendy – 'This is becoming a 'habit',' she said, posing for yet another photograph), and twins dressed as a pair of hunchbacks of Notre-Dame.

On chilly Sunday morning we toured haunted Scarborough

in an open-topped bus in swirling sea mist. Standing shivering, surveying Anne Bronte's grave, we all thought we would expire in Scarborough as she did.

At haunted Smugglers Museum, where the bodies of drowned sailors used to be laid out, the floorboards creaked and a dresser supporting a vase rocked up and down as we walked past. It has associations with sailors who went to America.

We photographed hilltop Scarborough Castle ruins, sat around the well listening to stories of the three ghosts, and went back to the hotel for a hot lunch of traditional roast beef and Yorkshire pudding.

Winners of the fancy dress competition, a quiz about Dracula, and the writer of the best short horror story, received copies of Dracula, signed by a bearded Bram Stoker look-alike actor, a fitting end to a 'frightful' weekend.

Press releases from Quality International and The British Tourist Authority went to the USA and an interview was syndicated to 800 US radio stations. Count Dracula Fan Club, New York, and Vampire Quarterly in New Jersey mailed members. And the Danish Vampire Society planned to come over to England – Danes in Drac.

So make a note of the next Dracula weekend: it costs about £90 per person, and is held at intervals through the year. Readers wishing to scare friends or enemies should phone *0723 373491* or contact:
Quality International, Piccadilly House, 33 Regent Street, London SW1Y 4NB, tel: 01-439 4955.

A television programme about Dracula was made at *Raven Hall Hotel, Ravenscar, Scarborough, North Yorkshire YO13 0ET, tel: 0723 870353.*

British Rail trains run from King's Cross to Scarborough (change at York). The clifftop Crown Hotel (some front bedrooms have good sea views) is a five minute walk uphill so I suggest sharing a taxi.

One last piece of advice – watch out for Dracula knocking on your hotel bedroom door! And ladies, don't forget to leave Scarborough late in the day for London. Count Dracula travelled on the 9.30 am train from Whitby to King's Cross!

CHAPTER 7
Odder Places for Eating and Sleeping

Leaving aside Murder and Dracula, there are a host of rather strange venues for that quiet meal or stopover.

The Black Bull Railway Restaurant (Richmond, North Yorkshire)
On your return to London from the north, about one mile from the Scotch Corner motorway junction, you will get lost along country lanes looking for the Black Bull Inn at Moulton, near Richmond, North Yorkshire. Do persist. It serves smoked salmon at lunchtime. Better still, go there for dinner, because in the evenings they open the adjoining railway carriage which once formed part of the old London to Brighton train, the Brighton Belle. Spinach soufflé is on the dinner menu.
Black Bull Inn, Moulton, near Richmond, North Yorkshire, tel: (032 577) 289.

Railway Carriage Hotel & Restaurant (The Sidings, York)
The world's first hotel and restaurant made up of five restored railway carriages (two make up the 90-seater restaurant, and three the bedrooms) is at Shipton-by-Beningbrough, five miles north of York on the London to Edinburgh railway line, ten minutes from York by road. Eight twin bedrooms in the wood-panelled carriages have private showers and television. One bedroom is fitted out as a honeymoon suite complete with a pine four-poster bed.

In the luxurious Pullman style carriages restaurant you can try English fare such as roast Duckling Flying Scotsman, Russian egg with smoked salmon and caviar, and fresh vegetables. Taped train noises are played in the restaurant, and passing drivers on the four railway lines running parallel toot as they pass.

The meal can be followed by coffee and liqueurs in the 'signal box'. The Sidings is filled with railway paintings, signs and nameplates. This venture fulfils the lifelong ambition of retired railwayman Bert Gemmell, who started on the railways at the age of 14 and retired in 1979 as Director of Public Affairs.

During the day you can play with the model railway and signal equipment or visit York. Railway enthusiasts could combine a stay in The Sidings with a trip to the National Railway Museum in York, or the North York Moors Railway and the Yorkshire Dales Railway.

Non-residents can eat à la carte or choose a set dinner at about £15 per person. One night's dinner, bed and breakfast in a twin bedroom (about twice the size of a normal sleeper compartment) costs a little over £55 for two, and in the four-poster under £70 for two including dinner and breakfast. For more information contact:
Bert Gemmell, The Sidings, Shipton-by-Beningbrough, York YO6 1B, tel: 0904 470221.

Railway Carriage Restaurant (The Marsden Rattler, Tyne & Wear)
While on a Catherine Cookson weekend we passed along the seafront and saw this restaurant in a railway carriage.
The Marsden Rattler, Sea Road, South Foreshore, South Shields, Tyneside, tel: 091 4553279/091 455 6789.

A little further along is a cave restaurant with a dramatic entrance and lift shaft.

Cave Restaurant & Bar (Marsden Grotto, Tyne & Wear)
A lift for which a small charge is made takes patrons from the clifftop to the public bar of The Grotto in a cave on the Marsden Bay beach. The lift which has an attendant operates only during opening hours. Going down the cliff steps takes five minutes. Climbing up, somewhat tipsy after closing time, takes what seems like five hours.

Although the limestone cliffs are naturally eroded these caves are man-made. Romans quarried here. A miner is said to have lived in the caves in the eighteenth century and in the mid nineteenth century a gamekeeper converted the dwelling into fifteen rooms and then into a cavern tavern.

Odder Places for Eating and Sleeping

Above the cave bar is the restaurant with a view over the bay. In the sea ahead of you is Marsden Rock, a one hundred feet high rock looking rather like a jagged Arc De Triomphe, with rows of little beaks pointing in the air, a seabird sanctuary supporting gulls, colonies of cormorants and other birds.

The cave is supposed to be haunted by the voice of a smuggler who tried, but failed, to betray a smuggling excursion to the excise men. You can hear the story if you take a Smugglers' Walk tour organised by Catherine Cookson Country. Contact: *Hazel Gray, tel: 0632 554321.*
The Grotto Public House, Marsden Bay, South Shields, Tyne & Wear, NE England, tel: 091 455 2043.

Four-poster Bar (Queen's Head Hotel, Lake District)
And there is a four-poster bed bar at the Queen's Head Hotel in the Lake District. Confusingly, the area has more than one pub called the Queen's Head, but you can stop at this one as you drive up the Troutbeck valley on the road from Windermere to Ullswater. You can amuse yourselves asking local people if they can recall the words of the old jolly folksong about fox-hunting, 'Do you ken John Peel with his coat so gay, he lived at Troutbeck once upon a day . . . diddy dum, diddy dum diddy . . . far, far away . . . from a view to a death in the morning.'

Four-poster on a Boat (Caprice afloat in Suffolk)
The luxury 32 foot cruiser, Caprice, is equipped with a four-poster bed and bathroom en suite. The cost for this two-person holiday is around £305 a week in high season, £185 in low season. The love boat is Hoseasons most romantic river cruise for 'messing about in boats', as you will remember Ratty recommended in 'Wind in the Willows'.

The Caprice is popular in high season. If you cannot get a booking additional luxury and less expensive boats can be hired on the Norfolk Broads, on the Thames near Stratford, as far north as Inverness in Scotland, and west near Llangollen in Wales.

Details of the Caprice and other boats are in Hoseasons brochure. They also supply a map of pubs on the canal routes. *Hoseasons Holidays Ltd, Sunway House, Lowestoft, Suffolk, NR32 3LT, tel: 0502 87373 dial-a-brochure, or tel: 0502 62271* for bookings. The US agent is *Camp Coast to Coast, 860 Solar Building, 1000 16th Street NW, Washington DC 20036, USA, tel: 202 466 6377.*

Riverside Pubs (along the Thames)
The Nicholson Ordnance Survey guide to the River Thames gives details of interesting riverside pubs including converted warehouses such as the *Samuel Pepys, 48 Upper Thames Street, London EC4, tel: 01-248 3048.*

Pubs with boats and nautical themes are described in this guidebook and it gives details of excursions along the Thames covering London, Hampton Court, Henley, Maidenhead, Windsor and Oxford. It has small print but is a very useful book for tracking down pubs when you remember the location but not the exact address. Similar guides cover other waterways. However, if you want a canal boat holiday with someone else organising your pub visit for you, this can be done.

British Boats for Eccentric Canal Cruises (Central England)
British Eccentric Cruises are organised by UK Waterways Holidays Ltd for parties of 2-8, lasting a week on board in the summer season, with two extra nights ashore. The five eccentric activities are an English Pub Visit, Ghosthunting, Morris Dancing, Bowls, and Tea At A Stately Home.

English Pub visits to a canalside pub are arranged. Your group leader can be elected landlord, pull the pints, and at closing time call 'Time, Ladies and Gentlemen, please' and ask people in the pub to return their glasses. Pubs chosen have weekend sing-songs, serve traditional ale from hand-pumps, and local teams which will challenge you to a game of pool or darts.

On a Ghosthunting cruise you are met by a psychic enthusiast who tells you spooky stories. Then you listen for ghostly shuffling footsteps of the former theatre director who wore slippers and was found dead in a room at the haunted Alexandra Theatre in Birmingham. Or look for a lady in black rustling along the ramparts at the haunted Elizabethan castle, Hartshill.

Aristocrats at Stately Homes welcome visitors, teach them to play croquet, and serve tea or sherry. Dinner can also be

Staff at Chilston Park, Kent (page 17)

Great Fosters, Surrey (page 83)

Burgh Island (page 13) [Photo: John Adrian]

Palm Court lounge at Burgh Island (page 13) [Photo: John Adrian]

Last Drop Village, Lancashire (page 23)

Flambards, Cornwall (page 183)

Odder Places for Eating and Sleeping

arranged if required. Settings are stone-built Swalcliffe Manor in Oxfordshire which has a Tudor Hall, Longdon Manor, and Stanford Hall where your host is Lt Col Aubrey Fletcher.

Prices for these various canal cruises are from £305, including a self-drive car from your airport to a hotel near the boatyard, a starter pack of food on board featuring British specialities, a cassette tape guide, the last night's hotel accommodation and a car for return to the airport. Train connections can be arranged instead for non-drivers.

Other cruises offered are Photography Cruises (you will be passing aqueducts and locks); Nature Canal Cruises, including nature trails; and History Canal Cruises, stopping at Stratford, Offa's Dyke, or Guy Fawkes' house. Cruise routes include Birmingham to Worcester and Stourbridge, Llangollen Canal, Oxford and Ashby Canal, Rugby to Stratford-upon-Avon.

Contact: *UK Waterway Holidays, Penn Place, Rickmansworth, Herts, WD3 1EU, England.* Booking office hotline in England, *tel: 0923 770040.*

Water Tower Self-catering Holiday (Cornwall)

The National Trust's water tower in Cornwall is a tall stone building rising to a conical roof with small arched windows. One room is on each floor, bathroom on the ground floor, lounge above that, kitchen on the third floor. It is pictured in their Cornish Holiday Cottages booklet. Contact the caretaker, *Mrs E Taylor, 14 Elm Grove, Feock, Truro, tel: Truro 865291.*

Bookings are for a minimum of one week self-catering, two weeks in high season, and National Trust members are allowed to start booking earlier in the year than the public.
The National Trust Regional Office, Lanhydrock Park, Bodmin, Cornwall PL30 4DE, tel: Bodmin 3880 (24 hrs) for provisional booking.

Artillery Tower Restaurant (Plymouth, Devon)

For an unusual evening out in Plymouth try the Artillery Tower Restaurant.

The waterside Artillery Tower is a crenellated octagonal limestone building, the small battlement roof terrace a superb setting in the right weather, says one of their leaflets. I don't know whether they mean for afternoon tea or sunset cocktails, but that was exactly what I thought when I saw it.

The tower is one mile from Plymouth city centre with waterfront views across the Sound to Drake's Island and Mount Edgcumbe. You glimpse it at a distance from passing boat rides on afternoon pleasure trips around the naval dockyards.

It is reputedly the oldest building in the city, constructed in about 1487. You first notice the stone, and the pointed arched windows, sometimes blocked by shutters. Upstairs there is a murder hole over the door. 'Useful for pouring boiling oil over enemy forces or unwelcome visitors,' comments owner Chris Neal humorously – 'such as late night drunks.'

Behind the bar is the original toilet in an alcove, wine bottles above the old seat. 'It was called a garderobe or wall closet, and it discharged into the sea,' explains Chris, 'when the tide was in, otherwise over passers-by!'

They serve shark steaks, and meals end with a bottomless coffee pot, which they say Americans expect. Meals average about £15 a head, ranging from £20 to £80 for two depending on what food and drink you order. Through 1987, which was the 500th birthday of the Armada, they were giving away one bottle of champagne every lunchtime and evening – 500 bottles to celebrate 500 years.

From the upper gun deck, seating about 25, a stone stair curves around the outside wall to the lower Gun Deck, seating about 30 for private functions.

You must book. My large group couldn't get in on Saturday night.

Artillery Tower Restaurant, Firestone Bay, Devil's Point, Durnford Street, Plymouth, PL1 3QR tel: Plymouth 667276 for reservations.

Chapel Pub (Plymouth, Devon)
An unusual stop going to or from the Artillery Tower would be a photograph or drink at the little Old Chapel pub on the corner of a road nearby. As you can see from the circular windows it is a converted chapel. The good God won't mind if you sip just one glass – a communion cup is permitted.

Chapel Public House, Devonport, Plymouth, c/o Ushers Brewery Ltd, Marshal Road, Cot Hill, Plympton, Plymouth, tel: 0752 339546.

Odder Places for Eating and Sleeping

Smallest Telephone Box Bar (Huddersfield, Yorkshire)
The Phone Kiosk Wine bar is pictured in the Guinness Book of Records as the smallest bar in the world. It stands in the Huddersfield Hotel, and was granted a licence despite being unable to comply with the Health Department requirement that it had to have two sinks and with the fire service asking them to provide an alternative means of escape!

Don't worry about whether they have enough stock of drink. The hotel has eight bars. To find the kiosk go to the middle of the beer garden. Other bars include the wine bar and the jungle bar with leopard skin walls, tigers' heads projecting from the wall and bamboo furniture. Upstairs there is a piano bar.

The hotel is used as a base by groups visiting the scene of the TV series 'Last of the Summer Wine', taking in the scenery and the Wrinkled Stocking Cafe in Holmfirth. Johnny's disco is another attraction in the hotel. And if it's your birthday they'll play a recording of happy birthday and present you with a piece of gateau bearing a sparkler.

This two star hotel is en route to Leeds, Bradford and York, via Knaresbrough where a cave petrifies hanging objects, turning bowler hats into solid stalactites.

Apart from drinking real ale, you can try out the hotel's spa bath and sauna, or stay in one of the two recently installed oak four-poster beds.
Huddersfield Hotel & Rosemary Lane Bistro, Johnny's Bar and Barrel Inn, Johnny's Night Club, 37-41 Kirkgate, Huddersfield, West Yorkshire, HD1 1QT, tel: 0484 512111.

Pub Dogs (Somerset)
Some people say the charm of the English pub is the characters you meet. Esther Rantzen's television programme featured the Soda Syphon Alsatians which put their paws on the bar and drink soda syphoned through the air into their jaws. Meet them at *The George Hotel, Castle Cary, Somerset, tel: 0963 50761.*

Sadie, the dog which shakes hands with you, is mentioned in Chapter 12 on royalty.

CHAPTER 8
Haunted Hotels

A natural step from the interest in bizarre breaks is the British interest in haunted homes. Now for some wonderful haunted hotels, a haunted castle, a haunted abbot's house and some haunted inns.

Lord Crewe Arms Hotel (Northumberland)
Within a remote walled village square is a former Abbot's house, Lord Crewe Arms, now a small, quiet, personally run hotel. The gently sloping hills of the Durham Dales were darkening as we drove through a stone gateway into the deserted square of Blanchland. The name means white land, recalling the white habits of the 12th century religious order. We stopped before the haunted Lord Crewe Arms Hotel.

Your footsteps echo like those of medieval travellers as you enter the atmospheric empty stone hall where a log fire crackles. A corridor leads to another stone hall, now a lounge which has a further grand empty fireplace with inviting wood-backed seating beneath it. Under the arch is a stone chimney stack rising three storeys high. Overhead, half way up, is a secret stone ledge supporting a rocking chair, marked: 'REPUTED PRIEST-HOLE'.

This is the ancient Priest's Hole where Jacobites took refuge during the 1715 rebellion. Tom Forster, leader of the local Jacobites in the uprising, hid in the house, presumably here.

The delightful dining room overlooks the garden and church through gothic arched windows. Proprietor Mr Oretti greeted everyone and explained that two of the medieval portraits in the dining room are of the former owner of the house, the Bishop of Durham, and his young wife, Dorothy Forster I. Her nephew Thomas led the local Jacobite rebellion of 1715.

It is Tom's sister, Dorothy II, who supposedly haunts the hotel. When he was captured, she rescued her brother from

London's Newgate Prison in time-honoured fashion, disguised as a servant, using duplicate keys. She brought him back here and shipped him overseas to safety.

Beyond the TV lounge is the reputedly haunted Dorothy Forster bedroom. Is it really haunted? 'I am a coward,' admitted smiling Mr Oretti. 'I have never slept there – in case it isn't!' The room has a draped headboard, shower cubicle, and a rocking chair by the window overlooking the church. This was the abbot's bedroom about 1235.

Our bedroom had an en suite bathroom with a bidet. Below our bedroom was another romantic room with a draped headboard, and a corner bath. We got talking to the occupants in the stone vaults of the underground Crypt bar (circa 1235) and they kindly showed us their bedroom and corner bath.

Before leaving we saw a further bedroom which has a four-poster bed and 300 year old antiques. The tariff for double rooms with bath, and special rooms, is over £55, with the annexe rooms at the lower prices. A two or more day breakaway (available weekdays nearly all year – please check) is about the same per person per day sharing a double room but includes dinner.

Daylight reveals the pretty village green in the silent walled square, where for the two shops the arrival of a single walker or car is a major event – the noise echoing off the stone walls. The church next door can be explored. John Wesley visited Blanchland and preached in the churchyard.

If you want to stay here, contact *The Lord Crewe Arms Hotel, Blanchland, County Durham, tel: (043 475) 251.*

Lumley Castle Hotel (Tyne & Wear)
We next tried 13th century Lumley Castle where banners wave from the high walls. You park in a flower-filled courtyard with a goldfish pond and garden. Low modern converted mews 'courtyard' bedrooms surround you on three sides, the tall Norman castle with haunted bedrooms being on the fourth. If you stay in the cheaper modern rooms of the converted mews, you can have breakfast amid the ancient stone pillars of the dining room. But I recommend that you stay in the castle, preferably in one of the four-poster bedrooms, at a weekend when lively medieval banquets are held in the cellars.

You enter on foot through the inner grass courtyard, admiring the shields carved up on the towers. At night white fairy lights glow among the trees; and a Scottish piper plays on Fridays, Saturdays, and some weekday evenings as guests arrive for the medieval banquets held in the crypt below. (See Chapter 9 on medieval banquets.)

The singers were excellent, some of them being professional opera singers. The song about opening the chastity belt with 'duplicate keys' sounds uncannily authentic after having visited Blanchland. (See above.)

Breakfast and normal dinners are held in the dining room which is supported by massive stone pillars – like dining in a cathedral.

Stone corridors with a central carpet lead this way and that. The piped music intrudes in the dining room and ground floor corridors. Sometimes hidden speakers haunt you with appropriate folk or Scottish airs, though more often with totally incongruous twentieth century jolly band music. Gothic shape wooden doors open onto corridors and the spiral staircases. Echoing stone spiral staircases in turrets wind up to the higher floor bedrooms.

There's a giant Queen Anne four-poster in an eerie high-ceilinged room, a bedroom with a shower over the haunted well, or a room with an en-suite wood-panelled bathroom hidden behind the walls. Keep looking, and eventually you'll find the entrance!

Our first twin bedded room, number 51, was beautifully decorated with paintings. Ruched curtains matched the bedcovers and the edging material on the tablecloths. Thick white pile carpet was in the bedroom, thick towels in the bathroom.

But the four-poster bedrooms are truly amazing. In room 49 if you tread on the creaking floorboards in the middle of the room a potted plant a few feet away wobbles uncannily. The four-poster rooms are fully booked on Saturday but we obtained one by moving rooms on Sunday. Our second double bedroom, number 50, had a high carved wooden four-poster on a dais. This is the room with the hidden bathroom (see Chapter 3 on clean weekends).

The castle's resident spook, your ghostess, is the renowned Lily of Lumley, wife of one of the Lords of Lumley, who was thrown down the well by monks because she dallied with others while her husband was away at the wars. And she wanders the corridors to remind everyone in residence that she has not forgiven or forgotten.

The haunted room has a draped headboard and a weird corridor (formerly an old toilet) converted into a modern shower-room. You step across the shower to reach the toilet. Under the shower tray space was the toilet/well-shaft which the medieval lady was thrown down. The night porter apparently did the rounds one night, turning off lights left on in rooms, accompanied by a chef, and in this room which was supposed to be empty they saw what looked like a body lying in the bed! The chef retreated in a state of shock. Shortly afterwards the night porter went back and, so they say, found the bed empty. Being both sceptical and nervous, I imagined I was writing a whodunnit, and maybe the porter wanted to frighten the chef who . . .

The present owner of the castle is a lord who lives elsewhere, and as the lady was one of his ancestors, the receptionist says, he is not too keen on playing up the haunted aspects of the hotel. Isn't he? The hotel brochure has a mock-up picture of a ghost over the library cum bar. On Hallowe'en night a local disc jockey records his programme in the castle.

Lumley Castle's best bedroom, and most expensive, is the King James four-poster bedroom suite, number 47. It may cost a lot but many people think it's worth the price for the experience, and brides who have their reception at the hotel receive a reduction.

What do they get? A Queen Anne four-poster about 15 foot tall, with drapes that high, almost to the 20 foot gothic arched ceiling. Is this the tallest four-poster in the world? The thick pile wall-to-wall carpet makes the room as sensual and comfortable as it is old and romantic.

There's a separate lounge hall as you enter. Different doors lead to separate little rooms. Off the bedroom is one concealing a washbasin. The next door reveals the toilet and telephone. Off the lounge, you discover first the basin, then the opulent bathroom with a corner spa bath, mirrors on both sides and plum coloured tiling. All very luxurious. There's a colour picture of the four-poster in the hotel's brochure.

The King James room costs around £125 for two including English breakfast, other four-posters over £80, cheapest rooms about £60, and weekend breaks about £65 per night for two sharing a room, including dinner and English breakfast.
Lumley Castle Hotel, Chester-le-Street, County Durham, tel: (0385) 891111.

The Bull Hotel (Peterborough)
Another supposedly haunted hotel is the Bull Hotel, Peterborough. Ghosts of a dog and somebody left in a dungeon haunt the bar, the duty manager Andrew Thomas told me, as well as ghosts of members of staff from 20 or 30 years ago – staff ghosts still drinking, I presume.

Interesting objects are everywhere, scrollwork arches over doorways, plants in urns on pillars, plates hanging on the walls, painted brickwork, carved wood, and tiles. Numerous antique chairs such as a wooden bath chair are in the eighteenth century building which is warmly decorated in gold and brown. Paintings of Mary Queen of Scots, Charles II and others adorn the walls, and you can sleep in an oriental bedroom suite.
The Bull Hotel, Westgate, Peterborough, Cambridgeshire PE1 1RB, tel: (0733) 61364.

THREE HAUNTED INNS

The Berystede (Ascot, Berkshire)
The Berystede country house inn dating back to 1886, with some turret bedrooms, is haunted by the ghost of a lady's maid who searches for her lost jewels. So watch your diamonds, they say. It is only 25 miles from London, and a good centre for visiting Windsor Castle and Ascot race course.
The Berystede, Bagshott Road, Sunninghill, Ascot, Berkshire, SL5 9JH, tel: (0990) 23311.

The Angel (Guildford, Surrey)
'The Angel' inn at Guildford has wood panelling, beams, a 13th century crypt, and a wooden gallery supported by timbers from old ships. When the inn was restored in 1948 a priest's hole was found. One of the exposed beams was discovered to contain a

bullet. A guest who saw an apparition in the mirror of room 1, dressed in continental uniform of perhaps 100 years ago, 'had the presence of mind to sketch it' on a handy red serviette.
The Angel, High Street, Guildford, Surrey, GU1 3DR, tel: 0483 64555.

The Dolphin (Southampton, Hampshire)
At the Dolphin Inn, Southampton, a ghost floats through the room at 2 am about two feet above the floorboards, where the old stable blocks would have been in her day. The Georgian facade of the inn, renovated in 1751, has attractive semi-circular bay windows and is a famous point in the main street.
The Dolphin, High Street, Southampton, Hampshire SO9 2DS, tel: 0703 26178.

BRADFORD'S SUPERNORMAL WEEKEND

Bradford, the Yorkshire manufacturing city, planned their first Psychic Sightseeing weekend for Hallowe'en. The tour visits haunted Bolling Hall where a wailing ghost dissuaded the Earl of Newcastle from slaughtering the people of Bradford during the Civil War. This shows that a good ghost does nobody any harm. But to provide a few thrills and chills and teases, programmes will include fortune-telling, riddle-solving, a visit to a 32 acre cemetery – I hope you don't get lost, rune-spotting on moortop rocks, and a lecture by an expert in psychic phenomena.
Details from: *Northern Heritage Travel, Salem Street* (yes, Salem Street),*Bradford, Yorkshire, tel: 0274 737318,* or *Bradford Economic Development Unit, 2nd Floor, City Hall, Bradford, West Yorkshire BD1 1HY, tel: 0274 753785.*

CHAPTER 9
Medieval Costume Banquets

Costumed banquets can be found in every region. Welsh banquets are held with singers and harpists in Wales, Old England banquets in the dungeons of ancient castles, a Nottingham banquet in what looks like a tent with games involving audience participation, and Scottish banquets with kilted pipers in Edinburgh.

WALES
Swansea (South Wales)
The first costume banquet I attended was held in Wales in a grand hall where trestle tables were laid out and we sat on benches. The Master of Ceremonies introduced the ladies of the court wearing colourful costumes, and a harpist.

Then six 'volunteer' members of the audience were selected and taken outside. They returned dressed in costume and clogs. During the evening they helped serve the food and performed a clog dance for us – with more or less skill and unison, to the great amusement of the audience. I can tell you exactly what happened because I bought the cassette of the evening's entertainment and play it regularly in my car. The songs included such traditional Welsh items as 'Men of Harlech' and 'The Ashgrove' and a few words of the Welsh language. The 'Hwyrnos' banquet is now held in Swansea, just west of Cardiff. Booking office:

Hwyrnos, Green Dragon Lane, Swansea, Wales, tel: 0792 41437.

The Swansea banquet is more Victorian than medieval, though the candle-lit trestle tables and ladies in long dresses give all these banquets a common element.

Ruthin Castle (North Wales)
A Medieval Banquet held at Ruthin Castle was along similar

lines. But this one included local acts such as a man playing music on a saw using a violin bow, and two young boys dancing in clogs. On this occasion I took my son who was aged five. His table manners did not matter because we all had bibs around our necks to protect our clothes. We also ate with our fingers assisted by a dagger-style medieval knife from wooden platters.

Ruthin Castle in the centre of the small town of Ruthin has a wood panelled hall, the obligatory suit of armour on the stairs and a ghost. And you can spend a weekend there in a four-poster suite – used by two princes – touring other sights in North Wales. The castle is an independently owned hotel, a member of the Best Western group. Getaway break prices are from about £25 per night including an allowance towards dinner or the medieval banquet when available; the four-poster suite for two nights is approximately £71 in winter, £79 spring, £89 summer. *Ruthin Castle, Ruthin, Wales LL15 2NU, tel: 08242 2664. Best Western phone number in London is 01-541 0033 weekdays and Saturday morning.*

Cardiff Castle (South Wales)

In South Wales medieval banquets are held in the centre of the capital city of Cardiff at Cardiff Castle. The arched stone medieval vaults are the setting. The ladies sing in harmony, sometimes with the jester or master of ceremonies. One of the songs is a lovers' duet in which the lady resists advances for several verses.

Do look around the rest of the castle if you get a chance. Exotic, oriental, amazing – it has something for everyone – an Arab style turret room, a roof garden with Hebrew inscriptions, and medieval murals depicting classical characters, biblical and historical scenes.
Cardiff Castle, Cardiff, Wales, tel: 0222 372737.

Caldicot Castle (South Wales)

Caldicot Castle is a few miles north of Cardiff and you can drive out for the Saturday evening banquet as I did. Arriving at sunset you approach through the trees and the appearance of the castle is quite atmospheric. The banquet price is £12-18. Again, you can buy a cassette of the banquet songs and commentary afterwards as a souvenir – or even in advance, but then it

wouldn't be a surprise.
Caldicot Castle, near Newport, Gwent, Wales NP6 4HU, tel: 0291 421425.

OLDE ENGLAND (in the north)
Lumley Castle Elizabethan Banquet
In the north of England near the Scottish border you find Lumley Castle, an old hilltop Norman castle with battlements and banners flying. As you enter the central courtyard to join the medieval banquet you are greeted by a kilted piper playing music on the bagpipes.

Being wise to the fact that most of the guests sit on benches, I asked in advance for a chair with a back and this was provided. Banquet prices are cheaper than in London, wine is included, and 'no offence is given' even by the song about the lady separated from her lover because she is locked into a chastity belt, the key being lost, until she is rescued by the character who appears with a duplicate key!

If you want to stay at the castle there are several four-poster rooms with a bathroom, or shower room and ghost! This is my favourite hotel – with flagstones, spiral stone staircases, huge columns in the dining room, luxury bedrooms with thick carpets and antique furniture or modern mews rooms. See Chapter 8 on haunted hotels for more on Lumley Castle.

For hotel booking: *Lumley Castle, Chester-le-Street, Co. Durham, DH3 4NX, tel: 0385 885326;* for banquet, *tel: 0385 891111/ 883267.*

Victorian Leeds
Merrion Hotel, Leeds, has Saturday night Victorian evenings in the Starlet Restaurant. The à la carte menu offers Mother's Ruin, homemade tomato soup laced with gin and cream, Oyster Chowder – oyster soup blended with Guinness, as well as steak and kidney pudding.

Merrion Hotel, Merrion Centre, Leeds LS2 8NH, tel: 0532 439191.

Medieval Manor (Manchester)
Worsley Old Hall in Manchester is a black and white timber-

frame 16th century manor house with gables and decorative brick chimneys. It holds a Jacobean Banquet in the candlelit baron's hall – a four course feast including wholemeal bread, spare ribs, and chicken, accompanied by red wine and Lindisfarne mead, a honey-based alcoholic drink made originally by monks in the north of England. Food is served on earthenware bowls in the Great Hall where Sir Thomas Egerton, Keeper of the Great Seal of Queen Elizabeth I, would similarly have dined. Again, there is a cassette of the songs and jokes.
Worsley Old Hall, Old Hall Lane, Worsley, Manchester M28 4GT, tel: 061 799 5015.

The same company which organises the banquets at Caldicot Castle, Lumley Castle, and Worsley Hall, also has a medieval banquet at *Dalhousie Courte, Edinburgh, Scotland, tel: 031 633 5155* (£12–18 for four courses) and another at Coombe Abbey near Coventry.

Moated Coombe Abbey has been associated with Lady Jane Grey, the Gunpowder Plot and the English Civil War. The four course candlelit banquet ends with apple crumble. *Coombe Abbey, Brinklow Road, Binley, Near Coventry CV3 2AD, (advance booking essential, tel: Coventry 452406).*

Nottingham's Merrie England
The Nottingham Medieval Banquet, held in a basement room with a tented roof, is different. All the guests are in medieval dress. The most convenient bit is that a costume hire company visits the hotel and for only under £10, and no nuisance of collecting or delivering costumes from the hire shop, you can have a medieval costume for the evening. They do try to persuade you by telling you that you'll be eating with your fingers, and you're better off messing up the hire costume than spending time and money having your own clothes cleaned. Other hire companies charge £15 or more, depending on the costume, and a deposit, so it's good value.

So almost the entire audience is in authentic costume. Take your camera and flash, because they don't have a photographer there.

Knights enter carrying candles. The Knights banter with the Lord who sits in the centre of the top table, and they encourage rivalry between the two main tables. There's a sword fight. I liked the audience participation. They asked for a volunteer to sit in the stocks. A little boy did so and later he was released and rewarded with a key ring.

Half a dozen volunteers have to race round the room, under the portcullis, over hurdles, riding a wooden hobby horse, take a drink, and wait for a girl dressed as Maid Marion in a tall wimple hat to pop up and say, 'Help me! Help me!' and then kiss her.

Each volunteer is a different character with a hat. The last one is the girl's own husband. And when he gets there she says, 'Help me! Help me!' from behind the chest, but when the hat pops up and he goes to kiss her there's a man in a beard wearing the maiden's hat!

Stakis Victoria Hotel, Milton Street, Nottingham, Nottinghamshire, England NG1 3PZ, tel: (0602) 419561.

STATELY HOMES

Several stately homes serve banquets to groups in sumptuous surroundings and suggest hotels where you can stay nearby.

Hatfield's History Show

The Old Palace, Hatfield Park, Hatfield, Herts AL9 5NE, tel: 07072 62055, is within reach of London, opposite British Rail's Hatfield station. The five course menu and show costs approximately £17 to £20 according to the day of the week. One show is Elizabethan, and another takes you through the ages with characters dressed as Henry VIII, Elizabeth I, Charles I, and diarist Pepys. The music is played on period instruments such as harpsichords and lutes.

Twelve different menus are offered on different nights, so you might have a main course of rabbit, venison, or pheasant. If you want to celebrate your birthday there as American friends of mine did at a banquet taking you through history, there is a birthday spot when anyone with a birthday is presented to Queen Elizabeth I.

Frames Tours, tel: 01-837 3111, and *Evan Evans, tel: 01-930 2377,* run coaches from various pickup points.

Medieval Costume Banquets

Warwick Castle celebrates 'our most glorious victory at Agincourt' with the Receiver General, minstrels, a jester, and servants who present broth, ribs of sheep, roast fowl, and lemon syllabub. Advance booking is essential.
Warwick Castle, Warwick, CV34 4QU, tel: Warwick 495421.

Leeds Castle in Kent offers six course dinners with entertainment, £18–£24.
Leeds Castle, Maidstone, Kent, tel: 0622 65400.

THE ARTHURIAN CONNECTION

Wessex Hotel (Somerset)
King Arthur weekends begin with a banquet at the Wessex Hotel in Street, Somerset. This three star hotel is near the Shoe Museum at the Clark's factory in the High Street. For details of future banquets contact:
The Wessex Hotel, High Street, Street, nr. Glastonbury, Somerset, tel: 0458 43383.
The Arthurian Adventure weekend package is bookable through *Rainbow Mini Holidays, Ryedale Building, Piccadilly, York YO1 1PN, tel: 0904 643355.*

Leaflets on following the King Arthur trail, and sampling A Taste of Somerset – local Cheddar cheese and cider, and weekend breaks in a thatched building or castle hotel, from: *Somerset Tourism, County Hall, Taunton, Somerset TA1 4DY, tel: 0823 73451.*

LONDON

Singalong Suppers, Cockney and Scottish evenings
In central London there are several singalong suppers. A Shakespeare Feast introduces jugglers, jesters, magicians and duellers during a five course feast held every night of the week. Knights and wenches supply continuous entertainment in Blackfriars Lane. A similar evening in the vaults of Ivory House Beefeater Club by the Tower of London includes the character Henry VIII.

The Cockney Club cabaret and music hall in Charing Cross Road's theatreland presents a pearly King and Queen (wearing traditional costume of clothes covered with pearl buttons), Honky Tonk piano music and a four course Cockney dinner.

If you would like to sample a Scottish evening without going all the way to Scotland there's a Scotch whisky reception followed by a 5 course Scottish banquet, ceremony of the haggis, complete with tartans and pipes – kilts supplied free to Men of Courage.

More information and reservations for all these from: *tel: 01-408 1001*. Prices are from about £25 per person.

Edwardian Piano
If you want the freedom to eat à la carte, and turn up any night of the week without booking, though booking is often advisable, try Flanagan's, at 100 Baker St, London W1, a restaurant with Edwardian piano entertainment. Make up your own table of four or six friends and sing along with the songs. Songsheets are handed out so you can join in with the words of Roll out the Barrel, or Cockles and Mussels Alive, Alive-O, and the pianist will play requests. Sawdust is on the wood floor and the girls who serve wear straw hats. *Tel: 01-935 0287 or 01-935 1053. Flanagan's, 11 Kensington High St, London W8, tel: 01-937 2519*, is similar.

BOOKINGS

Many of the above organisations can offer you medieval banquets or singalong suppers on additional nights for business companies, weddings or other private functions.

Please check all prices before booking. They may vary according to the time of the year, and the day of the week. Also sometimes discounts or free places are offered for group bookings.

PART III

The Taste of Tradition

CHAPTER 10
Olde Worlde Hotels

Stone spiral staircases create the chill of olden times, while timber-framed Elizabethan buildings have the warmth of colourful Tudor England. Nowadays hotels keep old restaurants candle-lit but carpeted and cosy. The nostalgia for the bygone Elizabethan era and buildings is not new. The olde worlde was nostalgically recreated in Victorian times by Chester's dramatic black and white buildings.

England's thatched cottages are equally picturesque from the outside, though people who live in them complain of insects. In England, Scotland and Wales castle hotels offer grand staircases and spooky suits of armour making you and your bank balance feel rather small. But the medieval black and white building is the easiest olde worlde setting to locate in every town. Here is a selection of olde worlde hotels, inns and pubs, starting with two older stone buildings with spiral staircases.

SPIRAL STAIRCASES AND OLD STONES
Llanthony Abbey Hotel (South Wales)
The romantic arched ruins of Llanthony Abbey were silhouetted

against the evening sky as we drove towards it through the remote darkening green Welsh hills. We stopped in the stillness where sheep grazed by the 12th century abbey, converted into a hotel.

The only remaining tower has a spiral stone staircase leading to two four-poster bedrooms. Our footsteps echoed as we dragged the suitcases up sixty-two steps. We arrived, dizzy, at the top floor room.

The unique tiny honeymoon room, complete with four-poster bed, has only a knee-high gothic window. Bend down and you see that you are overlooking the abbey ruins, where birds wheel and caw through the arches. The bedroom has monk-like simplicity, no built-in wardrobe, en suite bathroom or central heating. Just a one bar electric fire and some clothes hooks. The public bathroom is far below, near the ground floor. It is a long way down to clean your teeth, and a long way back up if you've forgotten the toothpaste.

If you don't like heights or suffer from claustrophobia, the more spacious bedroom below has another four-poster, and a normal size window at eye height looking out at the ruined walls. A ground floor room is nearer the bathroom.

Dinner is served by candle-light at wooden tables in the stone-flagged prior's parlour. You might expect a taste of Wales, such as seaweed soup, or home-made granary bread.

Distinctly memorable, the abbey is inexpensive, and an unusual place to spend a night before heading further west across Wales.

Abbey Hotel, Llanthony, Nr Abergavenny, Gwent, Wales, tel: 0873 890487/890559.

Dalston Hall Hotel (Near Carlisle, Cumbria): Spooky Spiral Staircase.

Dalston Hall near Carlisle is a fifteenth century mansion with a square 'pele' tower, rather like a castle. Pele is old border word for tower. Inside the hotel a minstrel's gallery is above the panelled dining hall. The spiral staircase leads past the gallery to the tower bedroom with mullioned windows and a four-poster bed.

I sat on the four-poster bed and my companion departed silently down the carpeted spiral staircase to fetch another suitcase. As the wind howled outside, branches of trees flapped against the mullioned windows and shadows crawled across the floor. I went cold. This room is not supposed to be haunted. But I felt the movement of my skin as my hair stood on end. In another twenty seconds I'd have died of fright!

I flung myself down the spiral staircase three steps at a time so fast I crashed into the back of my companion. This room is not for the nervous. My idea of romance is feeling relaxed, so I would only recommend it if your idea of romance is being so frightened that you cling to each other in a state of excited tension.

The double bath is sunken and created from tiles. The mirror on the ceiling overhead adds a touch of almost pornographic eroticism. Unfortunately, or fortunately, when I turned on the hot water the mirror steamed up!

Dalston Hall hotel has three more four-poster bedrooms, and a room haunted by a young boy – not a four-poster bedroom. I can't say I enjoyed the room on the spiral staircase, but I would not have preferred any other more ordinary room. It was definitely an interesting experience.

Togetherness breaks cost approximately £85 per person for 2 nights, £92 for the pele tower, champagne and fruit in the room on arrival. Two bedrooms have bidets. This is a Best Western hotel.

Dalston Hall, Dalston, (nr Carlisle), Cumbria, CA5 7JX, tel: 0228 710271.

MEDIEVAL AND TUDOR HOTELS
Strictly speaking the middle ages ended with the battle of Bosworth when the winner, Henry VII, Elizabeth I's grandfather, established the Tudor dynasty.

Great Fosters (Surrey)
Elizabeth I's Hunting Lodge, built in 1550, surrounded by a Saxon moat dating from about AD 800, is nowadays a country house hotel five minutes from the Thames. The hotel is at Egham only about six miles from Heathrow Airport, and 17 miles from central London. It takes 33 minutes by train to

Waterloo from Egham Station which is one mile away, so staying here is an easy detour for tourists from abroad.

The hotel's entrance was filmed in 'A Night to Remember' about the Titanic. Visitors arriving from nearby Windsor, driving cars up the old carriage drive, are immediately impressed by the magnificent gabled roof supporting twisted chimneys.

In winter welcoming log fires crackle in the old Jacobean fireplace of the entrance hall. Oak panelling surrounds you. Walking around the hotel you see antiques in every corner. An old grandfather clock stands in the quiet lounge. At the end of the panelled ground floor corridor you discover the dining room, a beamed 15th century black and white tithe barn, where banquets are often held. On Sunday cream teas are served in the barn from 4–5 pm at £5 per person for tea or coffee, sandwiches, fresh cream cakes and scones.

The main oak well staircase leads up to the panelled tapestry bedroom. One of the solid wood four-poster bedrooms overlooks the carriage drive. Another bedroom with a draped four-poster views the clipped yew trees of the formal garden.

Through mullioned windows I saw a springtime bride posing for photographs, first in the sunken rose garden, then on bridges over the stream as swans drifted by. In summer, from May to September, residents swim in the outdoor pool. Day visitors can buy a one month season ticket costing about £30 which admits a family of two adults and two children.

Famous visitors have included the Duke of Edinburgh, Elizabeth Taylor, Bette Davis, Sir Laurence Olivier, Rex Harrison, Vivien Leigh, Maurice Chevalier, Peter Ustinov, Olivia de Havilland, Hayley Mills, Noel Coward, Sir John Gielgud, and Ursula Andress. Noel Coward mentioned Great Fosters in his play Relative Values. Diana Dors used to pop in regularly, said the head receptionist. And Charlie Chaplin used the secret passage between the Tapestry Bedroom and Nursery Suite where the children slept.

Ginger Rogers had A Night to Remember when she slept here. Her furs were stolen by someone who climbed a ladder to the bedroom window. 'We don't leave ladders lying around now,' joked the Assistant Manager.

A four-poster bedroom costs about £85 for two including English breakfast. The Tapestry or Nursery Suite rooms are

£85 for two. The lowest price double room is over £60 for two.
 From May to September there's a Saturday night dinner dance at £17.50 per person. Friday dinner is £15.50 per person – no dancing. The hotel is privately owned.
 For more details, telephone the manager, *Egham 0784 33822. Great Fosters, Egham, Surrey.*

The Feathers Hotel (Ludlow, Shropshire)
The Feathers Hotel is one of England's most photographed timber frame buildings, with stunning black and white diamond shapes, triple gables, and numerous wood carvings.
 In an upstairs panelled lounge there is an elaborate fireplace flanked by wooden columns supporting a mantelpiece shelf. Above it a frieze of carved figures and arches rises to the ceiling. A framed picture shows a reproduction of Charles I's diatribe against smoking.
 The Feathers has seven four-poster bedrooms. In the new block a large bedroom suite is luxuriously furnished with every modern comfort, chocolates, fruit, coffee maker, and Malvern mineral water. Its newly decorated en suite carpeted bathroom had double basins with gold taps, foam bath and other toiletries, and a bidet behind a screen.
 The Feathers was a posthouse which hired horses to ride and for pulling vehicles. Later the 'post' was taken by horses driven by post boys from post to post. Coaching Inns were like modern bus stops and bus stations, requiring a large yard where the coaches could pull in and stop. The Feathers was merely a post house, not a coaching inn like the nearby Angel hotel.
The Feathers, Bull Ring, Ludlow, Shropshire, SY8 1AA, tel: 0584 5261.

The local blue badge guide showed us Ludlow Castle where Prince Arthur honeymooned with Catherine of Aragon. She was married less than six months when Arthur's demise caused her to become first wife of Arthur's brother, Henry VIII. Shakespeare plays are performed in summer during the June-July festival within the castle walls. Look inside the roofless circular tower, and climb up for a view of the countryside.
 'England's finest Tudor town', Shrewsbury, is a few miles north of Ludlow near the Welsh border. It is a good stopover if

you are going to northwest England or north Wales. Two equally attractive hotels are in the town centre.

Prince Rupert Hotel (Shrewsbury, Shropshire)
The attractive gables of the fifteenth century timber facade of the Prince Rupert Hotel are a local landmark. The Prince Rupert Hotel is named after the grandson of James I of England and 6th of Scotland. Rupert was a favourite at the court of his uncle Charles I, and supported the Royalists against the Roundheads during the Civil War. Part of this hotel was used as Rupert's headquarters. He lived abroad in exile under Cromwell's rule, but returned to England when the monarchy was restored in 1660. Later he was the first governor of the Hudson Bay Company in Canada. Sloping floors, old oak beams, and decorative wooden cartwheels abound. The privately owned Prince Rupert Hotel is in the Consort Hotels brochure.
The Prince Rupert, Butcher Row, Shrewsbury, Shropshire, SY1 1UQ, tel: 0743 52461.

The Lion Hotel (Shrewsbury, Shropshire)
The history of the Lion Hotel is equally interesting. Charles Dickens stayed in the Charles Dickens bedroom suite. The old room which all visitors can see is the public lounge. Here you drink tea underneath a large tapestry rising over the fireplace, almost reaching the high ceiling.

Wander to the back of the hotel and find the Adam-style assembly room where Paganini played. Prince William, later William IV, danced here. And the writer De Quincey slept in the ballroom because there was no room at the inn. He described it in *Confessions of an Opium Eater*.

This is a THF hotel.
The Lion, Wyle Cop, Shrewsbury, Shropshire, SY1 1UY, tel: 0743 53107.

Shrewsbury Town and Ironbridge
Shrewsbury's marketplace was filmed for a scene in Dickens' *Christmas Carol*, starring George C. Scott, Susannah York and Edward Woodward, who stayed at the Prince Rupert Hotel. Other famous people of the past are also associated with Shrewsbury. Notice the statue of Darwin who sits with his legs

crossed, and Clive of India, standing holding a sword.

On a walk around Shrewsbury our local guide showed us that after Elizabethan times the latest development, a new brickwork facade, had been used to smarten and they thought 'improve' the old-fashioned timber-frame houses. We could see the timber on the sides and back of a building. Later the Victorians reversed the trend, using a mock-Tudor timber facade to enliven a brick building.

From Shrewsbury you can visit the Ironbridge Gorge, birthplace of the industrial revolution. It is home of the world's first cast iron bridge, whose semi-circular curve is reflected in the river to form a full circle.

The nearby Severn Warehouse Visitor Centre has a video show covering all parts of the valley. A combined ticket enables you to visit the six other sites, including a tile museum, and Blist's Hill Open Air Museum which has a 19th century village where cobblers, plasterers and others work. *Ironbridge Gorge, Shropshire, tel: 095 245 3522 (recorded message).*

Chester

The town of Chester has even more, bigger, better, black and white buildings along the bustling pedestrianised shopping streets. The audio-visual slide show in the Chester Visitor Centre explains that the Victorians improved and rebuilt Chester's famous Rows – double-level walkways with a continuous line of balconies, providing shops in covered galleries at street and first floor level. (I must explain to any American readers who don't know, that this is what Americans call second floor.) The origin of these Rows goes back as early as the 14th century.

Take an interesting walk around Chester's walls, crossing a bridge over one of the streets giving you a view of gables stretching as far as you can see. Photographers get a lovely aerial view of Chester's streets by day, and illuminated at night.

A bearded town crier in medieval garb walks from the Visitor Centre (which is open until mid-evening to book accommodation) to a central crossing point. Ringing his bell, the town crier makes announcements about local shops, restaurants, and photographic stores – his sponsors. He also calls up British tourists and foreign visitors to say where they are from and join

in his act.
Chester Visitor Centre, Vicars Lane, Chester, Cheshire, CH1 1QX, tel: 0244 313126

Little Moreton Hall
This beautiful fifteenth century black and white half-timbered moated building with carved gable and plasterwork is preserved by The National Trust. The roofline and horizontal beams dip, undulate and slope alarmingly. Little Moreton Hall has a long gallery where the ladies used to take a daily walk for their health in the winter months. Excellent guided tours tell you about the 16th century wall paintings. Services are held in the tiny chapel on Sunday. There is a tea room, and the giftshop sells posters of Moreton Hall. Phone to check opening hours and tour times.
Little Moreton Hall, Congleton, Cheshire, tel: 02602 2018.

Maesmawr Hall (Mid-Wales)
If you want an olde worlde inn for a night, without paying for five star service and fancy bathrooms, unpretentious Maesmawr Hall is a budget stop-over about an hour into Wales from Shrewsbury. At the end of the tree-lined drive you glimpse the black and white timber front of the gabled building.

The pubby main lounge has an old carved wood fireplace, the twisting main staircase, and a carved wood bar, open both sides so you can see into the dining room beyond. Lorry driver John, who recently inherited the hotel from his late mother, stands behind the bar serving drinks to customers in both the lounge and dining room. Many of the winter weekend customers have arrived with vouchers from Thomas Cook or schemes such as Golden Key, Flexibreak, Keymark and Bonusbreak which gives you free accommodation, usually off-peak times only, if you have hotel meals.

In summer when they are fully booked take a torch so you can find your way in the dark to the modern annexe. In the main hotel most bedrooms have bathrooms en suite. There are carved wood doors, beams, and one wonderful four-poster bedroom reached by a twisting Y-shape staircase under an exposed cross-beam.

The old part of the hotel was once haunted by Bad Robin, who had a bull's head. He was overpowered by seven priests

who buried him in the Bulls Pool owned by John's neighbour.
  Mini-weekend breaks about £60 per person.
Maesmawr Hall, Caersws, Powys, SY17 5SF, Wales, tel: 068 684 255.

Red Lion Hotel (Salisbury, Wiltshire)
A hanging curtain of 150 year old green Virginia creeper – red in autumn – frames the view of the old gabled Red Lion hotel at Salisbury. Passing under the vine into the enclosed courtyard of the thirteenth century inn, you feel you are in medieval times. A red lion stands by the entrance.

  In the hallway is a huge old Skeleton Organ Clock, a floor-to-ceiling grandfather clock of triple width. Either side of the face are carved scenes. Above the clockface three skeletons strike the hour. The lounge has a Parliament Clock, with a huge clockface on a slender support.

  Pass through the oak archway to a dining room dating from about 1320 which has the original daub-wattle wall. It is beamed with a collection of old plates on the picture rail and arranged vertically against the white plaster background between the vertical beams.

  Naturally the Red Lion has a four-poster bed. It is a family-owned hotel in the Best Western marketing group.
Red Lion Hotel, 4 Milford Street, Salisbury, Wiltshire SP1 2AN, tel: 0722 23334.

The King's Arms (Salisbury, Wiltshire)
Another equally old hotel in Salisbury is the King's Arms where the four-poster bedroom is reached from an upstairs public lounge by a short flight of stairs.
The King's Arms, St. John Street, Salisbury, Wiltshire, tel: 0722 27629.

  From Salisbury you can visit Stonehenge which is about ten miles away. There is also a lesser known Woodhenge. Wilton House is a nearby stately home with a children's adventure playground. Details from the *West Country Tourist Board, Trinity Court, 37 Southernhay East, Exeter, Devon, EX1 1QS, tel: 0392 76351.*

Canterbury

Canterbury is associated with Archbishop Thomas à Becket, who was murdered by four knights in the cathedral in 1170, and canonised two years later, which has made Canterbury a pilgrimage centre for centuries.

The timber houses of Huguenot weavers have upper stories projecting over the water. Inside are displayed relics of the refugees who settled here in the 16th and 17th centuries.

The County Hotel in the High Street has a Tudor four-poster. The first recorded occupant of the house was Jacob the Jew in 1190, and his sons Samuel and Aaron. Behind the hotel is Jewry lane and the old synagogue was within walking distance of Jacob's home. Jacob the Jew's house was seized by Edward I in 1290 when he expelled the Jews and took their property. The building became an inn in the 1600s.
The County Hotel, High Street, Canterbury, Kent CT1 2RX, tel: 0227 66266.

The Falstaff Hotel has two old four-poster beds – alas without drapes. However this makes it easier to admire the carving. One bed has arches carved on the headboard, the other a frieze of leaves, and both beds have a solid wood roof.
Falstaff Hotel, St Dunstan's Street, Canterbury, CT2 8AF, tel: 0227 462138.

CASTLES

Several stately homes can arrange daytime conferences or banquets and suggest hotels nearby for accommodation.

Leeds Castle, 'Loveliest Castle in the World', offers banquets in the 17th century tithe barn and conferences can be held in the gate tower. Details from: *The Conference Office, Leeds Castle, Maidstone, Kent ME17 1PL, tel: 0622 65400.*

Belvoir Castle, home of the Duke and Duchess of Rutland, seats up to 200 in the State Dining Room. Belvoir means beautiful view, and it was the location of the films 'Little Lord

Fauntleroy' and 'Young Sherlock Holmes'. Medieval Jousting tournaments take place throughout summer, open to the public. It is one hour from London by train, and not far from Nottingham. Contact: *Conference Organiser, The Estate Office, Belvoir Castle, Grantham, Lincs, tel: Grantham 870262.*

Hever Castle

Hever was the home of Anne Boleyn, Henry VIII's second wife and Elizabeth I's mother. The Castle was bought by American William Waldorf Astor in 1903 and he built a Tudor village where guests can stay.

Henry VIII's Hever was filmed by the BBC in 'Six Wives of Henry VIII.' The BBC costume display of lifesize models in the long-gallery is open to the public. The grounds contain a maze, adventure playground, and topiary gardens. Conference guests receive their own private tour of the house. Henry VIII banquets are also held, at about £65 per person plus VAT! Cross over the moat by the working drawbridge, floodlit at night, under the portcullis to enter the castle.

For conference details and opening times contact:
Hever Castle, Near Edenbridge, Kent, tel: 0732 865224.

Kildrummy Castle (Aberdeenshire, Scotland)

In Scotland I recommend Kildrummy Castle Hotel. The yellow stone country mansion hotel has an olde worlde atmosphere inside with panelled walls and mullioned windows giving wonderful views of the thirteenth century ruined castle. It is worthwhile paying the entrance fee to visit the peaceful garden below, owned separately, where a bridge is reflected in the water.

Kildrummy Castle Hotel, Kildrummy, Alford, Aberdeenshire, Scotland, AB3 8RA, tel: 03365 288.

CHAPTER 11
A Classic English Weekend around Arundel

A typically British classic weekend is staying in a thatched hotel constructed for somebody famous, preferably occupying a four-poster bed in a beamed bedroom, ideally near a castle associated with King Henry VIII. If there is a seaside and an eccentric museum nearby, so much the better. Bailiffscourt Hotel near Arundel Castle on Britain's south coast fulfils all the requirements.

Bailiffscourt Thatched Hotel (West Sussex)
Bailiffscourt was built by the eccentric Lord Moyne of the Guinness family, before he was assassinated in the east. This building is a wonderful memorial to him, a perfect reconstruction, completed in about 1930, of a 13th century bailiffs' courthouse, and now a unique country house hotel with flagstone floors and beamed ceilings, warmed by log fires in winter.

To gothic stones from the old courthouse, were added pieces from a priory, a rectory, an abbey, a barn and a stable, put together by 300 craftsmen, at an undisclosed cost. No trees existed on the estate, but the medieval antiquarian in charge simply imported an entire wood of mature trees up to 25 years old, using cranes to lower them into gigantic holes.

The atmosphere is authentic but without the decay, so you experience a medieval manor in pristine condition, as it should be enjoyed.

Fireplaces, arched doorways and pointed gothic windows are edged with stone. Intricate and pretty black wrought iron candle-holders adorn the white walls.

You walk along creaking corridors whose mullioned windows overlook the central courtyard, through heavy wood doors studded with nails, to your bedroom.

The Thatch Cottage annexe along the path can be reached by an underground passageway in bad weather.

In the Thatch Cottage Lady Moyne's former bedroom has been divided into two bedrooms. One had an upside down V shape beamed ceiling. Other rooms featured wood panelling. Several rooms have four-poster beds with a carved roof to stare up at when you wake in the morning, or carved posts. Mattresses and pillows are very comfortable. Bedrooms are equipped with a tin of biscuits and bottled Malvern water.

Bathrooms have cotton wool, needle and cottons on the dressing table, a glass jug of green bath oil, and towelling bathrobes which you can buy if you take a fancy to them.

The carpet continues up the front of the washbasin, and a low tiled barrier separates the toilet from the bath. My bathroom had two basins. The best bedroom has two baths. I saw other bathrooms – all have different character. One was up a flight of steps with a tiny window by the lowest step.

Our evening entertainment was taking a sauna in the basement, down miles of spooky echoing corridors. Live-in staff have accommodation down here. Thirty five staff look after guests residing in 20 bedrooms. Eventually there will be 34 rooms.

The dining room has a solid wood ceiling and copper pans on the walls. A guest interpreted the tapestry as representing a betrothal because it depicted a couple standing between two trees, two his and hers family standards, a rabbit representing fertility, and a crawling baby. Dinner included hot bread, gravad lax, freshwater salmon, piquant lemon tart, coffee and petit fours. Dinner costs about £22, lunch about £15 per person, Auslese wine £10.50 a bottle, a glass of dessert wine £1.50.

Themed evenings are on offer including a twenties night and a Viennese evening. Medieval music is being specially composed for music evenings by Paul Lewis, who has worked for numerous TV series such as 'Swallows and Amazons' and 'Prisoner of Zenda'. You can meet the musician and composer, hear harp and harmonica music, and enjoy a buffet supper.

A walk down a muddy lane takes you to Climping beach which has sand dunes, a shingle shore, and sand underwater. The hotel also has an outdoor swimming pool and a helicopter landing pad.

Dogs are welcome, and dog basket and dog food provided for about £4 a day.

Double bedrooms cost from about £75 in a small room for two persons to £145 for the master suite. Details, including forthcoming music evenings, from:
Bailiffscourt Hotel, Climping, Near Littlehampton, West Sussex, BN17 5RW, tel: 0903 723511.

Arundel Castle (Arundel, West Sussex)

The massive towers and walls of hilltop Arundel castle dominate the scene for miles around, like Windsor castle. You enter the estate through the gatehouse at the bottom of the hill following directions, 'First right across the drawbridge'. Crossing under the menacing double portcullis, you are within the walls. The Duke is in residence if a flag is flying from the keep on top of a 45 degree mound which presents some problems to the lawnmower.

Arundel Castle has been owned by the Catholic Dukes of Norfolk for centuries. They are a fascinating family. Among the family portraits notice the notorious third Duke of Norfolk who was great-uncle of Elizabeth I. He was the ambitious uncle of both Elizabeth I's mother Anne Boleyn, and her cousin Catherine Howard, the two wives of Henry VIII who were beheaded. Don't feel sorry for their wily uncle Thomas Howard, I was told. To placate Henry, Thomas was callously shouting 'off with their heads' along with the rest of the crowd.

Later, outmanoeuvred by rival court factions, the third Duke himself was imprisoned, and due to be beheaded. But the day before the morning of his execution Henry VIII died! Henry's successor Mary, a staunch Catholic, naturally released lucky Thomas. So the Duke's prayers were answered. The Norfolk family chapel which you will see is very impressive too.

A dukedom is inherited by the eldest son of the Duke, who is an earl. The Earl of Shrewsbury didn't have a son, and his daughter married the 14th Earl of Arundel, taking to the Norfolks the property of the Shrewsbury family who had held Mary Queen of Scots captive. So souvenirs of Mary Queen of Scots can be seen – her prayerbook and rosary.

The important Dukes of Norfolk organise the coronation. Victoria gave the Norfolks her homage throne as a 'thank you' gift. You'll see it in the library, and in another delightful room is the gilded four-poster Victoria slept in when visiting her good friends the Norfolks.

In addition to the oriental desks with secret compartments, owned by any self-respecting British stately home or castle, Arundel castle has many other curiosities, such as an Armada chest with a hidden lock, and a wig cupboard lined with sandalwood to perfume the wig.

Arundel Castle is open to the public in summer and the Arundel Festival takes place in the Tilting Court in August. Banquets can be arranged, including a guided tour of the castle. *Arundel Castle, Arundel, West Sussex BN18 9AB, tel: 0903 883136.*

Around and About Arundel

Picturesque Arundel is an antiques centre. Have tea or meals at *Cafe Violette, 67 High St, Arundel, tel: 0903 883702*, which has a 16th century hand carved solid walnut and gold leaf ceiling.

The 14th century church is divided into two, one half Catholic, the other Anglican. And see the Catholic cathedral aisle decorated with a carpet of flowers for Corpus Christi in June.

You can enjoy birdwatching in comfort if you visit The Wildfowl Trust, where picture windows overlook masses of ducks waddling past and sitting on islands in front of the windows. Binoculars can be hired, but the birds can be seen all around you without them. The upstairs cafe serves gingerbread men. You eat overlooking the lake filled with black necked swans and geese. Ducks hop up the bank, waddling towards visitors and wait to be fed. Little children who have bought birdfood jump as birds poke their beaks briskly into little hands. The address is: *The Wildfowl Trust, Mill Rd, Arundel, West Sussex, BN18 9BP, tel: 0903 883355.*

Talking of birds, the International Birdman rally takes place at Arundel in August. And turning to boats, the Arun bath tub race, in which all kinds of craft except proper boats race along the river also happens in August.

The Clowns Convention takes place nearby at Bognor in April.

For an excursion in the area visit a working watermill at Michelham Priory, Upper Dickham, Hailsham, East Sussex, tel: 0323 844224. See the 14th century gatehouse and moat. A barn can be hired with medieval players.

OTHER HOTELS

Goodwood Park Hotel (Goodwood, Chichester)
Racing and clay pigeon shooting are two attractions at Goodwood Park Hotel in the grounds of Goodwood House. The hotel offers antiques, and clay pigeon shooting weekends, plus the opportunity to attend race meetings between May and September.
Goodwood Park Hotel, Goodwood, Chichester, West Sussex, PO18 0QB, tel: 0243 775537.

Crown Inn (Chiddingford, Surrey)
Driving down from London on the A3 or M25 and A320 via Guildford and Godalming to the A283 takes you to the medieval timber-framed Crown Inn at Chiddingfold. Stop for English tea, coffee or bar food and see the hall telephone fixed inside a sedan chair. The dining room has a magnificent plaster ceiling.

On the more romantic four-poster bed the posts are covered with soft material. The other medieval four-poster bed has elaborately carved arches above both pillows on the headboard, which reaches right up to the solid wood roof with carved interior. Both rooms are about £65 per night.
The Crown Inn, The Green, Chiddingford, Surrey, tel: 042879 2255/6.

If you want to sleep under thatch at quite a modest cost, you can choose a self-catering thatch cottage in Norfolk, available from Blakes Holidays. Details are in Chapter 25.

More information on events and accommodation in and around Arundel from *Arundel Tourist Information Centre, tel: 0903 882268, or Arun Tourism, The Manor House, Church Street, Littlehampton, West Sussex BN17 5EP, tel: 0903 716133.*

Within the 'Love Boat', *Caprice* (page 63)

Outside the 'Love Boat', *Caprice*

The Royal Scotsman (page 41)

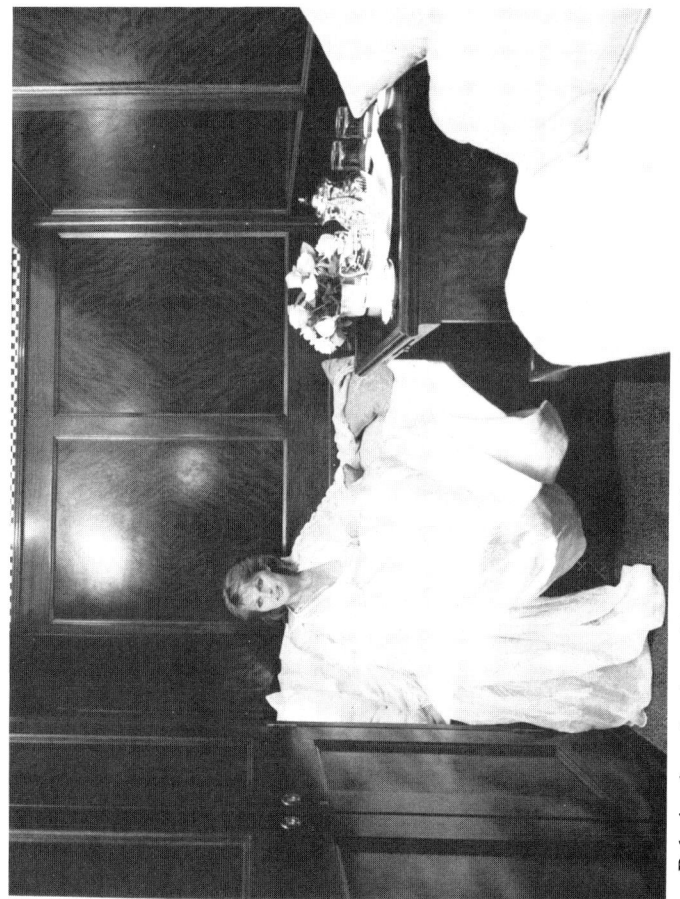

Relaxing in a sleeping cabin of one of the antique rail coaches of the Royal Scotsman

Studley Priory, Oxford (page 49)

Lumley Castle Hotel, County Durham (pages 69, 35, 76)

CHAPTER 12
Imprints of Royalty

"This is where Sarah Ferguson works," I learned on a Royal Wedding Tour. The organiser, Verite Baker, Managing Director of Ambassadors of Britain, stopped near BCK at 11, St George's Street, London, allowing us time to buy takeaway coffee and chocolate cake from the Queens Snack Bar where Sarah has often bought hers.

A Royal London Weekend
A royal sightseeing tour could include Westminster Abbey where Sarah and Prince Andrew married, as did Queen Elizabeth II, St Paul's where the Princess of Wales married, Buckingham Palace, and The Royal Mews, London SW1, to see the golden wedding coach, tel: 01-930 4832.

Sarah placed a wedding list at the General Trading Co, Sloane Street. You could have coffee or dinner in the elegant Cadogan Hotel nearby admiring the wood panelling and photographs of former owner Lillie Langtry, mistress of King Edward VII.

One of London's blue plaques marks Lillie's dates, 1854–1929. Her friend Oscar Wilde was arrested here. Pictures of her are in the hotel bar, where you can drink a toast to royalty, love and marriage. Single bedrooms about £85–105, doubles £105–125. *Cadogan Hotel, 75 Sloane Street, London, SW1X 9SG, tel: 01-235 7141.*

Central London has many luxury hotels with royal connections. The Queen attended a party at Claridges after Princess Diana's wedding. Lunching in the Causerie, as Sarah and her father did, costs from about £12 per person Sunday–Friday. *Claridges, Brook Street, Mayfair, London, W1, tel: 01-629 8860.*

'Royal-tea' in London
If you cannot afford a weekend, or wedding, you could take tea

in royal style.

THF's Brown's Hotel, which has entrances in Dover St, and in Albemarle St, in Mayfair, was opened by Byron's butler, Brown, and displays chairs where Queen Victoria sat.

Rudyard Kipling wrote at a desk in Brown's. Alexander Bell made the first phone call from Britain to America from one of the bedrooms. Theodore Roosevelt married Edith from here, and his nephew Franklin and bride Eleanor stayed here during their honeymoon.

I waited for tea with a colleague who wore an open-necked shirt, and a waiter wordlessly presented my companion with a tie. Tea 3–6 pm. £7.50 per person. *Brown's Hotel, Albemarle Street, London, W1, tel: 01-493 6020.*

Opposite Harrods is the Hyde Park Hotel, where as THF's brochure proudly announces, 'In the post-war years Her Majesty The Queen was known to frequent the hotel to take tea with her children'. *Hyde Park Hotel, Knightsbridge, London, tel: 01-235 2000.*

The bar of the Mountbatten Hotel displays news cuttings and cartoons about Mountbatten, great grandson of Queen Victoria. An alcohol-free cocktail is available in the bar and sandwiches at under five pounds make a meal. A porter in a grey top hat feeds the meter for you. Delicious lunch in the red and white Burmese temple restaurant costs about £10.50. Single bedrooms are from £90, and a luxury weekend including a Venice Simplon Orient-Express train to Broadlands (see following paragraph) near Bournemouth is £265. *Mountbatten Hotel, Monmouth Street, Seven Dials, London WC2H 9HD, tel: 01-836 4300. From the USA call 800 447 7011.*

Broadlands

The Princess of Wales spent the first night of her honeymoon in a four-poster bed at Broadlands, home of the late Earl Mountbatten of Burma, as did her mother-in-law, Queen Elizabeth I.

Following royal footsteps (and wheels), you can spend a royal weekend visiting Broadlands in summer, seeing Princess Diana's bridesmaid's dress, and Lady Mountbatten's wedding veil. *Broadlands, Romsey, Hampshire, tel: 0794 516878.*

If you are driving down, on your way stop at picturesque

Dummer, Hampshire, Sarah Ferguson's tiny home village, where the gabled local pub, Queen Inn, serves Fergie's Fizz.

Queen Slept Here
Romantic ladies who are not getting married can console themselves with the thought that Elizabeth I did not marry either. The 'virgin' queen slept with or without her lover at *The Spread Eagle, Midhurst, Sussex, tel: 073081 2211* where the White Room has secret passages, and The Mermaid Inn, which has a four-poster bed and linenfold panelled dining rooms: *The Mermaid Inn, Rye, Sussex, tel: 0797 223065.*

Royal Lover's Bedrooms
Lillie Langtry, Edward VII's lover, known as Jersey Lillie, got around. Nice girls go to heaven, says Helen Gurley Brown, but bad girls go everywhere. Bournemouth has Lillie's beautiful love-nest, Langtry Manor, built for her as a gift in 1877 by the Prince of Wales, later King Edward VII, Queen Victoria's son. Edward subsequently turned his attentions to actress Sarah Bernhardt, who had inspired Lillie's acting career. Lillie went off to tour theatres in the USA where she captivated the Americans. She was given a train by a Baltimore businessman and toured across the USA where she received a rapturous welcome and even had a town in Texas renamed after her: Langtry, Val Verde County, Texas. Before she returned to England she was granted American citizenship. Read all about it in the book 'Lillie Langtry' by Jeremy Birkett and John Richardson, on sale in hotels in England associated with Lillie.

Six-course Edwardian dinner parties, Edwardian dress optional, are available to non-residents at the Langtry Manor Hotel. They are held on Saturday nights in the hotel dining room overlooked by a minstrel's gallery where Lillie installed the motto, 'They say – what say they – let them say.'

The table d'hote menu includes Lillie's favourite sweet – meringue, fresh fruit, cream and a secret ingredient. During dinner there is a sound and light show featuring the words and story of Lillie and the people she knew well, such as Disraeli.

A beautiful Jacobean four-poster bed with elaborate carving faces a massive fireplace in the beamed Edward VII bedroom. In the en suite bathroom you use the bath with its gold-plated taps, and other conveniences, watched by the portrait of disapproving Queen Victoria. Lillie Langtry had another bedroom, of course. Lillie's bedroom is modern, with a four-poster bed, and a romantic heart-shaped corner bath.

Prices range from about £26 per person for bed and breakfast in a small double room, £37 in a four-poster room (supplement £8 per person for one night), £48 in the Edward VII Suite (with supplements of £12 per person for one night and reductions for a week). A four-poster room including dinner midweek is approximately £37, minimum two nights, weekend £40.

If you are a non-resident dinner à la carte is about £12–17 per person plus wine, £16 for the six course Saturday night dinner, and £10 the rest of the week. All week the dining room staff wear Edwardian servants dress of black outfits, with girls in white pinafores and white mob caps. Male staff wear bow ties all week, and black tail coats on Saturday nights. On Saturday the other staff also wear Edwardian costumes. You can hire Edwardian dresses with bustles from local shops. If you arrive late the hotel will have them delivered for you, the cost being about £10.

'What more romantic place to spend a honeymoon than in the lovenest of a King?' says the brochure. 'But you don't have to be a honeymooner to enjoy these suites. Indulge yourself on any occasion.' Contact:
Langtry Manor Hotel, Derby Road, East Cliff, Bournemouth, BH1 3QB, tel: 0202 23887.

Nearby you can visit Beaulieu Motor Museum whose latest addition, the 'wheels' exhibition, seen from a moving indoor train, was opened by Prince Charles. *Beaulieu, Hampshire, tel: 0590 612345.*

Windsor Weekends
A pleasant afternoon's drive from London is a visit to Windsor Castle, the largest inhabited castle in the world, according to the Guinness Book of Records, where Andrew and Sarah asked the Queen for permission to marry.

At Windsor station you can see Queen Victoria arriving in state at the Royalty and Empire Exhibition. The climax is watching a wax model of old Victoria rise, unsteadily, to her feet. *Royalty & Empire Exhibition, Windsor & Eton Central*

Station, Windsor, Berkshire, SL4 1PJ, tel: 0753 557837.*

Outside the castle walls in Frogmore Garden are the tombs of Victoria and Albert, as well at King Edward VIII who abdicated in order to remain with the woman he loved, the late Duchess of York, better known as Mrs Simpson, who came from Baltimore.

The royal calendar includes regular polo playing at Windsor Great Park, and Royal Ascot in June when racegoers see the Queen drive up the course *(tel: 0990 22211 or get tickets from Keith Prowse Harrods branch tel: 01-589 1101 or Obtainables Ticket Agency, tel: 01-839 5363.)*

Champagne lunch hampers for Ascot are provided for residents at Prestige's Pennyhill Park Hotel, near Windsor. Foreign royalty and company directors can arrive by helicopter. The hotel wedding package includes the bridal couple departing by helicopter for a honeymoon night at a sister hotel near Gatwick. An excellent nouvelle cuisine dinner (I celebrated a wedding anniversary here) is served under a silver dome. Double bedrooms from £65. Lunch about £1 per person. Tea and scones or sandwiches about £5. *Pennyhill Park Hotel, College Ride, Bagshot, Surrey, tel: 0276 71774.*

In Warwickshire
Earl Spencer, father of Princess Diana, unveiled the Heritage Panel at the Regent Hotel, Royal Leamington Spa, ten miles north of Stratford-on-Avon. This lists numerous royals who visited the hotel, which was illuminated for the arrival of the future Queen Victoria. Her statue stands in the street.

Guests are treated royally at Leamington's creeper-covered little Lansdowne Hotel and Restaurant, offering lovely decor, liqueurs and curios. Arched pelmets cover mirrors and every bedroom is different. If you like small beautifully decorated hotels, it is a good place to stay. *Lansdowne Hotel, Clarendon Street, Royal Leamington Spa, Warwickshire, CV32 4PF, tel: 0926 21313.*

For an eventful lunch I suggest you go to Clarendon House Hotel and Castle Tavern Restaurant. Armour recalling Cromwell's days is in the restaurant. The building features an oak tree supporting an internal wall. In the corner of the bar there is a deep well. And a sheepdog, Sadie, shakes hands with you.

Special guests get a card signed with Sadie's pawprint. *Clarendon House Hotel, (Old) High Street, Kenilworth, Warwickshire, CV8 1LZ, tel: 0926 57668.*

The current Earl of Warwick sold nearby Warwick Castle to Madame Tussaud's in 1978. Warwick Castle, the most visited stately home in the UK, displays Madame Tussaud's exhibition A Royal Weekend Party 1898. Wax figures sit in the castle rooms. Facing Edward VII there's Lord Curzon, who supposedly sinned on tiger skin with Eleanor Glyn. *Warwick Castle, Warwick, tel: 0926 495421.*

STATELY HOME HOTELS

Cliveden is the first National Trust property to be opened as a luxury hotel. It overlooks the river Thames near Maidenhead, 26 miles west of London. The bedrooms cost from £150 per night to £350 for the Lady Astor Suite. Nancy Astor was Britain's first woman member of parliament. Guests are attended by a butler, stewards, footmen and maids. The grounds are open to the public. Contact *Lord Crathorne, Blakeney Hotels, 52 Lower Sloane St, London SW1 8BS, tel: 01-730 9131,* or *The National Trust.*

Ripley Castle, at Ripley, Near Harrogate, North Yorkshire, tel: 0432 770152, is a mansion where Sir T. Ingilby, Bt, is the wine waiter, and Lady Ingilby cooks and helps wash up. It is also open midweek in summer to daytime visitors.

Drive just across the border into Scotland near Kelso and you can visit romantic Floors Castle (tel: 0573 23333 for opening hours), where Prince Andrew proposed to Sarah. This is the home of their good friends the Duke and Duchess of Roxburghe, whose Sunlaws House Hotel is nearby at Kelso. Sunlaws is a hunting, shooting and fishing place, furnished with antiques, where you can enjoy pre-dinner drinks and after dinner coffee sitting by the fireplace in the panelled library bar. Sometimes on Sunday mornings Prince Andrew was said to pop in. *Sunlaws House Hotel, Kelso, Roxburghshire, tel: 05735 331.*

PART IV

Breaks for Special Interests and Activities

CHAPTER 13
Sports and Activities

If you want to take part in a sport such as golf, horse riding, skiing, windsurfing, or fishing, you will find a good choice of opportunities in the British Isles.

There are many other kinds of activity weekends which can offer really stimulating recreational breaks to people from children to grandparents.

You can celebrate life on wheels in nostalgic or romantic ways, by hiring a classic or vintage car or indulging in a weekend Rolls. If your motoring needs are in other directions, you can sharpen up driving skills where special weekend instruction is laid on. Or you can enjoy being off the ground and take one of a variety of flying breaks.

There are some hotels which set out to offer a particularly wide spectrum of physical activities of one kind and another and of special recreations. There are also holiday organisations providing 'adventure' and activity programmes designed specially for children or for families. I will call these 'multi-activity' hotels and breaks and give details of them in the first part of this chapter.

MULTI-ACTIVITY HOTELS AND ORGANISATIONS
Peebles Hydro Hotel (Peebles, Scotland)

An example is the huge hilltop Peebles Hydro Hotel overlooking the picturesque Peebles river valley twenty miles south of Edinburgh. It has more activities than any other hotel I've seen. From the terrace above a flight of stairs you look down the grassy slopes to the tennis courts, putting, children's playground, and adventure playground.

The lovely indoor swimming pool has bird murals and a spa bath and is open late at night – no arriving back from Edinburgh at 5.30, and finding it has closed for the day. There is a poolside snack bar.

In the main restaurant there is a buffet breakfast. The menu choice includes Scottish delicacies and diet items marked with asterisks. The dining room manager greets everybody, and the hotel manager walks around saying hello to guests. In the busy season nannies organise sessions for children in the playroom and there's a children's high tea. The bedrooms are not particularly exciting, except for the views, but I rate this as Scotland's top hotel for family breaks, maybe the best in Britain. It has public rooms in one wing making it suitable for conferences.

A band plays dance music for Scottish dancing, and for ballroom dancing; everybody joins in music like the Birdie song, interspersed with a pop song or two, and the last waltz. You can join in the folk dancing on your own as it doesn't require a partner, sit having coffee in the lounge listening to the music, and chat to other people. Men are asked to wear ties at dinner, so the crowd is quite smartly dressed without being formal.

In summer, Easter and Christmas there's a programme of non-stop activity options and prices go up, but there are some off season special breaks. Two night breaks are about £65–70 according to season, and over £80 for the Edinburgh Military Tattoo, including a ticket to the Tattoo.

Other similar facilities are offered by Crieff Hydro Hotel at Crieff, and various Country Club Centres. Details are available from your travel agent.

You'll find these breaks in the Consort Holidays brochure. The other hotels offer golfing holidays, sea, lake and river

fishing, bridge, walking, skiing, riding, pony-trekking, tennis, painting, hunting, squash, rambling, flower arranging, sequence dancing, bowling, and windsurfing.
Peebles Hydro Hotel, Peebles, Scotland, tel: 0721 20602.

Aviemore
If you want to be in a large centre, the Aviemore Centre has a dry ski slope, ice rink, swimming pool, and a curling pond. Accommodation ranges from a youth hostel to major hotels such as the three star Stakis Colymbridge Resort Hotel, which has a sauna and indoor swimming, or the Four Seasons Hotel which has a sauna.
The Four Seasons Hotel, Aviemore Centre, Aviemore PH22 1PF, tel: 0479 810681.

The Selsdon Park Hotel south of London, has a tropical leisure complex, sauna, steam bath, mini gym, squash courts, tennis, riding, and an 18 hole golf course.
The Selsdon Park Hotel, Sanderstead, South Croydon, Surrey, tel: 01-657 8811.

There are many country club hotels. For example, the Redwood Lodge Hotel & Country Club outside Bristol offers a sauna and indoor swimming pool, table tennis, tennis, a children's adventure playground, billiards and pool, several squash courts, ladies' keep-fit sessions, and horse-riding.
The Redwood Lodge Hotel & Country Club, Beggar Bush Lane, Failand, BS8 3TG, tel: 0272 393901.

Camps, children's programmes, etc.
Butlin's has budget family centres.

PGL offers children's holidays with multi-activity facilities at numerous centres: *PGL Adventure Holiday, Young Adventure Ltd, Station Street, Ross-on-Wye, Herefordshire, HR9 7AH, tel: 0989 65556.*

So does Dolphin Adventure Holidays; in fact most children's camps offer popular activities like BMX bikes: *Dolphin Adventure Holidays, 34-36 South Street, Lancing, West Sussex, BN15 8AG, tel: 0903 765581.*

Camp Beaumont uses the prestigious Mill Hill School in north London and has a weekend summer open day. This gives children the chance to try out the activities and enables parents to see for themselves that children are kept behind a tape line when others are practising archery. *Camp Beaumont, Corpus Christi, 9 West Street, Godmanchester, Cambs, tel: 0480 56123, or 01-870 9866.*

Ardmore Adventure for those aged 7-27 and families has computer sessions, as do many other such companies. *Ardmore Adventure Ltd, 2 Osborne Road, Windsor, Berks, SL4 3EG, tel: 0753 850050.*

Note *Young Leisure Activity Holidays Ltd, Rock Park Centre, Llandrindod Wells, Powys LD1 6AE, Wales, tel: 0597 2021.* The organisers were active in promoting the foundation of the British Activity Holiday Association to establish standards for members running children's activity holidays.

Children's programmes are run in the summer holidays, and some companies offer Easter breaks and half-term breaks. Take insurance against cancellation of your holidays when the family are ill.

Youth Hostel Minibreaks

Multi-activity minibreaks are offered by the Youth Hostel Association. There is no upper age limit. You just have to be young at heart and prepared to share single sex bedrooms or dormitory accommodation.

Windsurfing, canoeing and sailing are combined in one action-packed Watersports Weekend at Bala in North Wales. Four night short breaks take place at Edale, Derbyshire, 2 and 4 nights in Yorkshire with as much rock climbing, orienteering, abseiling, caving, pony trekking, and cycling as you have time for, plus barbecues and discos in the evening.

Most two night breaks are nearer £75 than £100. Beginners' caving weekends involve crawling, dangling from ladders, 'abseiling down gloomy holes and generally enjoying yourself' they say. Climbing weekends, parachuting, and parascending, cost nearer £100 a weekend, staying at a clubhouse with a sauna. *The Youth Hostel Association, Trevelyan House, 8 St Stephen's Hill, St Albans, Herts AL1 2DY, tel: 0727 55215.*

Activity programmes of hotel groups

Trusthouse Forte has a brochure on special interest and activity breaks offered at dozens of different hotels. They cover fly fishing, rambling with local clubs or on your own using maps provided, clay pigeon shooting, birdwatching, riding, falconry, golf, parachuting, tennis, health and fitness, bridge, snooker, flying and gliding, driving, and the connoisseur breaks include painting.

THF (UK) Ltd, 24–30 New Street, Aylesbury, Bucks, HP20 2NW, tel: 01-567 3444. Other THF reservation centres are in major cities in England, Scotland and Wales.

Crest Hotels have designed a programme of special interest, hobby and leisure breaks such as antiques weekends, watersports, keep fit, bridge, cookery, crafts, snooker, astrology, and Trivial Pursuits.

Crest Welcome Breaks, Crest Hotels, Bridge Street, Banbury, OX16 8RQ, tel: 0295 67722 or 01-902 8877.

The Best Western independent hotel consortium has a 'Getaway Breaks' brochure. Many of their hotels are midprice three star hotels, although a few such as Kildrummy Castle in Scotland are distinctly grand. The breaks include ballooning, fishing, gliding, golf, beginners' golf, snooker, curling, riding, pony-trekking, bird watching, squash, bridge, chess, sailing, water-sports, video-making, shooting, parascending (parascending means ascending with a parachute; you are towed along until you take off).

Contact *Best Western Hotels, Vine House, 143 London Road, Kingston upon Thames, Surrey, KT2 6NH, tel: 01-541 0033.*

GOLF
Moor Park
From London you can visit the Moor Park Golf Club in parkland laid out by Capability Brown, who removed formal gardens to give what is now considered a typically English 'natural' effect. The clubhouse, which may be entered by the public to see the paintings, was owned in the 1600s by the Duke

of Monmouth, the Protestant, illegitimate son of Charles II, who tried and failed to take the throne from his Catholic uncle, James II. The Duchess was residing here when she heard that James II had beheaded the Duke.

In the early 1900s the house was bought by the soap king, Lord Leverhulme.

After admiring the Greek Portico you enter and see the painted ceiling by Thornhill, imitating the dome of St Paul's. The wall paintings depict the story of Io and Argus from Ovid's Metamorphosis. Other paintings are on the stairs and in the Thornhill room, as the handbook explains. It is open weekdays 10–12 and 2.30–4, and Saturday mornings 10–12, no charge.

The Four Stars National Pro-Celebrity Golf Tournament is held in the last week in May, and has been hosted by Terry Wogan, Bruce Forsyth, Henry Cooper and Jimmy Tarbuck. There is a small charge for watching.

Visitors can play on the two courses midweek, but not at weekends. *Moor Park Golf Club, Rickmansworth, Herts, WD3 1QN, tel: 0923 778020.*

Scotland
North of the Border one can visit the oldest golf club in the world at Muirfield near Edinburgh. It has the exclusive distinction of being started by Edinburgh bankers and judges. *Greywalls Hotel, Muirfield, Gullane, East Lothian, EH31 2EG, tel: 0626 842144.*

On the east coast about 50 miles north of Edinburgh is St Andrews Old Course, 'the home of golf'. It is the oldest course still in use and sets the golf rules for the world. The Old Course is owned by the citizens – but although it is a public course it is so popular that you must book year round. However, there are three more fine courses next to the Old Course. On the course itself is the expensive skyscraper Old Course Hotel, which has a rooftop restaurant overlooking the sea. Its modernity is in contrast to the town's miles of natural empty sandy beach, protected from commercial intrusions. The town is more lively when the university is in session. Golfing widows can visit the ruined cathedral. Real widows can play golf. Mary Queen of Scots did. She was reproved for playing golf only two days after the murder of Lord Darnley! Contact:

Old Course Hotel, St Andrews, Scotland, tel: 0334 74372.

Alternatively, Rufflets Hotel is a country house outside town with a lovely garden. You will probably need to take a taxi from the railway station.
Rufflets Hotel, Strathkinnes Low Road, St Andrews, Fife, KY16 9TX, tel: 0334 72594.

On the coast about 50 miles south west of Glasgow is Turnberry in Ayrshire. Golflink trains from Glasgow are laid on for major events such as the 1986 British Open. The course has associations with Robert the Bruce, who came from Brus in France and landed here in 1307, hoping to reclaim his throne in Scotland. He succeeded after his victory against English forces at the Battle of Bannockburn. A landmark at Turnberry is the lighthouse, which stands beside the ruins of Turnberry castle. The Turnberry hotel building was designed by Lutyens.
Turnberry Hotel and Golf Club, Turnberry, Ayrshire, Scotland, tel: 06553 202.

Perhaps the grandest golfing hotel is Gleneagles which has its own train station, leisure centre, restaurants, bedrooms with four-poster beds, shops and bank. It is almost a complete town, surrounded by four golf courses amid the heather, and probably the most interesting place if the golfer's partner is a non-golfer. £9 million has been spent on redevelopment. It has riding stables. Should you want to meet the famous in person, the weekend breaks have included Mark Phillips riding weekends, and Xandra Rhodes fashion weeks. Rail inclusive breaks are offered. Details from:
Gleneagles Hotel, Auchterarder, Perthshire, PH3 1NF, Scotland, tel: 07646 2231.

The Marine Hotel, Crosbie Road, Troon, Ayrshire, KA10 6HE, Scotland, tel: 0292 314444 serves another championship course. Details from the Scottish Tourist Board.

Many baronial style Scottish hotels offer both golf and fishing. Details from the Scottish Tourist Board which has brochures on golfing holidays and fishing holidays.

In England The Belfry Hotel near Birmingham has a golf course and non-golfers can enjoy the indoor swimming pool. It is described in Chapter 14. Several country club hotels offer golf. Details from the English Tourist Board or the regional tourist boards.

SKIING
While snow skiing takes place in winter at Scottish centres such as Aviemore, dry slope skiing practice can be tried all year round in London and at the Gloucester Hotel in Gloucester.

Activity Travel offers weekends, long weekends and midweek supersavers in Scotland. Children from the age of five are taught at the ski school in Glenshee near Perth. At Aviemore in the Cairngorms ski schools teach accompanied children, and the Aviemore Centre's entertainment includes go-karts. The Posthouse Hotel creche is supervised by a nanny. Colymbridge Hotel has a swimming pool, sauna and ice rink at The Woodshed Leisure Centre in the grounds. Write to:
Activity Travel Ltd, 19 Castle Street, Edinburgh, EH2 3AH, or phone their 24 hr London number tel: 01-541 5115.

At the London annual ski exhibition, a small steep, artificial ski slope moves continually uphill, while ski stars do acrobatic skiing and dance routines to music. After that it is quite a surprise to see the relatively long undulating artificial outdoor ski slope at the Gloucester Hotel and Country Club.

The Gloucester Hotel offers Learner Weekends and ski breaks, including free use of the sauna, two Poma ski tows, and hire of equipment. Learners must have three hours tuition which is offered at a discount to residents who must book three weeks in advance. Midweek breaks are available.

Other facilities are squash courts, a spa bath, an outdoor hot tub, snooker, pool, table tennis, darts, cards, skittle alleys, a golf driving range, and a putting green. There is an olde worlde restaurant, a chuck wagon lounge decorated with wagon wheels, and a sixteenth century farmhouse in the centre of the complex with a four-poster bed. The break of two nights is about £40 per person per night including dinner and English breakfast. Further details from: *Gloucester Hotel and Country Club,*

Robinswood Hill, Gloucester GL4 9EA, tel: 0452 25653, or *Embassy Hotels, 34 Queens Gate, London SW7 5JA, tel: 01-581 3466.*

Dry skiing preparation or refresher courses save time on snow skiing holidays. Here are a few of Britain's scores of dry ski slopes:
Alexandra Palace Ski Centre, Alexandra Park, London, N22, tel: 01-888 2284.
Watford Ski School, Woodside Playing Fields, Horseshoe Lane, Garston, Watford, Herts, tel: 0923 676559.
Hillingdon Ski Centre, Uxbridge, Middx UB10 9NH, tel: 0895 55183.
Others are at Brighton, Glasgow and Aviemore.

HORSE RIDING AND RACING

The game of badminton is named after the court at Badminton House which is equally well known for the Badminton horse trials. You can visit these for two or three days. You might choose which day would be more interesting. Stalls selling horse brasses, riding and walking clothes and accessories, tweed jackets for gentlemen, and sensible macs for ladies, as well as crafts, surround the lake around which some of the jumps are made. Take a camera with a telephoto lens or binoculars. Many people arrive equipped with shooting sticks or rugs to rest on, picnic hampers and umbrellas, and sit in a good position before the crowds mass. Coaches will take you from London to Badminton for the day. Contact *Badminton Horse Trials, High St, Badminton, Avon, tel: 045421 272.*

Races take place regularly at Ascot but the most interesting time to go is for Royal Ascot when the Queen arrives in her open carriage. This is not just a horse show. It is also a fashion show, with all the newspapers photographing the enormous or outrageous hats of Mrs Shilling, whose son runs a hat shop in London. Everybody would like to be in the Queen's enclosure, and each year it becomes more difficult to get in. My chosen hotel for Ascot would be Pennyhill Park described in Chapter 5 on gourmet food.

For weekends enjoying this spectator sport see the brochure on hotels offering weekend breaks pictured in 'Weekends in Beautiful Berkshire' from: *Beautiful Berkshire, Shire Hall, Shinfield Park, Reading RG2 9XD*, or *Thames & Chilterns Tourist Board, 8 The Market Place, Abingdon, Oxon, OX14 3UD, tel: Abingdon 22711.*

There is a race meeting somewhere in Britain almost every weekday throughout the year.

Horse riding is widely available in the countryside: there are riding schools where horses can be hired in every county.

Pony-trekking holidays are favoured in regions of open moorland, and facilities for them are well organised in parts of Wales and on Dartmoor and Exmoor and in some of the country of the Scottish borders and north of England. For information contact: *Ponies of Britain 1987, 56 Green End Road, Sawtry, Huntingdon, PE17 5UY, tel: 0487 830278.*

The national and local tourist boards have information on horse riding and golfing breaks.

MOTORING DAYS AND MOTORS
Nostalgia Motoring
You can travel in nostalgic style in Classic Cars of the 1950s ranging from a little Morris Minor (about £32 a week) to a luxury MKII Jaguar, a favourite criminal's get-away car in the old films (about £105 a week).
Nostalgia Motoring (Self Drive Hire), Higher Wiscombe, Southleigh, Colyton, Devon EX13 6JF, tel: 040487 408.

A vintage car can be rented from some museums such as Stratford Motor Museum, and are cheaper when you are already in Stratford, otherwise you pay the cost per mile for delivery of the car to London or elsewhere.

Motoring Events
The London to Brighton veteran car run takes place in November, with breaks offered at Brighton hotels.

The TT races, vintage car weekends and other car rallies are held on the Isle of Man in summer.

Sports and Activities

Contact *Isle of Man Tourist Board, 13 Victoria Street, Douglas, Isle of Man, tel: 0624 74323.*

Hire a Rolls

You can hire a Rolls Royce from major companies such as Hertz and Avis. If you don't drive or are feeling inactive, you can have a chauffeur driven Rolls Royce. Should you be fortunate enough to obtain a chauffeur trained by Rolls Royce, he wears the Rolls Royce chauffeur badge and follows the Rolls Royce rule book, wearing driving gloves. Guy Salmon charge over £150 for a half day tour of London by chauffeur driven Rolls Royce. A one day tour of up to 8 hours and 80 miles, including Windsor and Eton College (second oldest and most famous public school in England), Henley and Marlow on the river, will cost nearer £400. For details *Tel: 01-730 8571.*

A two-day tour of Stratford and the Cotswolds, stopping at Oxford would be over £750, plus accommodation which they will book for you if required at extra cost. A seven-seater Daimler is less expensive.

Rally Driving Instruction and Racing weekends

Ladbroke Hotels offer Action Extras Sporting Weekends. At the Rally Driving School registered with the RAC your skill at handling your own car is assessed. You also use the rally school cars for manoeuvres, high speed slalom driving and skid control. There are talks and lectures. The price is from £159 for one day instruction, £229 for two days, and under £50 bed and breakfast for non-participants.

Motor Racing

Ladbroke's motor racing weekends for budding Nikki Laudas are at the racing schools of Brands Hatch and Silverstone. The cost is from £87 at Silverstone, staying at a hotel in the university town of Oxford or the Ladbroke Hotel, Warwick, not far from Warwick Castle. The latter has an indoor swimming pool. The cost is £95 at Brands Hatch, under £50 for non-participants.

Practical, exciting and fun, another driver's weekend on offer costs about £70 including a three hour course on skid control. A six hour course ending with a test of skill is about £100 per person, for non-participants about £45.

Motoring Holidays

The Automobile Association's British Country Wanderer package is a go as you please voucher scheme for motoring holidays. You buy vouchers and can book your next night's accommodation ahead (one free phone call made at off-peak time between 18.00 and 22.00 hours) choosing from the list of nearly 500 hotels and inns. A free map and list of participating hotels is given. An extensive choice of nice hotels is included.

Prices for the accommodation voucher start from about £12.50 low season, £15 high season, for adults, with reductions for children sharing adult accommodation. Small supplements of approximately £2.50 per person per night are payable for single accommodation and private bathrooms. You only need to buy a minimum of four vouchers, which would cover two nights weekend accommodation for two people. Vouchers are valid all year except over Christmas. Unused vouchers are refunded less the administration fee of £2 per voucher. Contact your travel agents or *AA Travel (Argosy) Fanum House, Dogkennel Lane, Halesowen, West Midlands B63 3BT.*

Learn to Drive

If you can't drive, why not learn to drive? You can't expect to learn to drive in a weekend. You'll have to allow at least a week. Arel runs one and two week driving courses on manual or automatic cars to test standard, and refresher courses. Extra accommodation is available for families including children in cots.

They arrange for you to do a mock test and then a real one on Friday, returning to the school for a day at no extra charge if the Department of Transport cannot arrange the test on this date. Ideally you should have had eight or more hours instruction before starting the course if you want to take the test. Centres are at Bangor in North Wales, Brighton, Southend, and Whitley Bay. Courses for the hard of hearing and disabled are held in Llandudno, Wales.

For more details contact: *AREL Residential Courses, 5 Station Road, Llanfairfechan, Gwynedd, N Wales LL33 0AL, tel: 0248 680857.*

Sports and Activities

Driving Test Success Weekends
Celebration banquets for 10 to 500 people can be held at *Effingham Park Conference Centre & Motor Museum, Copthorne, West Sussex, RH10 3EU, near Gatwick, tel: 0324 713011.* The park contains a nine hole golf course and unusual fir trees, one of which has a soft trunk. A hotel and leisure centre is being built on this site. Alternatively you might wish to celebrate your first 100,000 miles of driving.

Motor Museums
See Motor museums such as *The National Motor Museum, Beaulieu, Hampshire, tel: 0590 612345* where you can ride on the monorail, and *Syon Park Heritage Collection, Brentford, Middlesex, TW8 8JG, tel: 01-560 0881,* about nine miles from central London. It closes at 4 pm in winter.

IN THE AIR
Ballooning
Ladbroke's sporting weekends include ballooning. You can help rig the balloon and take an early morning one hour balloon flight, floating over Bristol. Remember your camera. There is a glass of champagne on landing and you will be staying at the Ladbroke Dragonara hotel, known for the restaurant built around an old kiln used to fire blue glass. The cost is over £110, about half for non-participants.

Learn to Fly
A flying lesson for the budding Biggles is available staying at a Ladbroke hotel in Leeds. It is only a half hour lesson, but on these weekends you can try out a more expensive sport to see whether you like it before investing in buying equipment and a course of lessons.

Parachuting
If you feel like parachuting there's a day's instruction followed by an exhilarating jump and if you want you can pay extra and go back and do it again.

Gliding and Hang-gliding

A hang-gliding weekend includes a two day course of theory and ground training, practising low ground hops, ending with flying 15 to 20 feet off the ground for a distance of about 150 metres. This weekend is over £120. You pay roughly the same for a two day course in gliding. Alternatively for about half that price you can try gliding for twenty minutes, on a gliding weekend in another part of the country.

These prices include bed and breakfast. Details from: *Action Extras, Ladbroke Hotels, PO Box 137, Millbuck House, Watford, Herts, WD1 1DN, tel: 0923 38877*, or book through a travel agent.

Aircraft Museums

The aircraft enthusiast will wish to see the *Royal Air Force Museum and Battle of Britain Museum at Grahame Park Way, Hendon, London NW9 5LL, tel: 01-205 2266*.

Concorde 01 and a most important collection of civil aircraft can be seen at the *Imperial War Museum, Duxford Airfield, Cambridge, Duxford CB2 4QR, tel: 0223 833963 or 835000 (answering machine)*. Phone for dates of flying days. The museum also has a large collection of military aircraft and boats and land vehicles.

In Cornwall you can climb inside a model of the Concorde cockpit at *Cornwall AeroPark, Cornwall Aircraft Park, Nr Helston, Cornwall, tel: 0326 574549*. The museum park also has Flambards' Village with the sets and models of the TV series, and road transport from horse-drawn days onwards, as well as aeronautica.

Fly Joey

You can fly to Alderney in the Channel Islands and back to Southampton in a day on one of the little yellow planes made famous in the children's books. More details on this delightful and intimate air service by Aurigny airline are in Chapter 23 on islands.

WATERSPORTS

Waterskiing, and windsurfing and other watersports, are available

Sports and Activities

at various centres both on the coast and inland. Weekends based on these are available from Ladbroke hotels (address listed above).

Ladbroke hotels also do tennis weekends. Canoeing and rock climbing are arranged in the Fort William area of the west of Scotland.

More Information
The West Country Tourist Board issues a leaflet on activity holidays including horse riding, a three night walking holiday, with your luggage transported for you from one inn to the next, computer technology, brass rubbing, wood turning and other subjects.
Contact: *West Country Tourist Board, Trinity Court, Southernhay East, Exeter, Devon, tel: 0392 76351.*

CHAPTER 14
Water Appeal: Spa Baths and Beautiful Pools

The wet weather of Britain is well-known abroad, but to provide indoor entertainment all year whatever the weather seaside resorts and cities are building Leisure Centres all over Britain. Hotels, too, are installing indoor swimming centres and whirlpools to attract customers on weekends when business people have departed. The health craze has helped. Jacuzzis, they say, are 'good for tensed up skin, your circulation and your nerves'.

How to Spend a Wet Weekend
When it's wet weather outside, look for the wet inside, the hotel with a heated indoor swimming pool and, best of all, a Jacuzzi. Several companies offer weekend breaks.

The Italian Jacuzzi family emigrated to the USA and patented a water and air pump in 1925. Signor Jacuzzi, one of seven brothers in the San Francisco family firm, had a spastic son and developed a hydro-air massage jet which improved his son's condition. Thus the Jacuzzi pump company of America invented the whirlpool spa 25 years ago.

For a proper underwater massage strong jets are important. Whirlpools with teeny jets simply tickle you all over. The best whirlpools have a knob on the side enabling you to adjust the jet strength yourself. 'Larger and more powerful jets than any other whirlpool bath on the market', is Jacuzzi's claim.

A spa bath can tickle your feet, or massage shoulders aching after a long drive. Admittedly, some people prefer to be tickled all over, rather than pummelled in one place. Whirlpools which have strong jets need to have enough jets. Otherwise when several people get in a communal spa bath your neighbour gets the jet and you get nothing. Or there's no room to move around if the jet is in the wrong place! But in public jacuzzis the more the merrier. Socialising is part of the fun. One starts chatting when sitting opposite someone in a public whirlpool.

At most hotels, such as the THF group, the whirlpool attached to the swimming pool is free. However a few hotels have leisure centres run by other companies. Hotel guests get a discount.

Some hotels need extra business at weekends, and offer free use of the leisure centre as a bait. Others are inundated by weekenders who pop in for coffee, cocktails, or Sunday lunch and want to have a swim and whirl. The result is that people who have an all-year leisure centre club membership complain that on weekends the swimming pool is overcrowded, and the whirlpool is full. So Ramada Hotel, Reading, opens the leisure centre only to hotel residents or club members, while popular Last Drop Village, Bolton, with busy bars and restaurants at various prices, charge residents at weekends. Here are some of the hotels with good swimming facilities.

LONDON HOTELS

The Henry VIII Hotel has a small, warm indoor pool in the basement next to the bar area, though no Jacuzzi. See Consort Hotels listing at the end of this chapter or *tel: 01-262 0017*.

If you want a really luxurious weekend in London, try Le Meridien leisure club (formerly the New Piccadilly Hotel) which has a whirlpool and Turkish baths. The swimming pool is surrounded by blue tiles and white statues, overlooked by a poolside coffee shop. The centre is open to non-residents on a yearly basis for a hefty sum, but that lets you take in up to four visitors, so it might be worthwhile for a large family or business company. Back in the bedroom is your marble bathroom. See listing below.

Less expensive club membership is available at other hotels such as Holiday Inns. So for about £200 a year a family with three children could enjoy swimming, spas and saunas all day every Saturday, or Sunday, or both. Slimmers can exercise and swim two or three times a week after work.

The Sanctuary is a health club for women, a refuge from children and the man, with a tropical water garden, exotic birds, goldfish pond with fountain, sauna, Jacuzzi, Turkish steam room, and health food bar. Day membership costs about £20.
The Sanctuary, 11 Floral Street, London WC2, tel: 01-240 9635.

REGIONAL ENGLAND
Warwickshire
Ettington Park
A sumptuous stately home, surrounded by a massive private park with trees, is Ettington Park hotel. It features carved columns, wood panelling, and an indoor pool and jacuzzi too.
Ettington Park, Alderminster, Near Stratford-upon-Avon, Warwickshire, CU37 8BS, tel: 0789 740740.

The Belfry
Near Birmingham try the luxurious modern Belfry Hotel. It has a golf course, and a gourmet restaurant. A coffee shop overlooks the huge, luxurious swimming pool with dark wood ceiling and little wooden bridges. The spa bath is next to the pool, and a kiddies adventure playground is outside. And the hotel offers four-poster beds. A giant waterwheel adds character.
The Belfry, Lichfield Road, Wishaw, North Warwickshire B76 9PR, tel: 0675 70301.

The Holiday Inn in Birmingham has a smaller but pleasant brightly-lit swimming pool. It looks a bit like a pool under a greenhouse roof. There's no jacuzzi.

The **Albany Hotel** is my other choice in Birmingham, because the indoor pool is in a windowless basement.

Reading
Reading offers the elegant Ramada Hotel which has one of the prettiest pools I've seen. Blue tiles contrast with a white statue at one end and steps lead down into the shallow end, good for plump ladies who don't like descending, or ascending, ladders at the deep end.

It is a smart hotel with an ultra-modern presidential suite

featuring modern American furniture in pastel colours.
Ramada Hotel, Reading, Berks, RG1 7RH, tel: 0734 586222.

The Trusthouse Forte hotel in Reading is more of a family hotel with a children's playground adjoining the coffee shop and pleasant modern indoor pool with a jacuzzi.

Derby
The Swallow Hotel on the Derbyshire–Nottinghamshire border is a little way from Derby town by the motorway. It has an indoor pool and jacuzzi, prettily decorated rooms (swan theme net curtains) and bathrooms. There is an expensive gourmet restaurant, also a less expensive but not cheap second restaurant with lace decorations, Nottingham being a lace centre. Some bedrooms are designed with wide doors to take wheelchairs, and braille door numbers, though I couldn't see any way of getting a wheelchair downstairs to the pool area.
Swallow Hotel Derby/Notts, Junction 28 (M1), Carter Lane East, South Normanton, Derbyshire, D55 2EH, tel: 0773 812000.

The Lake District
When other lakeside hotels are full try the Lancaster Posthouse (THF), right on the motorway. Comfortable bedrooms are furnished with every convenience, though not much colour. A modern seating area is around the large indoor pool and jacuzzi. Separate saunas for each sex are inside their respective changing rooms, not ideal for romantic couples. 'Where have you been for the last half hour, in the sauna while I was in the pool? This was supposed to be a romantic weekend!'

The luxurious Pillar Hotel and Country Club in the Lake District is singularly attractive with its stream flowing through the restaurant, pub with waterwheel, swimming pool, spa bath and sauna. Breaks cost about £47 per night per person in the best available room including dinner and breakfast.
Pillar Hotel, Great Langdale, Near Ambleside, Cumbria LA22 9JD, tel: 09667 302.

Cheshire
At Chester the *Mollington Banastre Hotel on Park Gate Rd, tel:*

0244 851471 has a leisure complex and smart restaurant. Our family bedroom had an en suite kiddie bedroom with bunk beds. A Best Western hotel: see 'Hotel Groups' at end of chapter for details of address.

The Cottons Hotel, Knutsford, is rather uninspiring from outside, but beautifully decorated inside with rosewood furniture, a New Orleans style restaurant, a smallish indoor swimming pool and a spa bath.

The Cottons Hotel, Manchester Road, Knutsford, Cheshire WA16 0SU, tel: 0565 50333.

North West
Last Drop Village, Hospital Road, Bromley Cross, Bolton, tel: 0204 591131, has a leisure centre as part of the reconstructed olde worlde village.

The Royal Clifton Hotel, Southport, tel: 0704 33771, has an indoor pool and spa bath.

In Carlisle the String of Horses offers cosily romantic luxury. The beamed pub restaurant has lots of characterful clutter. Small bedrooms and bathrooms are filled with four-posters, Bonsack baths with gold taps, and all kinds of free bits and pieces from teeny sherry bottles to bubblebath. Down in the basement there's a unisex sauna – one of the few where couples can stay together, and a spa bath. Also an outdoor swimming pool for good weather.

String of Horses Inn & Restaurant, Heads Nook, Cumbria CA4 9EG, tel: 022870 297.

North East
At Scarborough the Royal Hotel in St Nicholas Street has a basement spa bath and indoor pool plus a mural and poolside bar. The grand staircase with pillars is most impressive, although it is a family hotel with a nanny service in summer.

Royal Hotel, St Nicholas Street, Scarborough, YO11 2HE, tel: 0723 364333.

In Huddersfield Cote Royd Hotel has a leisure centre including an indoor pool. The town centre Huddersfield Hotel has a spa bath.

Scotland

In Glasgow, the elegant Holiday Inn has an indoor pool, and spa bath. Bedrooms and bathrooms are nicely decorated.
Holiday Inn at Argyle St, Anderston, Glasgow G3 8RR tel: 041 226 5577.

The Holiday Inn, at Aberdeen Airport offers a Moroccan style entrance hall, with a log fire in winter, and a spa bath and large luxurious swimming pool surrounded by an elegant cocktail lounge.
Aberdeen Airport, Riverview Drive, Farburn, Dyce, AB2 0AZ, tel: 0224 770011.

In Edinburgh, Swallow Hotel's Royal Scot has a leisure centre with indoor pool and spa bath, *tel: 031-334 9191.*
  Carlton Highland Hotel, North Bridge, Edinburgh EH1 1SD, tel: 031-556 7277, has a leisure centre with a spa bath illuminated underwater, and children's activities.
  North of the city overlooking the Firth of Forth bridges, illuminated at night, is the Forth Bridges Moat House, South Queensferry, which has a pool and spa bath, *tel: 031-331 1199.*

The Mount Charlotte group's Hospitality Inn at Irvine has a Hawaiian lagoon. Tropical plants, palms and boulders surround the leisure complex which is one of the largest in the country. This four star hotel is on the west coast of Scotland – a pity it is not nearer the big centres.
Hospitality Inn, Irvine, Roseholm, Annick Water, Irvine, Ayrshire KA11 4LD, tel: 0294 74272.

The Peebles Hydro is conveniently just across the border into Scotland, and near enough to Edinburgh by bus or car. Family hotels, boring bedrooms and bathrooms but magnificent views across hills, lovely indoor pool with bird murals, poolside snack bar, jacuzzi, open till late evening (unlike other hotels which close at supper time, around 8), excellent for families. See Consort Hotels for address at end of chapter.

Wales

For Cardiff, The Inn on the Avenue on the motorway just before you reach Cardiff has a pleasant pool, spa bath and sauna.

tel: 0222 732520. You can also land a helicopter in the car park, on the H sign.

Cardiff also has a new Holiday Inn.

Holiday Inn Weekend breaks
Holiday Inns offer indoor swimming pools, and several have adjoining spa baths, e.g. Portsmouth.

A Manchester-based reader enthused about the Newcastle Holiday Inn, saying it was 'the swishiest hotel most ordinary folk like us will stay at'. Her family spent about £100 for two nights bed and breakfast for two adults and all offspring – children up to the age of 19 – yes 19! staying free, plus free 'Carvery' breakfast which would last you all day – eat your fill.

In addition the Newcastle Holiday Inn offers a programme of five or so stately homes, or gardens, free tickets for everyone, geared to summer or winter activities. Nylon zipper funbags were full of games, sweets, badges etc – all free, plus a tee shirt for one, free TV plus in-room movies, gym, sauna, and free swimming lessons in a super swimming pool! Breaks range from about £25 per person per night at Birmingham to £50 in Mayfair, London.

Crest Hotels
Crest hotels at South Mimms, Bristol and Maidenhead have Leisure Clubs with gyms, swimming pools, children's pool and play area, sauna, spa bath and games room. Annual membership is open to members of the local community and local companies for a fee. Overnight guests use the facilities free, except for solariums.

ADVICE

If you really want to know how often the water is filtered and recirculated, and how often entirely fresh water is used, ask the hotel or leisure centre manager.

One hotel owner pointed out that some people say you should not spend more than about 10 minutes in a jacuzzi anyway.

A strong jet massage is the main advantage of a jacuzzi,

making aches and depression disappear. But it's equally difficult to feel sorry for yourself sitting in a spa bath being tickled all over!

If you prefer the strong jet to the gentle tickle, many jacuzzis have a knob you can adjust. So if you're fussy, look into the leisure centre, ask, and twiddle the knobs, before investing in your weekend. If your main reason for picking the hotel is its leisure facilities, phone before you leave home and check what is working. I've been to hotels where the jacuzzi or sauna had broken down.

Also phone the leisure centre before eating in the restaurant and check whether facilities will be available later. In one hotel the sauna wasn't working after breakfast until the first customer turned it on and you had to wait for it to heat up. At another the sauna was not available after my early supper because they turned off the heat half an hour before closing time.

In some hotels the demand for saunas is so great that a charge is made and you have to book saunas in advance for 15 minute sessions. This applied when I was at Quality Inn's Beechhill in the Lake District, the Best Western Imperial Hotel at Hythe, and the Polurrian Hotel in the Lizard, Cornwall. I found that either I had to go without the sauna, or the day's outing started late, or the family's day out was interrupted by a dash back to claim the sauna.

SWIMMING CENTRES
London Swimming Pools
At least two London leisure centres offer warm water winter or summer fun to the general public. Among the half dozen or so wavepools in London are those at *Fulham Pools, Normand Park, Lillie Rd, London SW6, tel: 01-381 4494; Elephant & Castle Leisure Pool, 22 Elephant & Castle, London SE1, tel: 01-582 5505;* and *White City Pool, Bloemfontein Rd, White City, London W12, tel: 01-743 3401.*

A swimming pool with a giant spiral tube slide opened in 1987 at *Harrow Leisure Centre,* near Harrow & Wealdstone station, *tel: 01-863 9580.*

Wales Wave Pools

Swansea, the south coast town a little west of Cardiff, offers a public leisure complex with a wave pool and a spiral see-through tube chute or slide. *Swansea Leisure Centre, Swansea, South Wales, tel: 0792 49126.*

In North Wales, the seaside of Rhyl has an indoor leisure complex with kiddie slides, a wave pool and an indoor monorail. *Rhyl Suncentre, Promenade, Rhyl, North Wales, tel: 0745 31771.*

West Country centres

In the west country Butlin's Somerwest World, at Minehead, Somerset, TA24 5SH, opens the swimming pool, whirlpools, waves, fountains, 55 foot high enclosed slides, and amusement park to day visitors: admission about £5 before or after 6.30 pm, and £2 more for 10 am to midnight. For details ring *freephone 0800 222 555.*

Tropicana, Marine Parade, Weston-super-Mare, Avon

Giants and giant tropical fruit create a most unusual landscape and seascape at Tropicana, a large outdoor swimming centre. The surf pool washes you ashore on the artificial beach, and water chutes descend 130 feet, twisting and curving from a giant pineapple. Children can slide down the elephant's trunk or clamber over the alligator. In the activity garden they climb through the giant's head, slide down his tongue, and explore giant fruit. You can also take showers from the four huge fountains, or hire skates and glide around on simulated ice! Open April to October.
Tourist Information Centre, Beach Lawns, tel: 26838, 24 hour answering about the resort and accommodation.

HOTEL GROUPS

Best Western Hotels, tel: 01-541 0033. Public whirlpools, e.g. Selsdon Park, Croydon, and Grosvenor House Hotel, Stratford.
Consort Hotels, tel: 0904 20137, e.g. Peebles Hydro Hotel, Scotland, tel: 0721 20602, public whirlpool.
Crest Hotels, tel: 01-236 3242. Numerous hotels with bedroom

Spa Baths and Pools

whirlpools, e.g. Marlborough and Regent Crest Hotels, London, Gatwick Crest, and Crest Cardiff.
De Vere Hotels, tel: 0925 35471. Public whirlpools, e.g. Grand Hotel, Eastbourne, tel: 0323 22611 or Belfry Hotel, nr Birmingham, tel: 0675 70301.
Hilton Hotels, tel: 01-631 1767 (central reservations); e.g. Gatwick Hilton International Hotel, tel: 0293 518080, public whirlpool.
Holiday Inns, tel: 01-586 8111. Leisure centre whirlpools, e.g. Glasgow.
Intercontinental Hotel Corporation's Intercontinental Hotel, London, tel: 01-409 3131, has Jacuzzis in 8 bedroom suites. The Mayfair Hotel, tel: 01-629 7777, has 24 Jacuzzis in bedrooms.
Inter-Hotels, privately owned hotels, some with public spa baths, tel: 01-373 3241.
Le Meridien, formerly Gleneagles New Piccadilly Hotel, London. Leisure club with Jacuzzi, tel: 01-734 8000.
Norfolk Capital Hotels, tel: 01-581 0601, Norfolk Hotel, London. Some bedrooms have only shower rooms, but all 97 bathrooms have Jacuzzis.
Prestige Hotels, tel: 01-439 2365.
Queens Moat Houses, tel: 0708 25814, e.g. Forth Bridges Moat House, nr Edinburgh, public whirlpool, tel: 031-331 1199.
Sarova's Rembrandt Hotel, Knightsbridge, tel: 01-589 8100, has Jacuzzis in the Aquilla Health Club. USA tollfree 800 424 2862.
Shire Inns, tel: 0282 414141, who send courtesy cars to meet weekenders at railway stations, have a public whirlpool at Cottons Hotel, Knutsford, tel: 0565 50333.
Stakis Hotels, tel: 041-332 4343, Inn on the Avenue, Cardiff, public whirlpool.
Swallow Hotels, tel: 01-370 1595; eight hotels with leisure centres including the Swallow at Derby/Notts which has a spa bath.
Thistle Hotels, tel: 01-937 8033, Portland Thistle Hotel, Manchester, public whirlpool, also Gosforth Park, Newcastle.
THF (Trusthouse Forte), tel: 01-567 3444. Hotel leisure centre pools, whirlpools and saunas free to residents, e.g. Lancaster Post House Hotel, Cambridge Post House.

CHAPTER 15
Theme Parks and Special Interests

Theme parks like Alton Towers – the most ambitious visitors' and entertainment complex in Britain – offer all-day organised fun for families, or weekend packages. Daytime outings can be taken to leisure parks attached to historic stately homes. Theme evenings are arranged for groups at hotels and venues such as Windsor Safari Park. They will serve Italian and other ethnic food, with suitable table trimmings, decor, and music or entertainers if required.

There is also a vast choice of theme weekends ranging from the comic to the serious. Seaside towns offer maritime weekends, and it is easy to organise your own lighthearted trail on a sailing and smuggling theme. Complete pre-arranged theme weekends cover subjects as varied as clowns, music, gardens, ghosts, and Teddy bears.

For example, there is slapstick fun at the annual Clowns Convention on the south coast, or you could select serious culture provided by classical musicians at music weekends, or use your time in learning at holiday courses arranged by one of the universities.

THEME PARKS

Thorpe Park (London)

Just west of London not far from Heathrow airport is Thorpe Park, where you will meet characters in animal costumes, the way you do at Disneyworld. Thorpe Park redeveloped the site of an old gravel pit. It now has a Treasure Island, outdoor scale models of the world's famous buildings, and a thrilling ride through whirling white water along 'Thunder River'.

In the indoor cinema with a 180 degrees screen, your stomach yo-yos as you watch films of roller-coaster rides and high speed car racing. The car screeches around a corner then suddenly slams on the brakes as a woman with a pram steps into the road – the whole audience shrieks!

Computer-controlled lifesize puppets, a teacup ride, waterski shows and jousting are other attractions. Phone for the dates of shows.
Thorpe Park, Staines Lane, Chertsey, Surrey, tel: 09328 62633.

Alton Towers (Staffordshire)
One of Britain's most popular venues for a day out or package weekend is Alton Towers. More than two million visitors a year explore Britain's top theme park. There is always something new – the chair lift extended uphill in 1987, with rides on see-through gondolas.

The colourful gardens tumbling down the hillside appeal to grandparents and romantics, while teenagers brave turning upside down on the thrilling corkscrew ride.

Families with children love the new grand canyon rapids ride despite sometimes being doused in water. There is so much to do. See the wildlife and doll museums, acrobats at the circus, indoor fountains dancing to music, cinema, outdoor parades and Kiddies Kingdom. You could spend three days at Alton Towers and not try everything, though motorbus trains run you from one themed area to another.

There's fast food or an elegant pineclad Swiss restaurant and a moving waterwheel restaurant. Combined rail tickets and entrance fee are available for a summer day out from London.

Alton Towers supplies a leaflet listing the nearest hotels, budget breaks, guesthouses and campsites. Hotel group packages are available from THF, Crest, Stakis, Best Western, Thistle, Superbreak, Embassy, De Vere, Anchor and Swallow.

Admission is £6 or more for adults and children, with reductions for senior citizens and two-day tickets.
Alton Towers, Alton, North Staffordshire, tel: 0538 702200.

Alton has different theme areas such as the water section, but to the Americans its particularly British aspect is the way a leisure park is developed in the grounds of a former stately home. Alton Towers was merely a ruin. But previously other stately homes which could boast of intact buildings and priceless art treasures were in financial difficulties, and they opened leisure parks to bring in money for their upkeep.

Woburn Abbey (Bedfordshire) with its animals is known for being the earliest of the stately homes whose titled owner inherited death duty demands and started a safari park to meet tax bills. It is about an hour's drive from London. *Woburn Abbey and Park, Woburn, Bedfordshire, tel: 052525 666 (abbey) or 052525 246 (park).*

Longleat House (Wiltshire) is now as well known for its lions as its Elizabethan art treasures. The grounds were landscaped by Capability Brown in 1757. Whatever 'capabilities' he saw in the landscape, he could not have envisaged the tigers, giraffes, and camels. *Longleat House and Safari Park, Longleat, Warminster, Wiltshire, BA12 7NN, tel: 0985 3551.*

Lord Montagu's **Beaulieu Palace House** in Hampshire is famous for its motoring theme, with a National Motor Museum and monorail. *Tel: 0590 612345.*

Windsor Safari Park (Berkshire) offers a host of wildlife, seven drive-through reserves, and performing killer whale and sealion watershows. It also offers theme evenings such as medieval banquets, and Caribbean, or Country and Western, evenings. It can be reached on an afternoon out from London, or linked with a trip to Windsor Castle. *Windsor Safari Park, Winkfield Road, Windsor, Berkshire, SL4 4AY, tel: 0753 869841.*

Sudeley Castle (Gloucestershire): If you need to combine cultural interests for adults with activities having child-appeal, many stately homes offer adventure playgrounds. Sudeley Castle has a large log play fort, a toy collection, the tomb of Katherine Parr who was King Henry VIII's sixth wife, and falconry displays on summer Sundays. Phone to check dates and times. *Sudeley Castle, Winchcombe, Gloucestershire, tel: 0242 602308.*

THEME EVENTS AND WEEKENDS

Clowns' Convention (Sussex)

A popular weekend happening which everyone can join in is the Clowns' Convention. The World's first International Clowns' Convention took place in Bognor Regis, West Sussex in April 1985 and it looks like remaining an annual event. Clowns have a Grand Parade through the streets, local schools join in, and even the local police don red noses. Clowns stop the traffic, search buses for the best giggler, stop police cars and dust them down, escort elderly couples across the street, and shake hands with children while keen parents take photographs.

In the first year clowns from all over the world were invited, and TV and the media descended. In year two the postmen delivered mail, some dressed in motley clown costumes, all in red noses. Multiple chain stores put in special clown window displays and staff dressed up to serve customers in Clownsville.

The opening speech of welcome by Ron Moody was constantly interrupted by snatches of grand opera. Gala shows had full programmes remembered for numerous clown acts such as those by Christof of Austria and Vercoe from Southport. Clowns from all over Europe came.

In year three Virgin Atlantic brought the American and Russian Clowns to meet each other for a Clown Summit. A 3,000 seater big top tent was secured for a spectacular show. Who knows what the next year will bring?

For details of the Clowns Galore package with accommodation at all prices contact:
Dick Coen, Project Manager, Arun Tourist Office, Place St Maur Des Fosses, Bognor Regis, West Sussex PO21 1BJ, tel: 0243 823140 or Leisure & Tourism Department, Arun District Council, tel: Littlehampton (0903) 716133.

Theme evenings are arranged at hotels and restaurants around Britain.

If you are planning a party, the Granville Hotel in Brighton is willing to do any 'colourful' weekend. On one occasion their theme was pink, with pink champagne, pink ice-cream, and guests wearing clothes 'in the pink'.
Granville Hotel, 125 King's Road, Brighton, Sussex, BN1 2FY, tel: 0273 26722.

Most major hotel groups have brochures of pre-arranged theme weekends. But you could put together your own individual seaside tour, staying at small guesthouses or hotels, discovering smugglers' haunts.

Smuggling, pirates, restored ships, maritime museums and the sea are themes along the coast. You might follow a maritime England weekend theme, along Southern England or the Cornish coast, visiting harbours, lighthouses, and maritime museums. See Portsmouth and Plymouth maritime weekends described under city breaks (Chapter 24).

Smugglers' Hotel (Cornwall)
The small Smugglers' Hotel, down by Newlyn harbour, with its stone-walled cellar bar, and sheepdog, welcomes children and pets. Write to:
David and Deborah Reeve, The Smugglers' Hotel, Newlyn, Cornwall, tel: Penzance: 0736 64207.

Admiral Benbow (Cornwall)
In the once cobbled street of Penzance is the marvellous Admiral Benbow Restaurant. In olden times a tunnel used to lead into the courtyard of the 'sailor's lodging house of ill repute'. The tunnel was bricked up and earth-filled, perhaps to try and trap the Benbow ghost. If you still feel you are being watched, maybe that is because a spy-hole from the tunnel behind the fireplace looks into the Benbow.

The Benbow Brandy Men met here and one night the revenue officers came for them. The statue you see of a figure lying on the roof tiles pointing his pistol represents the heroic second-in-command of the brandymen who created a diversion to distract their pursuers. You'll be glad to know he lived to tell the tale.

When driving through Penzance you can stop to see and photograph the outside of the Benbow, but do try to see the inside. It is the best part. The Benbow's interior looks like an old low-beamed ship out of Treasure Island. The bronze bells and ship's wheels from numerous wrecks were salvaged from the sea by the Benbow's owner.

Bits of boats form the bars, ships' timbers are made into overhead beams and tables. Painted figureheads from shipwrecks guard doorways. Ships' copper lanterns hang on walls. And ropes, nets and tackle are draped across corners.

This is an ideal location for a pirate party. For groups pirate evenings can be arranged with local actors dressed as pirates staging fights and chasing a cabin boy who hides beneath the tables.

Potted plants surround the upstairs bar where you can lunch on spare ribs, sitting under the blackened beams, looking out towards the sea, reading the booklet on sale about the owner who dived and rescued all those figureheads in the old seafaring days. (Across the street is a maritime museum displaying more trophies rescued from wrecks).
The Admiral Benbow, Chapel Street, Penzance, Cornwall, tel: 0736 63448.

The tunnel into the Benbow's courtyard was probably made by a Cornish miner. Cornwall is known for its mines which you can visit, and savour the old stories revived in the Poldark novels and the Poldark TV series. The miner's safety lamp was invented by Sir Humphrey Davy whose statue is around the corner at the top of Penzance High Street.

MUSIC LOVERS' WEEKENDS

If you want to enjoy live music played by twentieth century personalities in splendid locations, Trusthouse Forte arranges seasons of concert weekends. Last season they invited Julian Lloyd Webber, the cello player who is brother of Andrew, and students from the Yehudi Menuhin Music School. The English Heritage Singers, whose programme comprises popular songs from Gilbert and Sullivan operettas, also sang love songs on St Valentine's Day. Numerous string quartets, harpists, pianists, choirs and bands of one kind and another appear at weekends around Britain.

The Lion Hotel (Shrewsbury)
One of my favourite hotels when music features is the olde worlde Lion hotel at Shrewsbury. Performances take place in the Adam ballroom, where Paganini played.
The Lion, Wyle Cop, Shrewsbury, Shropshire SY1 1UY, tel: 0743 53107.

Operetta (The Mansion House at Grim's Dyke, near London)
The Gilbert and Sullivan Sunday soirées are held in a hotel created from the Victorian mansion which was Sir William Gilbert's former home. The Grim's Dyke hotel is located in Harrow Weald, north-west of London in the 'Green belt', a ring of protected countryside encircling the city. In summertime Gilbert and Sullivan performances are held for a week in the gardens, viewed from seats on bandstands.

The hotel's Iolanthe Hall with its minstrel gallery, barrel ceiling, and Cornish Alabaster fireplace was Sir William's old music room.

The gabled black and white Victorian mansion now has a modern bedroom block in the grounds. But in the Gilbert Suite in the main building you can sleep in a four-poster bed in the room which was Sir William and Lady Gilbert's own bedroom. After the exertion of rescuing a young lady who was learning to swim in the lake, Gilbert died here in 1911.

You can hold a private dinner party in the oak-panelled Yeoman room where Sir William used to dine and it is said that by the window he wrote his last successful operetta in partnership with Sullivan, 'Utopia Unlimited'. Wedding receptions can be held here for anyone who is 'going to marry Yum Yum', as Gilbert wrote. For groups, English operettas, Victorian or Viennese evenings, and excerpts from American musicals can be arranged.

The autumn leaves along Old Redding are particularly spectacular. In good weather from the hilltop car park lookout point opposite the entrance to Grim's Dyke you can see across London suburbs to the peak of Harrow on the Hill. Drive up to visit the famous Harrow school, where Winston Churchill and so many others studied.

The Mansion House at Grim's Dyke, Old Redding, Harrow Weald, Middlesex HA3 6SH, tel: 01-954 7666 & 4227.

The Promenade Concerts (Royal Albert Hall, London)
Another very British musical occasion, a grand national event, is the Last Night of the Proms. The Promenade Concerts are held at the Royal Albert Hall, with ballots for the coveted Last Night tickets. The Proms were founded with the idea that those young

music lovers unable to afford seats could stand and walk about. 'Top' view is from the circular upper tier galleries. But the favoured cheap tickets are standing down in the centre, where some young people sit on the floor, but most stand. The Last Night is televised live. The audience links arms and sways to the music. They shout for the conductor to return for an encore and exchange banter with him. When the green light goes on over the TV camera window you know you are being filmed and there is a waving of jokey banners and teddy bears wearing union jacks. The programme ends with British patriotic favourites like 'Land of Hope and Glory', 'Jerusalem', and the 'Fantasia on British Sea Songs'. The audience joins in the choruses, singing with great gusto.

Male Voice Choirs (Wales)
Music lovers might also like the Eisteddfod International Festival at Llangollen, North Wales, held in the first complete week in July, at which choirs and dancers from all over the world compete. Hotels start getting booked a year in advance. The national Eisteddfod held in different Welsh towns each year takes place in the first week in August. Local tourist boards can arrange for you to attend a Welsh male voice choir rehearsal.

Male voice choirs sing at the Llanfyllin festival in Powys, Mid-Wales, and in the BBC's Choir of the Year competition held in Cardiff in the spring. Choirs perform in Cardiff and other Welsh towns in celebration of the national St David's Day, March 1st.

EDUCATIONAL COURSES
The Open University offers some short residential courses on a variety of cultural and educational subjects.

Some British universities and colleges offer study breaks and special interest holidays to the general public during university vacations, especially the long summer vacation. They accommodate their customers in college or campus accommodation.

Nine universities have grouped together to provide a range of summer vacation courses on art, literature, heritage, and the

countryside. Topics include Viking Britain, Music in Elizabethan England and The Marine Life of a Beach, with lectures and excursions. Locations are Birmingham, Canterbury, Durham, Exeter, Norwich, Sheffield, Liverpool, Swansea and Edinburgh. The cost is about £160 including accommodation, full board, and tuition.
Summer Academy of Continuing Education, The University, Canterbury, Kent CT2 7NX, tel: 0227 470402.

Children and parents can enjoy brushing up on computers at weekends run by Crest hotels.

The English Tourist Board publishes a guide to the subjects covered by Theme Weekend Breaks, ranging from bridge playing weekends to antiques.

To put together your own weekend consult the guidebook *Museums & Galleries in Great Britain and Ireland* which has a subject index covering everything you can think of from Advertising, Posters and Packaging to Zoology. Dozens of museums cover popular subjects such as archaeology, cinematography and photography, costumes, dolls and toys, medical, music, stamps, railways, science, sport, theatre, transport, and witchcraft.

Most local tourist boards have maps showing routes for suggested itineraries covering their area on specific themes.

GARDENS

The National Trust, devoted to preserving buildings, gardens, and landscape of special interest, has Meet the Gardener events. Annual membership tickets enable you to have free entry to properties every weekend. There is another National Trust for Scotland.

Best Western has garden weekends for gardeners. One of their gardening getaway breaks gives you the opportunity to visit the garden of Percy Thrower, the TV gardening expert. Contact *Best Western Hotels, Vine House, 143 London Road, Kingston-upon-Thames, Surrey KT2 6NA, tel: 01-541 0033.*

Escorted Garden & Heritage tours around Kent, known as

'The Garden of England', are in the Golden Gateways brochure. Contact *Kent Crusader Ltd, Freepost, Tunbridge Wells, Kent TN4 0BR, tel: 0892 28181.* No stamp required.

A useful reference book for outings is 'Historic Houses, Castles & Gardens' published by British Leisure Publications. 'The Ordnance Survey Guide to Gardens in Britain' has a colour picture of each garden and a description of it on pages interleaved with 60 maps. 'Gardens of England and Wales Open to the Public' published by the National Gardens Scheme is a guide to over 2,000 gardens which are not normally open to the public except on a few specific days of the year. Contact: *National Gardens Scheme, 57 Lower Belgrave Street, London SW1W 0LR, Tel: 01-730 0359.*

PART V

Weekends around the Regions

CHAPTER 16
Scotland

Scotland has been a favourite holiday destination for the British royal family since the time when Queen Victoria built Balmoral in the north east of Scotland, west of Aberdeen. The romantic royal history of Mary Queen of Scots and Bonnie Prince Charlie appears again and again in castles and stately homes all over Scotland.

A feature of Scottish architecture is that buildings in many parts are constructed from grey granite. Circular towers often project above ground level on the corners of fairytale castles, and are frequently seen decorating mansions and smaller detached houses too.

The character of the Scottish people and the wild scenery are complementary attractions. Pipers in swirling kilts and shops selling tartans abound in the busy cities of south Scotland. Most of the population lives in or near the big cities of Glasgow and Edinburgh, centres offering culture and entertainment.

The sparsely inhabited Highlands and Islands with their mountains and moors and lochs provide a totally different type of get away from it all holiday. There's golfing, fishing, and keeping warm by drinking whisky!

THE BORDERS
The nearest area of Scotland for visitors from England is, of course, the Borders. It is possible to drive here from London in a day, perhaps stopping for lunch or overnight at York or Carlisle. Overnight trains with sleeper accommodation go from London to Glasgow or to Edinburgh, and further north to Aberdeen or Inverness.

Abbotsford House (Melrose, Borders)
In the borders near Selkirk you can visit Walter Scott's mansion. See the wood panelled library and the desk where he wrote such famous novels as 'Waverley' and 'Ivanhoe'. His possessions included Rob Roy's gun, and a black mourning ring from Victorian times. *Abbotsford House, Melrose, Borders, Scotland, tel: 0896 2043.*

Traquair House (Innerleithen, Peeblesshire)
A Walter Scott Trail can be followed. Sir Walter Scott visited Traquair House in the border area eight miles from Peebles and used it as a setting in his novels. He said that Traquair House's Bear Gates were shut after Bonnie Prince Charlie left in 1745, never to be re-opened until the Stuarts are back on the throne. The bears face each other from the top of the plinths either side of the gate. Traquair House is the oldest inhabited house in Scotland. It is open to the public, and Mary Queen of Scots' bed can be seen, her son's cradle, and a secret staircase for the escape of Catholic priests. You might encounter the laird who lives here, and you can buy a bottle of the Traquair strong ale made in his brew house. *Traquair House, Innerleithen, Peeblesshire, EH44 6PW, tel: 0896 830323.*

Manderston (Duns, Berwickshire)
Another interesting stately home in the area is the Palmer family's Manderston Mansion which has a silver-plated staircase balustrade, and a collection of Huntley and Palmer biscuit boxes. Manderston, Duns, Berwickshire, tel: 0361 83450/82359.

John Buchan Centre (Biggar, Strathclyde)
West of Peebles at Biggar is the John Buchan Centre, honouring

the author who was also a statesman and distinguished public servant, and became Governor General of Canada. He was devoted to his native Scotland. 'The Thirty Nine Steps', filmed by Alfred Hitchcock, was set further south near Creetown. *John Buchan Centre, Broughton, Biggar, Strathclyde, Scotland, tel: 0899 21050.*

Hotels: Borthwick Castle (Gorebridge, Midlothian)

In the Borders and Edinburgh region you could stay at Borthwick Castle, Borthwick, associated with Mary Queen of Scots. When she and her husband Bothwell were beseiged here by an army her husband abandoned her, but she followed him by dressing as a pageboy and descending a rope! *Borthwick Castle, Gorebridge, Midlothian, Edinburgh, Scotland EH2 4QY, tel: 0875 20514.*

Other good hotels are aristocratic *Sunlaws at Kelso tel: Roxburgh 23303, see Royal*; and chic *Philipburn House Hotel, Selkirk, tel: 0750 20747*, which has pleasant pine bedrooms, a pine restaurant with gourmet food, and pine corridors; or jolly *Peebles Hydro* at Peebles, *tel: 0721 20602*, described in more detail in Chapter 13 on 'Sports and Activities'.

GLASGOW

Forty-five miles from Edinburgh is Glasgow. The city is larger than Edinburgh, and there is a feeling of rivalry between the two cities among the natives. Glasgow is a great Victorian city. In the centre there's now a lively modern outdoor pedestrian shopping precinct, and some major hotels (such as Holiday Inn, THF, and Skean Dhu) within walking distance. Around the city are several interesting museums.

The Burrell Collection

A major attraction is the Burrell Collection of art and antiquities and silver which opened in the 1980s. It is housed in a glass-walled museum admitting sunlight and views of trees in the park outside – a museum design which contrasts with older museums in Glasgow. A contrast to the light ultra-modern main section of the building is the dim interior containing traditional living rooms with wood-panelled walls brought here from the house of shipping magnate Burrell, who made his fortune from the River Clyde and formed the collection.

Nearby in the park is Pollock House which has paintings by El Greco and William Blake. *The Burrell Collection, Pollockshaws Road, Pollock Country Park, Glasgow G43 1AT, Scotland, tel: 041 649 7151.*

Hunterian Art Gallery (Glasgow)

The Mackintosh Room in the Hunterian Art Gallery at Glasgow University shows a reconstruction of the home of the great turn-of-the-century architect Charles Rennie Mackintosh, including his high-backed chairs. *Hunterian Art Gallery, Hillhead Street, Glasgow University, tel: 041 339 8855.*

Art Gallery & Museum (Glasgow)

In Kelvingrove west of the city centre, there is Glasgow's Art Gallery and Museum. The famous Salvador Dali painting of the crucifixion seen from above hangs here. It also houses the Museum of Transport collection, the Natural History collection and much more. *The Art Gallery and Museum, Kelvingrove Park, Glasgow G3 8AG, tel: 041 357 3929.*

Glasgow Cemetery and Cathedral

Finally, for something different, see Glasgow Necropolis, behind Glasgow Cathedral, one of the world's most startling cemeteries, on a hill crowned by a marble forest of the famous. Victorian statues of the departed stand proudly on giant columns surveying their city. *Glasgow Cathedral, Cathedral Street, Glasgow, Scotland, tel: 041-552 0220.*

David Livingstone Museum (Blantyre)

South of Glasgow at Blantyre is the birthplace of David Livingstone, showing the cramped conditions of the tenement in which he was born in 1813. There are accounts of how he studied to become a doctor and travelled as a missionary and explorer in Africa (where he was found by Stanley, 'Dr Livingstone I presume'), plus a complete Africa pavilion. *Livingstone Scottish National Memorial, Blantyre, Scotland, tel: 0698 823140.*

Glasgow Hotels

The Holiday Inn has a romantic bar, lounge and restaurant around the indoor swimming pool and whirlpool on the ground floor: a good place to meet a friend for a drink. Free transportation to and from the airport is available on request – it is next to the air terminal and bus station. *Holiday Inn, Argyle Street, Anderston, Glasgow, Strathclyde, Lanarkshire, Scotland G3 8RR, tel: 041-226 5577.*

One block away is THF's The Albany hotel, a bit grander and less intimate. It has a pricey suite with a four-poster. *The Albany, Bothwell Street, Glasgow, G2 7EN, tel: 041-248 2656.*

The most central large hotel, right in the shopping area is the Hospitality Inn. *The Glasgow Hospitality Inn, 36 Cambridge Street, Glasgow G3 7DS, tel: 041-332 3311.*

There are also five Stakis hotels, some of which are cheaper.

NORTHERN SCOTLAND — THE HIGHLANDS

Fort William

A museum in the centre of Fort William gives details of Bonnie Prince Charlie's campaign, and tartans, which were banned for several years after Charlie's defeat in an attempt to suppress Scottish nationalism and clan allegiances. See the secret portrait of Charles on a tray which seems to have an abstract swirling pattern. But the reflection in a polished cylinder placed on the tray distorts the image to reveal the face of Bonnie Prince Charlie. The tray would have brought whisky for a loyal toast 'To the King', normally referring to King George II, but the Scottish patriots would pause and then add, 'across the water' – the king across the water being Bonnie Prince Charlie. Charles Stuart's whirlwind march into England and initial successes so alarmed London that the national anthem 'God Save Our Gracious King' was composed for Hanoverian George II.

There is a memorable monument to Bonnie Prince Charlie at Glenfinnan at the head of Loch Shiel, 15 miles west of Fort William. A kilted highland figure is on the top of the circular tower, surveying the land Charles Stuart wished to reclaim as King. You can climb the circular staircase up to the parapet for a view of the lake and mountains west of Fort William.

Inverlochy Castle Hotel near Fort William: This is a grand hotel where Queen Victoria stayed. A huge rhododendron drive leads to the house where you alight to let a valet park your car, and are greeted by staff who have somehow seen you coming. Inside there are deer antlers on the walls. *Inverlochy Castle, Fort William, Scotland, tel: 0397 2177.*

Inverness

Inverness is a base for visiting the Loch Ness Monster Museum and Culloden. At Culloden a film show tells the story of the battle.

The Loch Ness Monster Exhibition Centre at Drumnadrochit is fourteen miles from Inverness. The museum provides a lot of scientific information about the depth of the loch and the difficulties involved in underwater exploration. The silliest but cleverest souvenir sold here and elsewhere in Scotland is three separate little bits of arched pottery representing the monster. *Loch Ness Monster Exhibition, Drumnadrochit, Inverness-shire, Scotland, tel: 04562 573.*

Near Inverness, Dunain Park Hotel has peacocks, and a four-poster. The food includes herbs freshly picked from the garden. A booklet of their recipes is for sale.
Dunain Park Hotel, Inverness, Inverness-shire, Scotland, tel: 0463 230512.

Another famous, very grand hotel in the north is the Culloden House House where Prince Charlie stayed before the battle. It has a four-poster bed and sauna.
Culloden House Hotel, Culloden Moor, Inverness, Inverness-shire, Scotland IVI 2NZ, tel: 0463 790461.

I felt at home in the Clifton Hotel, Nairn, on the north coast near Inverness. Although the hotel has a sumptuous seaview dining room it is like a large rambling suburban house, the corridors crammed with paintings and curios. The four-poster bed in one bedroom has heavy drapes and a fringed canopy.
Clifton Hotel, Viewfield Street, Nairn, Nairnshire, Scotland, IV12 4HW, tel: 0667 53119.

Inland is *Kildrummy Castle Hotel* (see end of Chapter 10); and on the west coast is *Summer Isles Hotel*, a gourmet hotel (see Chapter 5).

Driving all the way around the Scottish coast north of Inverness, you will be amazed how empty it is, nothing for miles, not a cafe offering a cup of coffee and a toilet, nor a museum or shop with a postcard, just scenery.

Skye (Western Isles)
Regular ferries leave from the west coast to take you to the Western Isles, 'Over the Sea to Skye' like Bonnie Prince Charlie. On Skye Dunvegan Castle has a lock of Bonnie Prince Charlie's hair, and tells the story of Flora Macdonald. The Clan Macdonald museum shows tartans and clan history.

Fingal's Cave (Island of Staffa)
Boats also go to Fingal's Cave on the isle of Staffa which inspired Mendelssohn's overture. Find out the boat schedule and allow extra time if you particularly wish to go because the boats do not depart in bad weather. Trips can be taken when you are based at west coast hotels such as the *Taychreggan Hotel, Kilchrenan, Argyll, tel: 08663 211*, which is by the water's edge on Loch Awe, just near the more expensive Ardanaiseig Hotel.

Aberdeen
By car from Aviemore or by train inland from Aberdeen you can visit the Glenfiddich Distillery at Dufftown, tel: 0340 20373.

On the main road north of Aberdeen is the Baxter's jam factory. A tour goes around, watching jam and soup making, ending by the old Baxter's shop with its wooden counters and sacks of goods, and a modern souvenir shop.

Numerous castles are beautiful to photograph and have interesting interiors. To name only one, Craigevar Castle (National Trust for Scotland) near Aberdeen has circular turrets with conical rooftops. Alcove beds have been reconstructed and the guide explains that maids would sleep sitting up for protection against attack and because it was feared that one might die by sleeping down!

The Holiday Inn (Aberdeen Airport): at one time confusion was caused by the fact that two Holiday Inns were very near each other at Aberdeen Airport. This one is the larger of the two with a huge indoor pool and whirlpool encircled by pillars.

Adjoining is a large elegant lounge. The hotel entrance hall is Moroccan style with pointed arches and one of the bedrooms has a big corner bath with mirrors. Nearby is another hotel with a smaller pool. *The Holiday Inn, Aberdeen Airport, River View Drive, Dyce, Aberdeen, Scotland, tel: 0224 770011.*

Aberdeen's Stakis Treetops Hotel which served chicken stuffed with haggis is described in Chapter 5 on gourmet treats.

Crieff Hydro Hotel has wonderful views of the multi-coloured forest and the valley, at its best in early autumn. It is excellent in all weather because there is plenty to do indoors. At the indoor swimming pool children's competitions are held. There's table tennis, evening dancing with competitions, putting, and supervised children's entertainment in summer and school holidays. While adults eat their evening meal upstairs children are kept away having high tea followed by a video film.

Wine can be ordered with meals, but there is no bar. This ban on drinks and drunks is not related to the fact that certain towns in Scotland are 'dry'. The hotel itself was founded by the church. The hotel is enormous, almost a city. Their full time maintenance staff paint it like the famous bridge. By the time they get to one end the other end needs repainting. So a smart conference centre is on one side, a tattier area elsewhere.

Accommodation ranges from smart executive rooms to plain rooms where kids can safely scrawl on walls protected by perspex sheets. Self-catering in pleasant pine cabins among the trees suits people wanting budget accommodation and large family get-togethers. Alternatively it appeals to those who want to avoid the mass dining hall and prefer to arrive with stocks of their own food and their own wine.
Crieff Hydro Hotel, Crieff, Scotland, tel: 0764 2401.
See also Peebles Hydro (Chapter 13).

BURNS' COUNTRY

Burns Cottage (Alloway, Ayr)
Back south in the Lowlands you can follow The Burns Trail starting from Ayr where you see a monument and his thatched birthplace. Burns, who wrote 'my love is like a red red rose',

seems to have been rather fond of the lassies. Alloway which is about two miles from Ayr also has the Brig o' Doon arch described in Burns' poem 'Tam o' Shanter'. *Burns Cottage and Museum, Alloway, Ayr, Scotland, tel: 0292 41215.*

Culzean Castle (Ayr)
On the south-west coast near Ayr wonderful gardens surround magnificent Culzean Castle. It was designed by Scotsman Robert Adam and has a round drawing room. There is also an exhibition about Eisenhower. *Culzean Castle, Kirkoswald, Ayr, Scotland, tel: 06556 269. Kirkoswald Tourist Information tel: 06556 293.*

More Information
A pre-paid voucher scheme is available for holidays in Scotland. Major tourist sites sell maps pinpointing Scottish tourist attractions, and posters of the Scottish royal family tree so you can sort out which royal personage lived when and where. A quick résumé of Scottish history is in the pocket size Berlitz travel guide of Scotland. The Scottish Tourist Board book 'Scotland 1001 Things to See' has an index of castles according to the century in which they were built. More details from the Scottish Tourist Board and British Tourist Authority.

CHAPTER 17
Wales

Wales is known for coalmines, waterfalls, steam trains, Welsh dressers, and Welsh male voice choirs.

The Wales of coalmines is inland from the south coast, easily reached from London by the M4 motorway to the capital of Cardiff and nearby Swansea, possibly stopping off at Monmouth. Further west are the seaside town of Tenby and the cathedral of St David's.

The north coast's busy seaside resorts such as Rhyl, Colwyn Bay and Llandudno are popular with holidaymakers from the Midlands. Going south inland there's music at Ruthin Castle medieval banquets and Llangollen's Eisteddfod music festival, waterfalls at Bettws-y-Coed, and slate mines in Blaenau Ffestiniog.

For a quiet countryside holiday go to Mid Wales. Mid Wales is a region which is hard to define. It has no capital, and no symbol. But it covers the majority of Wales. You can start by touring the pony-trekking country of the Brecon Beacons in the east, going west through the hilly Snowdonia National Park, then north up the west coast to the town of Harlech, or south to Aberystwyth where steam trains start.

SOUTH WALES

South Wales is easily reached from London. The train to Cardiff takes only two hours, but you can drive there for a long weekend.

Big Pit Coalmine (Blaenavon, Gwent)
The Big Pit coal mine is typically Welsh and near to England making a good starting point, although many people drive as far as they can into South Wales, perhaps to a Cardiff hotel for

Friday night, tour around that area over the weekend, and see the Big Pit on the way back.

After queuing to don the miner's helmet and cap lamp and heavy waistbelt, you wait to descend, a few people at a time, in the small, slow creaking lift. Stumbling along the cold black tunnels with their uneven floors and roofs you reach the coal trucks. Wear stout shoes and a warm old coat, preferably coloured black. Your guide is usually a miner, since 1000 men were employed here until 1980. Although I wouldn't have missed it, the best part of this trip to the pits was getting back to ground level again!

Big Pit Mining Museum, Market Street, Blaenavon, Gwent, South Wales NP4 9XP, tel: 0495 790311.

SWANSEA
Penscynor Wildlife Park (Cilfrew, Near Swansea)
No children under five are allowed in the Big Pit for safety reasons, but a family outing can be taken to the Penscynor Wildlife Park with its penguin parade and toboggan rides down the hillside, north of Swansea.

Penscynor Wildlife Park, Cilfrew, near Neath, South Wales, tel: 0639 812189.

Families can also visit the Dan-yr-Ogof showcaves, where lifesize dinosaurs are on the hillside.

Dan-yr-Ogof Caves, Abercrave, Glyntawe, Swansea, South Wales, tel: 0639 730284.

In winter or wet weather there's Swansea's indoor leisure centre with its spiral tube slide dropping you into the swimming pool.

Swansea Hotels
West of Cardiff near Swansea The Georgian Norton House Hotel has its view of the sea obscured by housing; however, the interior is charming. And you can sleep in a reproduction of the giant Elizabethan four-poster bed of Ware (the original is in the Victoria and Albert Museum, London).

Norton House Hotel, Norton Road, Mumbles, Swansea, South Wales, tel: 0792 404891.

North of Swansea at Llandeilo, the three star Cawdor Arms

Hotel boasts the Howard Hughes room where Howard Hughes stayed because of a forced landing after flying across the Atlantic in 1927. It has two four-poster bedrooms, one with pink drapes called the rose room decorated with roses, and residents receive a glass of sherry on arrival.
Cawdor Arms Hotel, Llandeilo, Dyfed, South Wales, SA19 6EN, tel: 0558 823500.

TENBY

Beyond Swansea is picturesque Tenby, a typically Welsh small seaside town where terraces of neat guesthouses with tiled entrances and flower-baskets surround the harbour. The sandy beaches, small hotels and fashionable shops in a busy but pretty resort make Tenby ideal for a family or budget holiday. Enter through The Five Arches gateway which looks like a circular tower with five arches set into it. This was the original south west gate through the old 11th century stone walls leading into the pedestrian area of town. Elizabeth I rebuilt the wall in preparation for the arrival of the Spanish Armada. At the far end a statue of Prince Albert stands on the headland between the two bays which back onto each other.

Caldey Island, three miles out at sea, is a 29 minute boat ride away, boats plying only on weekdays, in summer, when the sea is not rough. See the Cistercian monastery, the farm owned by the monks, and a shop selling perfume that the monks make. Men can go into the monastery, and ladies into the chapel gallery viewing the chapel from above.

Tenby Hotels

There are two midprice clifftop hotels. A local landmark is the Imperial whose restaurant windows seem to overhang the cliff, giving spectacular views of sandy South Beach and St Catherine's fort on St Catherine's Island, which you can walk across to when the tide is out. *Imperial Hotel, The Paragon, Tenby, Dyfed, SA70 7HR, tel: 0834 3737, central reservations, tel: 01-541 0033.*

In a quieter position overlooking the harbour is the Park Hotel which has a heated outdoor pool and a sauna. *The Park Hotel, Northcliff, Tenby, Dyfed, South Pembrokeshire, Wales, tel: 0834 2480.*

A few miles inland is a relatively isolated countryside hotel, The Court, which has an indoor swimming pool. Again, it is a midprice family hotel, though the white column portico looks rather palatial from a distance. *The Court, Lamphey, Pembroke, Dyfed, Wales, tel: 0646 672273, reservations, tel: 01-541 0050.*

ST DAVID'S
Continuing along the south coast, on the far west point of South Wales is the 12th century St David's Cathedral in Britain's smallest city. It looks hardly bigger than a village. Beyond the triangular green an alley leads down steps to the enormous cathedral hidden in a quiet valley to protect it from attack, instead of the more usual hilltop position. On Sunday mornings you can watch the bellringers. Behind the cathedral across a small stream is the beautiful lichen-covered ruin of the Bishop's Palace with arched parapets.

The major hotel is the Warpool Court, which is on a headland with sea views, so this is most people's first choice for accommodation, though often fully booked in high season. The hotel is also known for its food. *Warpool Court Hotel, St David's, Pembrokeshire, Dyfed, Wales, tel: 0437 720300.*

Good food for a snack lunch is available from a restaurant on the 'village' triangle. An excellent dinner can be obtained at a smaller hotel with a friendly owner, *The Old Cross, The Cross Square, St David's, Dyfed, SA62 6SP, Wales, tel: 0437 720387.*

The south west coast of Wales is good walking country. Hardy youngsters can also sleep in a sleeping bag in a cave on an outward bound course. Bargain and luxury weekends including golf, fishing, pony-trekking, festivals, coach tours, and go-as-you-please motoring, are organised by *City Travel Ltd., 13 Duke Street, Cardiff, Wales, CF1 2AY, tel: 0222 395317.*

MID WALES
The major routes into Mid Wales are the southern route driving through the Wye valley, or north by road or British Rail to Shrewsbury then west via Welshpool, Newtown, and Dolgellau, to the coastal town of Barmouth and Harlech. The moment you cross over the border from Shrewsbury you know you are in

Wales because the buildings are in stone, not brick, and there are all those white Welsh sheep, some with black faces, and black Welsh cows.

Taking the southern route you can cross the Severn Bridge, see the arched ruins of tranquil Tintern Abbey and lunch in Monmouth.

MONMOUTH

To get to the town you cross a bridge over the blood-red river, under an old arched gateway complete with portcullis. There is a statue showing Rolls of Rolls Royce fame holding a model aeroplane, and another of Henry V.

King's Head Hotel (Monmouth, Gwent)

Henry Vth who was born in Monmouth was the victor of Agincourt and he is commemorated in the name of Agincourt Square and this 17th century King's Head inn. But in the bar you see a more interesting memento of a later royal visitor, King Charles I. A plaster panel depicting the king is said to have been placed there by the landlord to please his patron, or so that the vain king could sit looking at himself! In the town's Nelson Museum you can see relics of Nelson and Mr Rolls. Weekend breaks are offered. Like many other Welsh hotels The Kings Head serves 'A taste of Wales'.

Kings Head Hotel, Agincourt Square, Monmouth, Gwent, Wales, tel: 0600 2177.

From here you can explore the Wye valley surrounded by grassy hills, reminiscent of the book 'How Green Was My Valley'. Tours entitled How Green Was My Valley based on Richard Llewellyn's book and the TV series, including a mining museum or coal mine visit, are organised by: *Cardiff Travel Centre, 9 Upper Clifton Street, Cardiff, South Glamorgan, tel: 0222 492362.*

HAY-ON-WYE

An unusual stop in the Wye valley is at Hay-on-Wye near the Welsh border to see the biggest second-hand bookshop in the world, an entire small town of shops fitted with shelves of secondhand books. There are more books (a million) than people (a thousand).

A converted cinema is only one of the many buildings filled with old books. To locate any section such as history, biblical, music, poetry, travel, sports, or children's books simply follow the town map they supply.
Hay Cinema Bookshop, Castle Street, Hay-on-Wye, Powys, Wales, HR3 5DR, tel: 0497 820071.

LLANDRINDOD WELLS
Further into the heart of Wales is Llandrindod Wells, whose name recalls the fact that it was a spa many years ago as the small town museum explains. The water still appeals to wildlife. By the lake signs warn the motorist to slow down for toads crossing the road. Remembering its heyday, this small town holds a late summer Victorian costume week.

A family hotel with an indoor swimming pool is the *Commodore Hotel, Spa Road, Llandrindod Wells, Powys, Wales, tel: 0597 2288.*

WELSHPOOL
Powis Castle
Visit pretty Powis Castle at Welshpool which has connections with Clive of India (1725-1774) and his son, the second Lord Clive (1754-1839). The collection of Indian relics includes jewels, a hookah, and Lady Clive's ivory dressing table. The most remarkable room in the building is the one with the state four-poster bed, whose drapes draw around to conceal it completely. The bed alcove is separated by an old wooden balustrade, the only one in Britain, probably prepared for Charles II who never came here, following French etiquette of the day. Only lords and ladies with the closest royal connections could cross the wooden barrier through the gate to the king's bedchamber.

The castle stands above terraced gardens. The tea-room which is open in summer serves lunchtime quiche and bara brith – Welsh currant bread.

Powis Castle, near Welshpool, Powys, Wales, tel: 0938 4336.

Trelydan Hall Hotel (Welshpool, Powys)

Bara brith can be sampled at Trelydan Hall, Welshpool, a black and white timbered manor house with many gables, which specialises in Welsh food. Sandwiches contain herbs from the garden. Groups can book daytime or evening entertainment including Welsh harp music, clog dancing and singing. Mrs Iona Trevor-Jones who lives here used to play the harp with her late aunt, and she owns a small harp which was used to teach Edward VII – the carved royal feathers prove it.

Individuals who book accommodation but miss the live entertainment can buy a cassette of Welsh male voice choir music, and a copy of Mrs Iona's book, which she will sign for you in English and Welsh, about how she organised flower arrangements using daffodils for the Royal Investiture banquet.

In the timbered attic is a priesthole where a skeleton was found, believed to be that of a man who claimed to be a priest seeking refuge, who the Catholic householders realised was a Protestant spy sent to betray them.

More details about bedrooms are in Chapter 3.

HARLECH AND AROUND

On the west coast is the town of Harlech dominated by the hilltop red sandstone Harlech Castle. The well-known marching song 'Men of Harlech' probably recalls the valiant attempt to defend the castle during the Wars of the Roses. From the higher roads near Harlech Castle you can see that beyond the sand dunes there is a very pleasant sandy beach, which is invisible from the lower roads. When the late Lord Harlech died Jackie Onassis visited Harlech for the funeral and stayed at a hotel on land adjoining Lord Harlech's.

Maes-y-Neuadd Hall Hotel (Harlech, Gwynydd)

Maes-y-Neuadd Hall where Jackie Onassis stayed is a 14th century stone manor house. Stone alcoves in the beamed bar contain Roman glass bottles dug up on the site. The lounges have leather chairs and log fires but the dining room is particularly light and bright, combining touches of the old amid the very modern. Lunch might be served to you by one of the four owners, perhaps finishing with Welsh Amber Pudding, made with marmalade, followed by petit fours. The hotel is in the Welsh Gold Country House Hotels brochure. Welsh male voice choirs perform here one weekend in November and one in February.

The bedroom Jackie Onassis stayed in is also very modern with a piece of fabric on the wall behind the bed suspended diagonally above the pillows by a curtain rail. A bedroom allocated to those requiring quiet is separated from the adjoining room by walls several feet thick containing two back to back fireplace chimneys. And another bedroom has a bed specially made for back sufferers. The hotel has the kindly ghost of a children's nanny and one guest who was in bed sick reported that a strange lady entered the room and mopped her brow!
Maes-y-Neuadd Hall Hotel, Talsarnau, nr Harlech, Gwynedd, North Wales, LL47 6YA, tel: 0766 780200.

Portmeirion Italian-Style Village (Gwynedd)
The prettiest place on the west coast of Wales is the idyllic pastel-coloured Portmeirion village, setting for the TV series 'The Prisoner'. It was built by an architect on one of the west coast's warm promontories. Sloping paths wind through trees between Italian-style houses and follies around the wide sandy estuary beach where shells can be gathered. Shops sell the Portmeirion pottery and accommodation is available. Honeymooners would like the busy high season when it is pretty and lively, the retired might prefer the peaceful off-season.
Portmeirion Village Hotel, Penrhyndeudraeth, Gwynedd, Wales, tel: 0766 770228/770453.

Maes Artro Craft Village (Llanbedr, Near Harlech)
Further south Maes Artro craft village has a museum section incorporating a medieval street, like Jorvik's with sounds of crowing cocks and galloping hooves. In summer you could eat on the outdoor wooden terrace over the water. There is a children's adventure fort outside, including a hammock bridge and wooden horses.

Maes Artro Tourist Village, 2 Maes Artro, Llanbedr, Nr Harlech, Gwynedd LL45 2PZ, tel: 0341 23 497.

Centre for Alternative Technology (Machynlleth, Powys)
'Alternatively' eat at the wholefood cafeteria in the Centre for Alternative Technology, Machynlleth. It demonstrates organic gardening, solar power and energy conservation in housing. You can try tools and operate a hand-driven waterwheel. Also visit Tywyn centre for alternative technology taking honey farm tours.
Centre for Alternative Technology, Panterthog, Machynlleth, Powys, tel: 0654 2400.

ABERYSTWYTH
Aberystwyth has a Victorian funicular railway which rises up the cliff giving a view of the town and shore. On the clifftop there is a Camera Obscura, tel: 0970 617642.

From seaside Aberystwyth the Rheidol Steam Railway runs inland to Devil's Falls, a spectacular wooded gorge spanned by three bridges. *Rheidol Steam Railway, Aberystwyth Station, Aberystwyth, Dyfed, tel: 0970 612377.*

NORTH WALES
Llangollen
The North Wales coast of the land of song and steam trains is a favourite holiday area for people travelling from the Midlands.

Alternatively, journeying from London allow a minimum of about five hours driving via the half-timbered English border town of Shrewsbury. By Friday evening you can reach Llangollen which is best known for the annual July music Eisteddfod, though the bridge is one of the Seven Wonders of Wales.

A signpost directs you uphill to see stunning black and white Plas Newydd, decorated with elaborate woodcarvings, more carved wood, and leather walls inside. It was formerly the home of two famous eccentric Ladies of Llangollen, who entertained Wordsworth and Wellington. Now it is a National Trust property. *Plas Newydd Museum, Hill Street, Llangollen, Clwyd, Wales, tel: 0248 714795.*

Bettws-y-Coed – Waterfalls

At the picturesque village of Bettws-y-Coed you can see three waterfalls, of which the largest and noisiest is dramatic Swallow Falls. The pretty Faerie Glen waterfall is framed by trees. This was a Victorian honeymoon spot. Notice Telford's Waterloo bridge decorated with leeks and shamrocks. There is a small charge to take the walkway to some of the waterfalls. *Swallow Falls, tel: 06902 236; Conwy Falls, tel: 06902 696.*

Ruthin's Two 'Castle' Hotels

Ruthin Castle hotel, a castle which holds medieval banquets is nearby. Confusingly named Castle Hotel, Ruthin, in the main square is a smaller medieval hotel with antique stocks and other attractive medieval features. We spent a few minutes trying to persuade them that we had a booking, before the receptionist realised we should have been at Ruthin Castle.
Ruthin Castle, Corwen Road, Ruthin, Clwyd, Wales, LL15 2NU, tel: 08242 2664.

Down a Slate Mine in North Wales

Continuing through the grey hills you reach two equally interesting rival slate mines at Blaenau Ffestiniog. 'Biggest in the world', claims Gloddfa Ganol, which has a dramatic view over a valley created when the mine caved in. You can watch slate-splitting demonstrations. The award-winning Llechwedd Slate caverns on the opposite side of the road offers a train ride through the largest 'working' slate mine in the world – so says the guide, an ex-miner.
Gloddfa Ganol Slate Mine, Blaenau Ffestiniog, Gwynedd, tel: 0766 830664.
Llechwedd Slate Caverns, Blaenau Ffestiniog, Gwynedd, Wales LL41 3NB, tel: 0766 830306.

British Telecom has an information service on festivals, events and attractions; What's on Wales, tel: 0222 464120; What's on Cardiff, tel: 0222 394424; What's on South Wales, tel: 0792 466330; What's on West Wales, tel: 0348 874525; What's on Mid Wales, tel: 0654 2040; What's on West Wales, tel: 0492 34455.

CHAPTER 18
North East to Catherine Cookson country

Hadrian's Wall and Washington's ancestral home have been known to tourists for many years, but now just south of there the poverty-stricken area of South Shields has found a new way of attracting visitors. The life story of their most famous resident, author Catherine Cookson, who has described South Shields in many novels, is the basis for a Catherine Cookson trail.

The rags to riches story of Catherine Cookson, who writes under the names of Catherine Marchant, Catherine Fawcett, and Katie McMullen in the USA, and whose sixty four best-selling books (85 million copies) are also the books most borrowed from public libraries, is set in the mining area of South Shields in the North East.

Catherine Cookson was the illegitimate daughter of Kate, brought up as Kate's sister by her grandparents. To this day Catherine won't allow her name to be associated with pubs or any form of alcohol, which featured so strongly in the bad old days vividly recalled in her books. Her step-grandad sent Catherine to the pub to carry home a heavy gallon stone jar of beer as a child, and her mother Kate died at the early age of 45. There is still unemployment in the area but today Catherine Cookson is helping to bring some prosperity from the local tours to which she has given her name.

At the Gambling Man Gallery, named after her novel and run by ex-miner Bob Ollie, tours and coach groups are likely to hear two musicians on fiddle and flute playing Geordie music of jigs and reels. Kids' parties are held at the Gambling Man Gallery on a cowboy ranch theme. *The Gambling Man Gallery, Wapping Street, South Shields, Tyne & Wear, NE33 1LQ, tel: 091 4540360.*

Signposts alert you to sites associated with Catherine Cookson. The South Shields Museum in the pedestrian High Street shows a photo history of South Shields and Catherine Cookson.

A reconstruction of her street with her real front door is there, the Olde Sweete Shoppe readers will recall from the book 'Our Kate', and the turn of the century kitchen.

There are many interesting sights in the area. St Hilda's church has a gilt replica of a non-capsizable boat hanging from the ceiling and a pretty red and white interior. A full size lifeboat is on show at the end of Ocean Road. How times change. Ocean Road once led to the German Ocean which had its name changed to the North Sea. Ocean Road is now known colloquially as Asian Road.

Along the seafront are Marsden rock, the Grotto bar-restaurant and the railway bar-restaurant which I have described under bizarre buildings in Chapter 7. I lunched overlooking the bay at the *Water's Edge* restaurant and bar, *Trow Lea, South Shields, tel: 091 454 0140*. It serves wine and a delicious ice cream with ginger and crushed brandy snap.

The beach is not safe but there's lots of fun at Temple Park swimming pool which when built had the biggest waterchute in Britain. You can hold a children's birthday party here. On many weekends it is possible to spend Saturday seeing Catherine Cookson country and Friday or Saturday night at a Northumberland or Geordie evening with a dinner and a glass of local Lindisfarne mead. The honey-based mead is popular with Japanese lady visitors because they consider honey to be healthy.

Washington's Ancestral Home
I drove seven miles west to see Washington Old Hall, the gabled family home of several generations of ancestors of George Washington, who became the United States of America's first President in 1789. George Washington's father was educated in England although he lived in Mount Vernon and his family was trading in wool with England.

Astonishingly you can hire the Hall for just £12 an hour. There is no drinks bar in the building so you start with sherry on the lawn outside, where wedding photographs are taken in the sunlight. Wine can be served for the toast with the meal.

A reconstructed bedroom setting made of pieces brought together with the aid of generous American donations includes an extraordinary 17th century bed of the period. A hidden compartment overhanging the pillow contained a gun, as did a chest at the foot of the bed. The original beams and arches date back to 1183, restored in the early 17th century. Displays include a raffle ticket signed by George Washington, two letters, and a fan given to George Washington's wife Martha by General Lafayette who fought for the Americans in the war of independence. Also notice the wooden cradle, and a wooden baby walker – not a twentieth century invention; it dates from the 17th century.

Washington Old Hall, The Avenue, Washington, Tyne & Wear, NE38 7LE tel: 091 416 6879.

Roman Remains
Another trip I made on the Catherine Cookson weekend was to see Roman remains. Further north towards the border with Scotland is the spectacular Hadrian's Wall, where several Roman sites are open (mostly half the day only on winter Sundays). I saw Housesteads Roman fort, where 1000 Romans were stationed from the years AD 122–130.

A museum centre is at the base of the hill at Housesteads. The path and Roman steps lead up to what looks like a small stonebuilt city, encircled by a wall, all reduced to knee-height remains. The most famous building is the Roman bathhouse and latrine, with two stone baths and the gulleys between the rows where circular toilet seats were cut into a long shelf.

Embleton's colour drawing sold as a poster and postcard here and at Vindolanda shows how the Romans in their togas would have sat along the toilet benches talking to each other. They wiped their sponges, used like toilet paper, in the gulley in front of their feet. How different from our modern notions of privacy – very much a Roman army with its camaraderie.

I remarked, 'The most astonishing thing is the way they all sat together.' My guide, an unemployed ex-miner who is an unpaid voluntary guide, agreed.

'Yes, just like we did in the mines before they closed,' he said. 'Exactly the same system. No cubicle walls. The water flows all the way along under the bench. We used to put things in the water and float them from one end to the other for a joke.'

'When was that?' I asked. 'In the 1950s,' was the reply. I was silent.

Housesteads Roman Fort, Bardon Mill, Northumberland, tel: 04984 363.

During the return journey by British Rail to London I was able to read a copy of Catherine Cookson's book 'Our Kate', her autobiography. On the Catherine Cookson weekend you are given a copy of one of her books, containing a facsimile signature, and a stop is made at a souvenir shop where other books can be bought.

Catherine Cookson country is ten miles from Newcastle and Newcastle airport, and twenty miles from Durham.

Hotels and package tours
Luxury hotels in the area are Lumley Castle, Chester-le-Street (See Chapter 8 on haunted hotels), and *Linden Hall Hotel, Longhorsley, Morpeth, Northumberland NE65 8XF, tel: 0670 56611.*
Hotels with leisure centres are *The George at Chollerford, Northumberland NE46 4EW, tel: 043 611,* and *The Gosforth Park Thistle Hotel, High Gosforth Park, Newcastle-upon-Tyne, Tyne & Wear, NE3 5HN, tel: 091 236 4111.*

Rainbow Holidays and Enterprise Travel offer Catherine Cookson breaks.

More details about the organised Cathering Cookson Country weekend costing from under £50 are available from *The Press and Publicity Office, Town Hall, South Shields, Tyne & Wear, NE33 2RI, tel: 091 455 4321.*

Blanchland, Northumberland, with the Lord Crewe Arms Hotel (page 68)

Washington Old Hall, ancestral home of George Washington (page 158)

The Edward VII Suite at Langtry Manor, Bournemouth (page 100), with Lillie Langtry's picture above the fireplace

Brighton Pavilion (page 174)

Joey, the plane of Aurigny Air, flies to Alderney in the Channel Islands (page 198)

Battle of Flowers, Jersey, Channel Islands (page 193)

The Mansion House at Grim's Dyke (page 134): Iolanthe Hall, once the music room of W.S. Gilbert

CHAPTER 19
England's Lake District

Spectacular scenery of mountains and trees is reflected in lakes in the north west of England. The Cumbria region on the borders with Scotland includes the Lake District and offers 'the most beautiful corner of England' says the Tourist Board, and most visitors agree.

The Lake District National Park is over 800 square miles and the mountains include Scafell, highest peak in England. The west of Britain is subject to rainfall on the mountains – hence parts of the Lake District are the wettest in England, so if possible take your holiday in the driest months of the year.

The journey by car from London to the Lake District takes about five hours. There are sixteen main lakes. The largest, in fact England's largest lake, is Lake Windermere, which is over ten miles long but only one mile wide. There are many small museums based on the picturesque homes of famous former residents. And numerous fairytale hotels with towers have been built on promontories, enjoying the views around Lake Windermere and at the pretty lakeside resort named Windermere in the centre of the east side of the lake.

A motorway from London takes you via the town of Lancaster to the Lake District. The road then goes through the bustling market town of Kendal and up to lively Windermere where the road forks. The left side of the fork is the popular route continuing around Lake Windermere, through Ambleside in the north up to the busy town of Keswick on the Derwentwater Lake. The right hand fork goes to quiet Ullswater.

You could easily spend one or two weekends motoring around Lake Windermere and another of the lakes to see the major sights, Windermere being the obvious choice of base for a first visit. On subsequent trips, leaving lakes for the mountains, many hours can be spent walking or taking the mountain passes such as Hard Knott pass along narrow roads, around hairpin bends, and up inclines with one in three gradients.

Many well-known artists and writers lived in the Lake District, but the most famous of all was the Romantic poet Wordsworth.

I am assuming that most motorists are going north to the Lake District, but starting from Scotland you might stay at Keswick, and follow this route in reverse.

Southern Lake District

First stop near the Lake District would be Levens Hall, an Elizabethan stately home famous for its topiary gardens. *Levens Hall, Kendal, Cumbria, LA8 0PB, tel: 05395 60321.*

A long stop can also be made at the award-winning Museum of Lakeland Life and Industry which has gallery after gallery of interesting displays of craft workshops and farmhouse rooms, and a Marks & Spencer penny bazaar. *The Museum of Lakeland Life and Industry, Abbot Hall, Kendal, Cumbria LA9 5AL, tel: 0539 22464.*

Windermere

If you want to 'wander lonely as a cloud' like the poet Wordsworth, take an off-season break to avoid the crowds of tourists. His crowd of golden daffodils are seen in spring. However, in summer boat trips are available from Windermere, and lakeside cafes open near shops selling woollen jumpers, anoraks and climbing gear, posters of Wordsworth's poem, guidebooks and the usual tourist souvenirs.

On the road around the lake you will come to *The Lake District National Park Visitor Centre at Brockhole, tel: Windermere 2231,* which has exhibitions, a shop, and events on the hillside on summer weekends.

Windermere Hotels

Cumbria has at least sixty hotels with four-poster beds for spring honeymoons or autumn anniversaries.

Beyond the town of Windermere is Miller Howe, an expensive lakeside gourmet hotel offering delightful views of the lake by day, and spotlight kissing cupid statues at night. An afternoon tea of scones costs only £3. Dinner is £22 per person for a five course meal, with bottled Malvern water already on your table, and butter shaped like a swan. More details are in the chapter on gourmet food.

Elegant bedrooms contain large umbrellas, a cassette player, and cookery books written by the owner and TV personality John Tovey. One room has a four-poster bed. Autumn and spring breaks are available at reduced prices. *Miller Howe Hotel, Windermere, Cumbria, tel: 09662 2536.*

A midprice hotel of character on the road above Windermere is the Wild Boar which has a rock wall in the restaurant and a very pleasant lounge for after dinner coffee. I stayed in the old oak four-poster, but preferred the more colourfully decorated modern rooms. *Wild Boar Hotel, Crook, nr Windermere, LA23 3NF, tel: 09662 5225.*

For families with children wanting activities within the hotel I suggest one of two hotels at Bowness-on-Windermere just down the road from Windermere, either a THF hotel: *Belsfield Hotel, Bowness-on-Windermere, Cumbria, tel: 09662 2448/2444*; or a Quality International Hotel: *Beech Hill Hotel, Newby Bridge Road, Bowness-on-Windermere, Cumbria, tel: 09662 2137.*

Ambleside

En route between Windermere and Ambleside stop at the Queen's Head Hotel, Troutbeck, to see the inn's bar made from a four-poster bed.

Notice the Bridge House built over the river at Ambleside. Your destination here is Wordsworth's last home from 1813–1850, Rydal Mount, which overlooks a lake. *Rydal Mount, Ambleside, Cumbria LA22 9LU, tel: 05394 33002/09663 3002.*

On a forest road outside town is an expensive hotel with a lovely landscaped pool and spa bath. *Pillar Hotel and Country Club, Gt Langdale, Nr Ambleside, LA22 9JB. Tel: 09667 302.*

Grasmere

The other house associated with Wordsworth is nearby at Grasmere. Dove Cottage was Wordsworth's home from 1799–1808, and in the adjacent Wordsworth Museum you see two versions of his famous poem. *Dove Cottage and Wordsworth Museum, Town End, Grasmere, Ambleside, Cumbria LA22 9SG, tel: 09665 544.*

Wordsworth himself specified the traditional lakeland round chimneys for Lancrigg Hotel, which is a historic listed building. It offers log fires and luxury suites with a four-poster bed and whirlpool bath. It serves vegetarian cheese, fruit wines and organic French wines. *Lancrigg Vegetarian Country House Hotel, Easedale, Grasmere, Cumbria LA22 9QN, tel: 09665 317.*

Western Lake District
Children would also like Beatrix Potter's House at Sawrey, where she created her animal characters such as Peter Rabbit. It is a National Trust property: *Hill Top, near Sawrey, Cumbria, tel: 09666 269.*

West of Lake Windermere and running parallel to it is the relatively deserted pencil shaped lake Coniston Water, where Ruskin's House is on the hillside overlooking the lake, and a museum about Ruskin is down in the village.

Coniston
You can see lovely views from Brantwood, John Ruskin's home at Coniston. Ruskin was Professor of Art at Oxford and 'if Venice ever fell down, it could be rebuilt from Ruskin's drawings,' said Kenneth Clark. Ruskin boosted Turner's paintings and influenced Gandhi. Ruskin lived here from 1872 to 1900. There is a nature trail around the grounds.
Brantwood, Coniston, Cumbria LA21 8AD, tel: 05394 41396/ 0966 41396.

Taking a detour into the empty and rather desolate area south of here you could also visit the small Laurel and Hardy Museum at Ulverston, perhaps continuing on to the hillside holiday village of Grange-over-Sands and then to Cartmel. An inland mid-price sister hotel to the Miller Howe is Uplands, which has pretty modern decor – silver and pink, and gourmet food. *Uplands Hotel, Cartmel, Cumbria, tel: 044 854 248.*

North Lake District
Cumberland Pencil Museum has an exhibition of the history of pencil-making machines, working conditions for workers in the factory's early days, and the world's largest pencil. The factory shop sells coloured pencils and novelty sharpeners. *Cumberland*

Pencil Museum, Southey Works, Keswick, Cumbria CA12 5NG, tel: 07687 72116.

Stop to climb the big Boulder Stone with a staircase up the side, on the way to Lodore Swiss Hotel and Keswick. The stone inspired the hymn 'Rock of Ages'. Indoor swimming pools are at lakeside Lodore Swiss Hotel, which backs onto a cliff. A dramatic waterfall can be seen from the hotel's car park, unless there is a summer drought when it reduces to a disappointing trickle. *Lodore Swiss Hotel, Borrowdale, Nr Keswick, Cumbria, tel: 0596/07687 84285.*

Wordsworth was born at Wordsworth House, Cokermouth in the far north of the Lake District. *Wordsworth House, Main Street, Cockermouth, Cumbria, tel: 0900 824805.*

Sharrow Bay Country House Hotel in a remote lakeside location on Ullswater is nonetheless so well-known for its gourmet cuisine that there is a bustle of visitors looking at books on shelves in the corridors and eating in non-smoking dining rooms crammed with antiques. Tea including scones is about £5, weekday lunch approximately £15–19, £21 Sunday lunch, dinner £29. *Sharrow Bay, Howtown, Nr. Penrith, Ullswater, Cumbria, tel: 08536 301.*

Detour to Hadrian's Roman Wall

If time allows, go north to Hadrian's Wall, and the Roman forts, such as Vindolanda and Housesteads. The wall was the northern boundary of the Roman empire, keeping marauding Scots at bay, with forts at approximately five mile intervals along the 90 miles from the west coast to the east coast.

In theory you could drive right the way along beside the wall. In practice it is a narrow country road with little to see, no-one to ask the way, and it is easy to get lost and disheartened. So visit one or two of the western forts as a side trip from the Lake District, and the other eastern forts from the North East. I have described Housesteads in the Catherine Cookson Country section.

Along the remote sections of Hadrian's Wall separating England from Scotland is the old Roman Fort of Vindolanda. To get there follow signs, with difficulty, from the B6318 road, or use the Ordnance Survey Map of Hadrian's Wall. By the time you arrive you know why the sensible Romans built straight roads. So they didn't get lost in remote areas where they couldn't even find a Latin-speaking sheep to tell them the way.

The 3rd century remains of the old fort are mysteriously excavated walls and foundations which make sense only to archaeologists. But a reproduction built alongside shows you exactly how the fort was constructed, with high wooden walls on stone foundations. From here the Romans would have watched, surveying the rolling hills, supposedly for approaching attackers – more likely for local thieves.

The most informative museum is a further walk towards the other end of the the three and a half acre site of Vindolanda. Here you see lifesize wax models in the reconstructed kitchen of a Roman house. A well-paid Roman soldier made a good mate for a local girl. She would have prepared a breakfast of fruit and porridge, and cooked dates in oil. The baby is in a woven wicker cradle, and commentary includes the sound of the baby crying and the fort bugle call waking the Roman family. The soldier's diet would include venison. A favourite food was mouse. I resisted the temptation to buy a Roman recipe book.

So life in Roman times was very different. Fortunately modern tourists can enjoy the 20th century entertainment of a video film and eat modern food in the snack bar. Afterwards, returning through pretty ornamental gardens and walking back across the lumpy grass, you may pity the tired Roman footsoldier, as you reach the car park to collect your twentieth century motor vehicle.

The site is open from 10 am daily (except two weeks at Christmas); until 4 pm in January, February, November and December; until 5 pm in March; 5.30 April to October; 6 pm in May, June and September; and 6.30 in July and August. Sixty minute guided tours are offered.

For details contact:
Vindolanda Trust, Bardon Mill, Northumberland NE47 7JN, tel: Bardon Mill (049 84) 277.

More information on Cumbria and the Lake District from:
Cumbria Tourist Board, Ashleigh, Holly Road, Windermere, Cumbria, LA23 2AQ, tel: (096 62) 4444.

CHAPTER 20
Stratford 'Shakespearience' and Oxford and Cambridge

Stratford-upon-Avon, Oxford and Cambridge evoke the atmosphere of past centuries, and every building tells stories of the characters who inhabited them, the world-famous writers and philosophers of yesterday.

STRATFORD-UPON-AVON

The river Avon flows past the Shakespeare Memorial Theatre and the beautiful parish Church where Shakespeare is buried. Stratford's medieval half-timbered buildings with their gabled upper storeys overhang the streets as they must have done in Shakespeare's time.

Street entertainers still go from town to town, and on the spring and late autumn holidays you will probably see Morris Dancers performing. Bells jingle on their feet as they dance, waving white handkerchiefs in the air. When I stopped to photograph them, they insisted on linking arms with me and blackened my face like theirs!

You can book a weekend Stratford Stop-over, including theatre tickets, an evening meal at the theatre, and a hotel reservation all arranged for you. Just make one phone call.

Driving from London early one Friday afternoon we reached Stratford while it was still light enough to see Shakespeare sitting on his pedestal in the park by the theatre.

'A Midsummer Night's Dream' was probably first performed in the grounds of gabled, beamed Alveston Manor Hotel. Book early to get a reservation in one of Stratford's popular half-timbered medieval hotels, of which Trusthouse Forte has four. These were full on a bank holiday weekend.

So we stayed at family-run Grosvenor House Hotel, a couple of minutes walk from the theatre. The management sent up chicken sandwiches very quickly for us to gulp down before we raced over to the theatre for the 7.30 performance.

'As You Like It' was performed by the Royal Shakespeare Company in modern clothes, with the verve and pace of a TV thriller. Every word was clear. Whatever your grasp of Elizabethan vocabulary, the play's meaning is made comprehensible by the facial expressions and gestures of Britain's leading actors. 'All the world's a stage . . .'

Afterwards we ate our pre-booked three course dinner upstairs in the theatre's elegant Boxtree Restaurant. The pretty pink decor was echoed by the pink grapefruit and Ogen melon with pink champagne sorbet on the menu, about half of the choices being within the meal voucher price.

We walked back to the hotel. Stratford is so small that most major hotels are within walking distance of the theatre.

Next morning I sampled the Grosvenor hotel's spa bath, losing most of my hairdo in the steam. Despite this I emerged pink-faced and grinning from the sauna, where I dried off in the warm air because I had forgotten to take a towel! The sauna and spa charge is under £5, and residents pay less than non-residents.

Before the hotel's Saturday guests arrived I managed to see the modern brass and lace four-poster bedroom which has a bathroom with a bidet. But I prefer the real olde worlde carved wooden four-posters which are in the best bedrooms of the medieval hotels.

Opposite the theatre is the World of Shakespeare which has a 25 minute audio visual show. In the three-storey high octagonal hall the tableaux of lifesize talking figures are illuminated, one by one. Lights traced Elizabeth I's journey from London to see her lover Robert Dudley at Kenilworth Castle where she had such a good time that she stayed an extra week!

Queen Elizabeth's rendezvous was no secret. Four hundred members of court and traders from miles around gathered, probably including Shakespeare's father, a glovemaker, and his family. Dioramas of waxworks both above and below stairs in medieval buildings told the story of what little William Shakespeare, aged, seven, probably saw. Elizabeth's visit included a pageant culminating in fireworks, and other spectacles which Shakespeare mentioned later in his plays.

Next from the Guide Friday desk in the foyer shop outside we booked a two-hour Stratford trip on the 'topless' open-top bus. This took us past the town's timbered buildings such as

Shakespeare's Birthplace and Tudor hotels, giving keen photographers aerial views.

Then it drove from Stratford for a mile through the fields to Anne Hathaway's Cottage. The picturesque thatched building was Shakespeare's wife's property when the well-to-do 26-year-old girl married 18-year-old William. He left for London, and made good.

Finally, the bus moved on to Mary Arden's House three miles from Stratford. Mary was Shakespeare's mother. The guide's fascinating commentary revealed that husbands were allowed to beat their wives twice a week in those days.

The Guide Friday bus tour cost under £5, plus small extra admission charges for Anne Hathaway's Cottage and Mary Arden's House. Independent tourists can get a combined entrance ticket for five properties, but you'll need a couple of days to visit them all.

I had a glass of wine and ice cream at the theatre foyer's riverside bar which is open all day, and then discovered that a tempting strawberry tea was being served in the panelled lounge of Alveston Manor.

A brief shower of rain sent me into the nearby Queen's Moat House, formerly a Hilton, which despite its ultra-modern exterior has a corridor of old-style boutiques.

Being a spa bath addict, on the way back to London I stopped to see Ettington Park Hotel, newly-opened in 1986, in its own forty acre park just five miles from Stratford. It must be unique. How many hotels offer you the modern convenience of an indoor swimming pool and spa bath complex, in a converted stately home? Carved pillars dominate the entrance hall and staircase. Wood-panelled dining room walls are adorned with marquetry shields. And conferences can be held in the library under a vast, vaulted wooden ceiling. Double bedrooms start at £99, suites from £135. A weekend break minimum two nights costs about £125 for dinner, bed and breakfast per person sharing. *Ettington Park Hotel, Alderminster, near Stratford-upon-Avon, CV37 8BS, tel: 0789 740740.*

Arriving home, my view of Shakespeare had changed. I no longer saw William as an actor who wrote absurd plays about twins for no apparent reason. I knew that his own children were twins, and that he was an astute man who had observed royalty and court life since childhood. So I recommended a weekend Stop-over in Stratford.

The Shakespeare play theatre season runs from April to January, and other plays are performed in different theatres. Shakespeare's birthday was April 23rd and every year street bands parade with international delegates on the nearest Saturday.

Stop-over Theatre Package
Stratford Stop-over luxury accommodation such as the modern Moat House costs different prices according to the date chosen. Cheaper Stop-over packages are available with accommodation at more modest hotels. The packages include the theatre ticket and a full dinner at the theatre's Box Tree Restaurant. The one-night Stop-over costs from £38 to £66, and a two nighter is offered from £64.

For recorded information about the Stop-over Package telephone *0789 295333* (24 hours); credit card bookings tel: 0789 67262, 9.30 am–9 pm, telex 317424; or write to Stop-over, Royal Shakespeare Theatre, Stratford-upon-Avon, CV37 6BB.

Travelling by train you can read a copy of the play you are going to see. Discounted rail fares are offered to those booking a Stop-over, including coach links to Stratford railway station at certain times. Phone *0727 34475* for details.

Alternatively, when you get to Stratford drop into the World of Shakespeare foyer and for a charge of about £1 they'll phone around and find you a hotel room. Guest houses start at about £10 per head for bed and breakfast.

Don't let having young children stop you going to Stratford for a weekend. Kids can try the adventure playground at Ragley Hall, or look at the Stratford Motor Museum – and some Stop-over hotels will arrange baby-sitting.

Stratford has many historic buildings within a small area. You can see the residences of four generations of Shakespeare's family. Shakespeare's Birthplace, we presume, was in his father's house in the 1500s. Hall's Croft was the home of Shakespeare's daughter Susanna, and Shakespeare's son-in-law, Dr John Hall. It displays the doctor's apothecary jars in the dispensary, old surgical instruments, and records of cures, deaths and diseases of the day.

The garden and foundations are all that remain of New Place where Shakespeare died in 1616. But adjoining here is Nash's House which was the home of Shakespeare's grand-daughter Elizabeth, his last direct descendant, and of her first husband Thomas Nash.

Shakespeare's family is buried in Holy Trinity Church. The grammar school where Shakespeare learned to read and write is nearby. And there's Harvard House, the home of the mother of John Harvard who founded the American university. Many other interesting sites are a short drive from here, such as medieval Warwick Castle only eight miles away. No wonder that after seeing London, many tourists go straight to Stratford.

Further details from:
Best Western's Grosvenor House Hotel, tel: 0789 69213.
Trusthouse Forte (UK) Ltd, 24–30 New Street, Aylesbury, Bucks HP20 2NW. London, tel: 01-567 3444.
Tourist Information Centre, Judith Shakespeare's House, 1 High Street, Stratford-upon-Avon, Warwickshire, tel: 0789 293127.
Living Shakespeare Secretary, The Shakespeare Centre, Henley Street, Stratford-upon-Avon, CV 37 6QW. Details of 3 day breaks on themes such as houses and gardens of Shakespeare's England, Shakespeare and his theatre.

OXFORD

Many politicians and future Prime Ministers, such as Gladstone, Macmillan, Heath and Harold Wilson have spoken as undergraduates in the Oxford Union debating chamber, where scenes of 'Another Country' were recently filmed. A video in the union shows you what student life is like through the year.

In this 'city of dreaming spires' as Matthew Arnold described it, visit the Ashmolean Museum, Beaumont Street, tel: 0865 512651; the Balfour Building, 60 Banbury Road, tel: 0865 512541, housing the world's largest collection of musical instruments; and the British Telecom Museum, Veteran Cycle Museum, Museum of the History of Science with Einstein's blackboard, Uffington's Tom Brown's School Museum, and numerous other museums.

Buy Frank Cooper's Oxford Marmalade in the Frank Cooper Shop, 84 High Street, Oxford, tel: 0865 245125. Or simply glide along the river enjoying yourself as little Alice did when The Professor of Mathematics at Christ Church entertained her with the story of Alice in Wonderland.

If you want to stay in Oxford, one possibility is Studley Priory Hotel, described in the gourmet chapter.

More details from: *Thames and Chilterns Tourist Board, 8 The Market Place, Abingdon, Oxfordshire OX14 3UD, tel: 0235 22711.*

CAMBRIDGE

Cambridge is liveliest when university students are cycling through the narrow streets in term time. But individual visitors have more opportunity to walk around the quadrangles in the vacation when the students are not resident. Group guided tours are arranged.

First see the cathedral size King's College Chapel which has 'soaring spires' and interior fan vaulting. King Henry VI founded King's College and Eton School at Windsor. Until 1850 only Old Etonians were accepted as scholars and fellows at King's College.

Trinity College chapel displays statues of Sir Isaac Newton, Francis Bacon and Lord Tennyson, and busts of the famous are along both sides of the library designed by Sir Christopher Wren.

Samuel Pepys studied at Magdalene which owns his diary manuscripts written in shorthand. Milton was at Christ's College, founded by Henry VIII. St John's college hall has portraits of students William Wordsworth and William Wilberforce. If you want your own memorials, go to the brass rubbing centre. Town maps are available from the tourist board information office.

From April onwards in good weather you can hire a boat and go punting along the river Cam under the covered stone Bridge of Sighs at St John's College. With luck you will see a student pushing too hard on the pole and either losing it or following it and landing in the water!

Look for the wooden 'Mathematical' bridge built without any nails across the river at Queens' College.

Right on the riverbank is the smart modern four star Garden House hotel, which has a pretty garden with a little bridge. Ducks and boats pass a few yards from the lounge and bedroom windows.

Garden House Hotel, Granta Place, Mill Lane, Cambridge CB2 1RT, tel: 0223 63421. US rep Distinguished Hotels, tel: toll-free 212 661 3210.

Beyond Mill Lane you can reach the thatched village of Grantchester where poet Robert Brooke composed in the vicarage garden the poem 'Grantchester': 'Stands the church clock at ten to three? And is there honey still for tea?'

If you can't find honey, try the delicious date crumble at Carrington's coffee house, 23 Market Street, Cambridge, tel: 0223 61792.

Cambridge is just over an hour from London by British Rail train.

More details from: *East Anglia Tourist Board, Topplesfield Hall, Hadleigh, Suffolk IP7 5DN, tel: 0473 822922.*

CHAPTER 21
Prince Regent's Brighton

A popular day out from London is to the south coast resort of Brighton, where nodding heads on Chinese statues welcome visitors to Brighton Pavilion, one of the most exotic buildings in England, indeed Europe. How impressive it must have been when well-dressed Beau Brummell and the Prince of Wales entertained here.

Regency Brighton and the Pavilion
The Prince began building his fantasy in 1787, starting with the Chinese interior. An exhibition shows designs for Chinese exteriors which were rejected. John Nash, the architect of London's Regent's Park terraces, rebuilt the pavilion's exterior in domed Indian style.

George IV became Prince Regent in 1810 when his father King George III was declared mad. On his father's death in 1820, 60 year old George IV finally became King. 'Regency' however, describes the fashion until King George IV himself died in 1830.

George IV introduced to the pavilion the mod con of a flushing WC, and in the colourful domed music room the latest technology – thin cast iron pillars, entwined with spiralling snakes to imitate Coleridge's poem about Xanadu where Kubla Khan 'a stately pleasure dome decreed'.

In the banqueting room of swirling serpents and dragons see the first gas-lit gasolier. Beyond is the kitchen with its palm tree columns where Chef Carême, inventor of caramel, prepared a banquet of 112 dishes for the plump Prince.

Prince George, aged 23, secretly married the twice-widowed Mrs Fitzherbert in 1785. Being Catholic and a commoner she could not be Queen, wife of the head of the Church of England. In 1795 Parliament settled extravagant George's debts on condition that he married to have an heir. So he married

German Caroline, whom he met only three days before the wedding. They disliked each other on sight and soon separated.

In later years George was confined to the ground floor in his wheelchair. Notice the 'secret door' without an architrave in his bedroom which enabled his last lady love whose bedroom was upstairs to 'come down and see me'.

When 18-year-old prudish Princess Victoria became queen she was appalled to find the town centre pavilion overlooked by neighbouring houses! She eventually sold the pavilion to Brighton council, who own it now. It is open all year 10–5, till 6.30 in summer, and can be hired for a wedding reception or company dinner, tel: 0273 603005.

Seaside Weekends
The man who invented the fashion of visiting the seaside was Dr Russell of Lewes. From 1750 he sent patients to drink seawater and bathe in Brighton's sea. More details are in an information sheet obtainable from the Brighton Art Gallery and Museum just outside the Royal Pavilion. This museum has a Moorish arched entrance, Victorian tiling and art deco and art nouveau exhibits.

Brave swimmers still race across the shingle and plunge into the sea all year. The rest of us prefer to use the King Alfred Leisure Centre, tel: 0273 734422, with tropical pools, badminton, paddling pool, palm trees, and sauna. Or the Prince Regent Swimming Complex, Hove Lagoon, which has a playground for children, and windsurfing, near a naturist beach.

Old seaside postcards by Donald McGill and Mabel Lucy Atwell can be seen in an old house which offers afternoon guided tours of the collection, Pastimes, 22 Charles Street, Brighton, tel: 0273 687183.

Outings
Good outings for children are Brighton Aquarium and Dolphinarium, Madeira Drive/Marine Parade, Brighton BN2 1TB, tel: 0273 604233, featuring a flight simulator ride, Hove Toy Museum, and the British Engineerium, Nevill Road, Hove, E. Sussex, tel: 0273 559583 which displays lots of models.

From Easter to October The Volk's Seafront Electric Railway,

Britain's first public electric railway, runs from the aquarium past the Peter Pan funfair to the Marina where you see HMS Cavalier, sole surviving World War II destroyer involved in Arctic convoys.

There's the National Museum of Penny Slot Machines, tel: 0273 608620, and Punch and Judy are on the Palace Pier which is illuminated at night. Take an excursion to Drusillas Zoo Park, Nr Alfriston, East Sussex, tel: 0323 870234, or Rottingdean Windmill Museum. Teenagers would be interested in Sussex University.

Everybody enjoys treading the red bricks in the narrow, sloping, twisting pedestrian-only Lanes, looking at antiques and clothes boutiques.

HOTELS
Grand Hotel
The Grand Hotel, where Mrs Thatcher stayed where a bomb exploded during the 1984 Conservative Party Conference, reopened in 1986, redecorated. The white wedding cake glistening front has a large glass conservatory on the ground floor either side of the arched entrance. There is a leisure centre in the basement.
The Grand Hotel, King's Road, Brighton, E. Sussex, BN1 2FW, tel: 0273 21188.

Important hotels are in the few hundred yards between the Palace Pier and the old broken West Pier by the grass which marks the start of Hove.

Norfolk Resort Hotel
The Norfolk Resort Hotel is owned by Conservative Councillor Albert Feldman and his wife Lily Feldman, former mayor and mayoress of Brighton, who entertained Mrs Thatcher. The hotel is ideal for family holidays, aiming to be a complete 'resort' with a disco on the rooftop, and a basement leisure centre with swimming pool, sauna and whirlpool – £2 per resident per stay, £5 per family, £1 to hire a swimming costume.

The Corner Counter coffee shop is open until 7 pm in winter, later in summer, but children and latecomers can have sandwiches in the bedroom 24 hours a day. The pretty rooftop restaurant, decorated with plum colour canopies and pink glass lights, serves an excellent melon starter with ginger flavour grated apple filling. At breakfast you can watch waves breaking on the beach below.

Seafront bedrooms were being refurbished in early December. I stayed in a delightful modern back courtyard extension. Two storeys of bedrooms with a communal gallery balcony are built around a Taj Mahal style oblong pond and fountain, illuminated with parallel lines of white globes in the evening.

Some rooms have a fridge and 2 electric rings, useful for those whose dietary rules require self-catering, and coffee makers are also in the room.

A family room for two parents and a child costs approximately £75 a night, but there are also dinner, bed and breakfast breaks at about £30 per person per night for a minimum of two weekend nights, or 3 midweek nights. You can keep your dog in your bedroom for £4 a day, not in public rooms.
Norfolk Resort Hotel, King's Road, Brighton, East Sussex, BN1 2PP, tel: 0273 738201.

The Gorgeous Granville Hotel

The Granville is run by extrovert Mrs Audrey Simpson (psychology background), her university husband, son (the chef) and receptionist daughter (actress). It has a Les Routiers plaque, AA red 'B' for beautiful bedrooms, and is mentioned in the 'Lovers Guide to Britain'.

The main charm of this hotel of character is the decor of bedrooms and exotic bathrooms – even the downstairs ladies cloakroom has floor length Laura Ashley curtains matching the tablecover. Apart from four-posters and spa baths there is an art deco room based on Noel Coward's bedrooms, a Japanese room, and an offbeat black bedroom. The best four-poster, made of wood, is in one of the grander suites.

I stayed in the honeymoon pink Brighton Rock bedroom, named after Graham Greene's novel. The modern spindly four-poster looks pretty, but when you move around in bed the little lacey frills shake with excitement. The chief delight of this room is the silver wallpaper bathroom with two washbasins, and arched mirror L-shape around the corner bath.

Delightful cocktails can precede dinner – excellent for romantic couples. It is also convenient for conference delegates using the Metropole Hotel conference centre next door. Perfect for those who prefer small personal hotels, provided you are amused when friendly staff tell your spouse phoning from London what time you left the hotel, and ask why you stayed out so late.

I opted for the à la carte menu at breakfast and ordered porridge with whisky and a curl of butter in the centre, aromatic, heady, and tasty.

Granville Hotel, 125 King's Road, Brighton BN1 2FA, tel: 0273 26302.

Flying
THF's Curzon Hotel organises flying weekends with the Flying Club at Shoreham Airport. *Curzon Hotel, Cavendish Place, Brighton, BN1 2HW, tel: 0273 25788.*

Murder Weekends
Murder Weekends are held at the centrally situated Royal Albion Hotel where Prime Minister Gladstone stayed. Can you spot the Brighton hotel where the murders take place in the recent film Mona Lisa which starred Bob Hoskins? It's this one. You can have a four-poster bedroom suite at £80 a night for two including breakfast, though the film murder scene was shot in a studio. You'll recognise the pier outside, anyway.

Royal Albion Hotel, Old Steine, Brighton BN1 1NT, tel: 0273 29202.

The Old Ship
The Old Ship, rather pubby for my taste, is where the Prince Regent and his secret bride Mrs Fitzherbert stayed. The bridal suite has a four-poster bed. There's a weekend creche with nannies and videos, children's tea, and a kiddie outing to the Dolphinarium.

The Old Ship Hotel, King's Road, Brighton, BN1 1NR, tel: 0273 29001.

Dickens
The Bedford Hotel frequented by Dickens, has his letters in the bar, and his characters painted in the restaurant.

The Bedford Hotel, King's Road, Brighton, Sussex, BN1 2JF, tel: 0273 29744.

Getting There
By car or National Express from Victoria coach station to Brighton takes about 2 hours. British Rail's fastest trains from Victoria take only about 1 hour. In the rush hour slower trains allow commuters to alight at more stations along the line.

Tours
Ex-Londoner and London Blue Badge Guide Glenda Clarke of Southern Tours and Guides welcomes individuals and small groups who can have a car tour with driver guide for a morning from about £25 to £50. Her guides can take clubs and other groups on a Brighton walkabout for 25 persons minimum, at approx £1 per person. Subjects are 'The Lanes and Royal Pavilion', 'In Famous Footsteps', and 'Fisherman's Brighton'.

The 'Rich and Famous' or 'Jewish Connection' group coach tours cost about £30. Guides tell you about streets recalling Jewish baronet Goldschmid, and the Sassoon family who were host to Edward VII. Their mausoleum was turned into a pub.

Groups can be met at the airport or docks and escorted anywhere in London and the South East.
STAG (Southern Tours And Guides), 24 Pembroke Crescent, Hove, Sussex, BN3 5DD, tel: 0273 737748.

More Information from: *Brighton Tourist Information Centre, 54 Old Steine, Brighton BN1 1EQ, tel: 0273 29801.*
South East England Tourist Board, (East and West Sussex, Kent and Surrey) 1 Warwick Park, Tunbridge Wells, Kent TN2 5TA, tel: 0892 40766.

CHAPTER 22
The Far South-West – Cornwall

Sandy coves, thatch cottages, and gardens with gnomes where cream teas are served – these aspects of the warm south-west create England's top summer holiday resort area.

The tip of the toe of England is Land's End, beyond the picturesque artists' holiday village of St Ives with its sloping streets, and the romantic causeway leading to the mysterious tiny island of St Michael's Mount.

Tintagel Castle, on the Atlantic coast, associated with King Arthur, offers a spectacular steep U-shape walk along a way between two adjoining mounds. Further up the coast, 30 miles north in Devon at cobble-stoned Clovelly, crowds of tourists take the steep path down between rows of cottages to the tiny harbour. Looe and Polperro, on the gentler south coast of the English Channel, are quaint little fishing villages with narrow streets where cars get stuck on corners.

If you're taking an early season break try to see the Floral Dance or Furry Dance during May in the streets of Helston. There's a children's dance, a mid-day dance in morning suits, like a wedding, and a late afternoon dance which visitors can join, to the furry dance tune which was in top of the pops – remember 'dum de dum . . . on The Big Bass Drum', which Terry Wogan liked to hum on the radio.

Goonhilly and the Lizard
If you only have a weekend, you might like to stay in Cornwall's heel, called the Lizard. It is the most southerly point on mainland Britain, therefore the warmest, both summer and off-season. Cornish Palms sprout in roadside front gardens.

Because of the rarity of snow and ice, British Telecom's Goonhilly satellite dishes are set up here, a manifestation of modern science amid the land of novels, pixies, and paintings.

Driving along you see the large white dishes reflecting the

sunlight. In the summer high season you can take a tour around the site. Allow two hours. A bus travels past the dishes which are made of stainless steel and aluminium alloys. While waiting your turn (you buy a numbered ticket) you watch a sound and light display. This tells you how telephone calls from London are transferred via the GPO tower to Goonhilly, and then up to satellites and sent around the world (or alternatively through undersea cable across the Atlantic to America).

Viewing screens in a control room show how television programmes are continuously transferred by satellite to the major USA stations so they have up-to-date transmissions from Europe.

Goonhilly Satellite Earth Station, Goonhilly Downs, Helston, Cornwall TR12 6LQ, tel: 03265 4141.

Marconi chose this area for his first transmission to America. A clifftop obelisk at Poldhu Cove has plaques on four sides explaining how he first sent Morse code sounds from Cornwall to Newfoundland in 1901 – later proper speech. Imagine the excitement of being the first to hear someone communicating signals across space without a wire, then later actually talking to you from the other side of the Atlantic.

The sandy beaches in small coves are Cornwall's main attraction for families in summer. Off-season waves crash spectacularly over the harbour wall at tiny Mullion Cove. In October there can be brilliant sun one day, swirling white sea and land mists the next.

The waves and rocks are a summer pleasure and a winter hazard for ships and seals which give birth to their young in the winter months.

Seal Sanctuary
Keith Jones, a former Welsh miner, who began saving seals on the north coast, now has a Seal Sanctuary here on the south coast at Gweek. Babies start in the indoor hospital, are transferred to an outdoor hospital, and then to a convalescent pool. Other pools include maternity pools, for expectant seals. Those which recover completely and can feed themselves are released into the sea.

Twice a day at 11 am and 4 pm all year, you can see the seals

being fed by Mr Jones. Naturally he knows all the seals by name, tosses each one a few fish, and gives an amusing running commentary to camera-clicking tourists who watch. The site shop sells Keith Jones' book 'Seal Doctor' at £1.95. If you buy it he'll sign it for you. Entry to the site costs £2 for adults, £1 for children, including a safari bus from the entrance and hospital down to the pools. Picnic tables are set up by the riverside.
Keith Jones, Cornish Seal Sanctuary, Gweek, near Helston, Cornwall, tel: 032 622 361.

Victoriana
Mr Jones also has an interesting Victoriana Plus Museum at Mullion, near the 'Mullionaires' shop. It contains a copy of Queen Victoria's wedding dress made to fit a woman of the same size, only 4 foot six inches tall with a tiny seventeen inch waist. A miniature fairground turns to the sound of a tiny organ playing punched piano music rolls. Even more unusual is the miniature working mine, constructed by a retired Cornish miner, built of matchsticks. Tiny clockwork miners work at machinery and one has a moving mouth munching lunch.
Victoriana Plus, Mullion Old School, Mullion, Cornwall.

Poldark mine
You can visit a real Cornish mine, Poldark mine, after the novel of the same name. And dark it is. You walk into the mine down sloping tunnels, past the noisy waterwheel which has to be kept pumping the mine free of water every day of the year. The mine closes to the public in winter, though tours go until late afternoon early and late summer after other tourist sites have closed down.

Around the former tin mine's entrance is Ha'penny Park. The cost is 10p for adults, one penny for children, and you all get a reproduction old halfpenny coin token to pay for the amusements which each cost an old half penny. More tokens can be bought for use at the park or as souvenirs. Pretty gardens are by the outdoor slides. Indoors are the usual video games and a ballpond for the under 12s to bounce in. Parties can be held here, with children bouncing in the ballpond.
Poldark Mine and Ha'Penny Park, Wendron, nr Helston, Cornwall, tel: 03265 3531.

Flambard's Triple Theme Park

A robot's talking head greets you at Flambard's where up to six hours could be spent. A return visit costs only 10p. 'Britain in the Blitz' is an indoor exhibition, showing living rooms, shelters, a pub which has run out of draught beer, a car with covered headlamps and other displays. You hear snatches of radio broadcasts playing Vera Lynn singing 'We'll meet again', the original news broadcasts, and the whine of air-raid sirens and approaching planes as lights flash and a bomb explodes in the distance.

Undercover Flambard's village was featured in Yorkshire TV serial 'Flambards' based on Kathleen Peyton's trilogy about the early days of flying. It is a delightful reconstructed turn of the century Georgian and Victorian village, larger than the ones I've visited in York and elsewhere. Exploring the two levels, you enter a shop smelling of boiled sweets, and even see a hotel entrance hall, where characters in cloaks stand by huge trunks.

Outdoors, helicopters and other planes are distributed around a park with rides. You can go inside a helicopter and the wooden prototype of Concorde.

A space age simulator, 95p, shows a film of a big dipper ride, while jolting and tilting you!

Flambard's Triple Theme Park, Culdrose Manor, Helston, Cornwall, TR13 0GA, tel: 0326 574549.

Shipwright's Inn (Helford)

In good weather you should lunch at an inn overlooking one of the many creeks along the Helford river. The best known is Frenchman's Creek, which gave its name to Daphne du Maurier's novel. The Shipwright's Inn, Helford, is in a typical tiny village so small that cars cannot enter. You park outside and walk past thatched cottages to the inn. Here you can sit outdoors watching the boats which are for hire. A typical Cornish ploughman's lunch of bread and cheese can be followed by a chocolate dessert. (It's in the Les Routiers 'Good Value Guide 1987'.)

Shipwright's Arms, Helford, Cornwall, tel: 032 623 235.

Penzance

In poorer weather lunch indoors at the 400 year old Admiral

Benbow inn, Chapel Street, just past the statue of Humphry Davy who invented the miners' safety lamp, in the bustling town of Penzance. On the Benbow's roof is the model of a pirate who climbed the roof to shoot a warning shot at customs officials and save his smuggling friends. Inside are several bars and restaurants, constructed from bits of shipwrecks. (More details in Chapter 15.)
Chris Baker, Admiral Benbow, 46 Chapel Street, Penzance, tel: (0736) 63448.

Opposite is a Nautical Museum including items saved from shipwrecks, and four decks of an 18th century man o' war.

Cliffside Minack Theatre
A steep cliffside overlooking the sea near Land's End is the setting for the outdoor Minack Theatre at Porthcurno where Shakespeare and other plays are performed in good summer weather. Semi-circular tiers of seats are built into the cliff. You look down on actors performing with their backs to an arched stage, their voices competing with the sound of the waves behind them.

HOTELS
Smart Lamorna Cove Hotel in a quiet location on a clifftop is built of granite and has a four-poster bed, sauna and outdoor swimming pool.
Lamorna Cove Hotel, Lamorna, Cornwall TR19 6XH, tel: 0736 731411.

The small Smugglers' Hotel on the Penzance harbour road is described in Chapter 15.

Polurrian Hotel
Clark Gable who starred in 'Never Let Me Go', filmed at Mullion Cove in 1952, stayed at the clifftop Polurrian Hotel, Mullion. It now has a new leisure centre providing a warming diversion at the end of the day off-season. The jacuzzi costs about 50p for a 15 minute session for the family and the sauna costs about £1.50. You have to book a sauna session, and allow half an hour for the sauna to heat up in non-busy periods. The seaview from back bedrooms reveals the outdoor swimming

pool and children's playground.

This is not a plush five star hotel, but a family hotel in an area which is a favourite with families. The resident proprietor, Mr Robert Francis, plans to update his three star hotel's old fashioned bathrooms next. Meanwhile he's been mentioned in the 1986 Ashley Courtenay's Hotel Guide as well as the Good Hotel Guide, probably because of the personalised touches. e.g. a glass of sherry is poured out waiting for you in your bedroom on arrival.

The dining room has a sea view. Leisure breaks are offered at about £30 per person per day. Apartments are from £9 per person per day November until March while the main hotel is closed, but the leisure club remains open.
Robert Francis, Polurrian Hotel, Mullion, Helston, TR12 7BR, tel: 0326 240421.

GUESTHOUSES

Cornwall is one of the best areas in Britain for guesthouses. Signs hang outside garden gates along the main road, a bit noisy, and in the quieter side roads. But there will be difficulty getting accommodation over the bank holidays. Cheap rooms are available in tiny terraced guesthouses in the narrow streets of St Ives. A most picturesque view is obtainable in Seaview Road from the lounge bay windows overhanging beaches where the breakers smash below you in the sun.

Farm

I stayed at Polcoverack Farm, a short walk or drive down a lane from Coverack. In the morning children can follow the farmer taking the cows for milking. In summertime children play in the haybarn. Take wellies for winter or summer rain which turns field and cowyard into mud. The various converted farm buildings now used as self-catering holiday units have practical lino floors, with carpet in the centre of the living room.

A building of great character is Porcorum, a beamed one-storey converted pig-sty, sleeping six. A woodclad bungalow is dark and mysterious, and a barn has a sleeping platform overhead. Some cottages have baths, others merely showers. One entry in the visitors' books said a bidet and pay telephone would improve amenities. Most families of parents, grandparents and two children praised the relaxing holiday and were very pleased with the simple life.

The cost is from about £22 per person per week. Porcorum itself costs from about £92 to £250 according to season. Fortnightly bookings are made in summer holidays, running from midweek so you don't travel at busy weekends.

Farmers Jimmy Yeats, wife Olive, and son Alex, will show residents their inglenook fireplace. They will also describe the mystery smugglers' hidey hole, an internal gap between the walls of two rooms which they've never uncovered. Apparently in the olden days almost every isolated Cornish house had one! *Olive and Jimmy Yeats, Polcoverack Farm Cottages, Coverack, Cornwall, tel: 032 6280 497.*

Jamaica Inn
We returned across Bodmin Moor. On the main road is Jamaica Inn, made famous by Daphne du Maurier's novel, and the setting for two films. A parrot and a continuously burning fire are features of the old beamed bar. Food is obtainable from the self service snack bar at the back. There's a souvenir shop, and a children's playground.
Jamaica Inn, Bolbentor, Launceston, Cornwall, tel: Pipers Pool 250.

Getting There
By car it takes about five hours from London plus a meal stop on the motorway. The slow part is beyond Exeter, depending on traffic and which route you take to the far south-west. Side roads meander along lanes just wide enough for one car.

Alternatively stay overnight beyond Exeter in the Torquay area of Devon, known as England's Riviera.

You can also fly by Brymon Airways from Heathrow to Newquay on the north Cornish coast.

Polurrian hotel arranges fly drive, or meets your British rail train. National Rapide buses go along the M4 motorway from London to Exeter. And British Rail trains go to Redruth where you can be met by car, or you can use the Motor Rail, putting your car on the train to Penzance.

Cornwall

Brymon Airways, Newquay Airport, tel: St Mawgan 860551.
National Travel (bus) services to Penzance/Exeter from London Victoria and London Heathrow, tel: enquiry centres: Penzance (0736) 69469, or 01-730 0202.
British Rail, Paddington Station, London: enquiries for trains to Exeter and Penzance, tel: 01-262 6767.

More Information
Most of the sites mentioned above are marked on the Cornwall Tourist map and illustrated guide of places to visit, £1.95.
West Country Tourist Board, Trinity Court, 27 Southernhay East, Exeter, EX1 1ON, tel: 0392 76351.

CHAPTER 23
Offshore Fairy Islands

The sunny Channel Islands, Queen Victoria's favourite Isle of Wight, and the tax haven holiday Isle of Man – all are delightful overseas holiday destinations where the pound is welcomed and the passport is not required when arriving from mainland Britain.

ISLE OF MAN

The Isle of Man has its own parliament and makes its own laws. As a result it is a tax haven, and unlike mainland Britain pubs stay open all day. Manx licensing laws allow children to be admitted providing parents are eating meals.

It is very much an old-fashioned children's holiday paradise, famous for one of the largest waterwheels in the world, but great fun for nostalgic adults too. The landscape is as scenic as Devon and Cornwall, with steam trains chugging up hills, steep-sided valleys and wooded glens with lovely waterfalls where you can walk along dappled paths – areas of natural beauty unaffected by mass tourism.

Douglas

After flying by Manx Airlines from Heathrow to Ronaldsway airport you drive to the capital, Douglas, over the Fairy Bridge. As you cross the Fairy Bridge by bus the passengers to avoid bad luck shout 'Good morning, fairies!' Alternatively take the ferry to Douglas where a horse-drawn tram meets passengers. You can load your suitcases on the tram for a trot along the promenade where many hotels are situated, and photograph your child holding the horse's reins.

Bustling Douglas promenade borders a sand and shingle bay where colourfully painted terraced houses and hotels have arched windows. Douglas offers sophisticated evenings at the Casino, or The Palace hotel Lido which holds laser shows. The Gaiety Theatre has an amazingly elaborate interior with domed boxes and a curtain showing an oriental scene.

Restaurants in Douglas
The circular Crows Nest restaurant with its central spire looks like an orange squeezer on top of the ferry terminal and bus station. The Crows Nest bar gives panoramic views of bobbing boats on the sea in all directions by day. Romantic window tables view the night-time promenade illuminations. The plump, jovial Italian manager keeps up a constant patter. I said, 'The weather's better now.' 'Oh yes,' he replied, 'last month we played Spot the Tourist and nobody won.'
Crows Nest Restaurant, Sea Terminal Building, Douglas, Isle of Man, tel: 0624 75009.

Boncompte's gourmet restaurant is near Douglas at Onchan. Vegetarian meals are served if they are given notice. Eschewing the local delicacy of 'queenies' (small scallops), I had a delicious meal which ended with a meringue cooked when ordered. My companion merely wanted an apple for dessert. It arrived cut into slices arranged in two concentric circles going in opposite directions, on a bed of ice.
Boncompte's, King Edward Road, Onchan, Isle of Man, tel: 0624 75626.

ATTRACTIONS AROUND THE ISLAND
Manx Cattery
The Isle of Man is known for its tailless Manx cats. In Nobles Park, Douglas, you can visit the Manx Cattery which was set up to breed tailless Manx cats ensuring they do not die out. Cats can be bought – join the waiting list.

Laxey Waterwheel
The Isle of Man's famous waterwheel has a 72 ft diameter making it the biggest in Britain, probably the largest in the world. At Laxey you climb the spiral staircase to the top of the stunning red and white wheel for a wonderful view. The Manx three legs symbol on the wheel is accompanied by a Manx motto meaning, 'Whichever way you throw me I stand'.
Laxey Wheel, Laxey, Isle of Man, tel: Laxey 781136.

A three day Rail Rover allows one journey on Snaefell Mountain railway to Laxey, and unlimited travel on the Douglas-Ramsey electric railway and the Douglas-Port Erin steam railway.

Steam Train South

The steam train sets off from Douglas and you can see it as you take the road alongside from Castletown to Port Erin.

The toast-rack steam train with its smoky smell jolts south from Douglas to Port Erin along delightful dappled cuttings. Families with children should get off at Ballasalla to try the water-powered merry-go-round. Pull the lever to tip water over the wheel which sets it in motion. There is a boating lake, and under the cafe is the Gnome Grotto where gnomes with moving heads and hands pour tea, hammer nails, and pan for gold. You could also alight at Castletown to explore Castle Rushen's numerous staircases and towers.

Your destination, the tiny pollution-free bay of Port Erin has a sandy beach. At Port Erin's small Aquarium you can identify the plaice and cod everyone eats. The sea is cold for outdoor swimming, but the Cherry Orchard Hotel is open to non-residents for morning and afternoon indoor swimming sessions.

Just uphill The Manx Open Air Folk Museum at Cregneash has thatched buildings and spinning and smithying demonstrations. A lady cooks soda bread made with currants and tears off a piece for you to taste.

The Folk Museum, Cregneash, Port St Mary, Isle of Man. For opening times contact *Manx Museum, Douglas, Isle of Man, tel: 0624 75522.*

Vikings

Other links with the past are four replica Viking ships resting in Peel harbour alongside Odin's Raven boathouse museum. The fifty foot long wooden replica boat was featured on TV by Magnus Magnusson. The bearded curator looks very much as you imagine a Viking would. He wears Viking gear and poses with visitors for photographs, equipping everybody with shields and Viking helmets.

Odin's Raven Boathouse, The Quayside, Peel, Isle of Man, tel: 0624 843300.

Isle of Man

On the opposite side of the harbour is Peel Castle where an archaeological dig has uncovered Viking remains. More Viking carvings are in the north of the island.

Sheep and Souvenirs
At Tynwald Craft Centre, St Johns, there are horned Manx sheep, weaving demonstrations and Manx tartan rugs for sale. Other typical souvenirs are Manx coins and stamps. Manx kippers are sold at the airport flower shop for about £5 as you depart, and Glen Kella whiskey. The island has its own brands of tea, coffee, real ale, and ice cream.

Events
During the TT motorcycle summer races, and car rally, certain roads are closed, causing detours, and it is difficult to get accommodation, hire cars, or obtain car spaces on ferries.

In July Parliament is opened for one day outdoors on Tynwald hill, where laws are read and petitions presented.

There's also a tin bath boat race, and in August there is a Victorian festival week.

HOTEL ACCOMMODATION ON ISLE OF MAN
Hotel Admiral (Douglas)
Staying in busy Douglas is convenient if you don't have a car. A small exclusive romantic hotel is Admiral House which has a giant four-poster in the Tudor suite, a romantic sunken oval bath, and a pink Pompadour suite, about £70 for two.
Admiral House, Loch Promenade, Douglas, Isle of Man, tel: 0624 29551.

Sefton Hotel (Douglas)
The large smart Sefton Hotel has a new shallow indoor pool with a spa pool, and a bar next to it so you can sit and watch youngsters swimming. Children's menus are available in the seaview Carvery restaurant. At dinner time the family's first child under age 9, accompanied by two paying adults, gets a free meal. Bedrooms are newly decorated. Book a month ahead to be sure of getting free child accommodation.
Sefton Hotel, Harris Promenade, Douglas, Isle of Man, tel: 0624 26011.

Mannin Hotel (Douglas)

The small Mannin Hotel has a delightful Italian restaurant with a 45 degree mirror on the ceiling. The newly built arched downstairs buffet bar is attractive and when the charming new owner (Italian with handlebar moustache) redecorates all the bedrooms it will be a lovely hotel.

The Mannin Hotel, 12 Broadway, Douglas, Isle of Man, tel: 0624 75335.

Grand Island Hotel (Ramsey)

Several smart bedrooms are available at Grand Island Hotel, a mansion with lawns sloping down to the seafront, and bed with draped headboards. Winter weekend breaks are offered.

Grand Island Hotel, Ramsey, Isle of Man, tel: 0624 812455.

Cherry Orchard Hotel (Port Erin)

Cherry Orchard Hotel is in a side road near Port Erin Station and orchard trees are on the carpet. It is a good hotel for anyone with babies because there is a toddlers' playroom, baby listening, and a coin-operated launderette. Children get a free trip on the steam railway in summer and one free pony-trekking session. Suites with high chairs and maid service are available. The Penthouse apartment for two people costs about £33–45 per day according to season, two bedroom apartments for 1–6 people, about the same price. Bed and breakfast in the hotel is from about £20 per person.

Cherry Orchard Hotel/apartments, Port Erin, Isle of Man, tel: 0624 833811.

Package Deals

Package holidays including fares are offered in the Island Magic Offpeak Holiday brochure. A package with an average grade hotel bedroom (called Grade A) such as one at the Mannin Hotel, Douglas, with en suite bathroom, costs from about £70 each adult for two nights, and £45 for a child sharing the bedroom.

A package with a superior hotel (called Super A) such as the Sefton Hotel in Douglas or the Cherry Orchard at Port Erin costs from about £90, plus about £50 for one child sharing. Add £50 offpeak to take your car.

Inverlochy castle, near Fort William (page 143)

Cowes sailing events off the Royal Yacht Squadron premises and cannons (page 199)

View over Lake Windermere from Miller Howe (pages 23, 46, 142)

Haworth, Yorkshire, home of the Brontës (page 206)

The Feathers, Ludlow (page 85)

Getting There

The Heysham car ferry, near Lancaster, takes four hours. A 60 hour excursion ticket allows two nights on the island.

Ferries operate from Liverpool all year and other ports in high season. The boat's video sometimes shows children's cartoons. A passenger only adult day excursion fare costs about £15.

For motorists there's a 120 hour summer excursion fare, car plus 2 adults about £150 plus £18 per child; economy fare Monday-Thursday; winter fare about £110 for the car and two adults plus £13 each child.

Manx Airline, a subsidiary of British Midland, operates flights from Heathrow. Fares vary, e.g. from Heathrow about £104 budget return, £49 off peak one way; Liverpool fares from about £44 return, £28 return child under 12. Flights are available from other cities. For Valuebreak inclusive holidays brochure tel: 0624 73613.

Manx Airlines Ltd, Isle of Man, Ronaldsway Airport, Ballasalla, Isle of Man, tel: 0624 824313. Send for the Easyway Guide.

Return rail fares from London range from about £57 to £62 in the peak period, child fares about £17 and £9. Tel: 01-493 0803.

Tourist Information

The Tourist Information office sells a cassette of Manx tourist commentary, and a book called 'The Manxmen are Coming' for a child's bedtime story, plus leaflets on beaches and sightseeing. *Isle of Man Tourist Board, 13 Victoria Street, Douglas, Isle of Man, tel: 0624 74323.*

THE CHANNEL ISLANDS

One of the attractions of going south to the Channel Islands is good weather. Spring starts earlier in the Channel Islands, which are a group of islands off the coast of north-west France which belong to Britain. The two largest islands are Jersey and Guernsey, and three minor ones are Sark, Alderney and Herm.

You can fly direct, fly-drive, or reach them by ferry. On

Jersey and Guernsey little coves are glimpsed between ivy-clad trees as you drive along narrow lanes – leave the big car at home. You pass stone-built bungalows and houses, no bricks, because you are in the Channel Islands. No VAT or high excise tax means cheap wine, beer, cocktails, and perfume. The French food in the supermarkets is inexpensive.

JERSEY

Jersey is the biggest, busiest, best known British Channel Island. You can drive across the island in an afternoon day from anywhere, or spend all day on the north seeing only Jersey cows, prehistoric tombs and sandy bays. But bustling St Helier, the capital, is the liveliest place to stay. The clifftop Fort Regent Leisure Centre which dominates the town is a complex containing museums and leisure activities.

Visit Jersey Museum at 9 Pier Road, St Helier, which has Lillie Langtry's travelling case. Boat trips and flights go from St Helier to Guernsey, Sark, Herm and Alderney.

Around the Island

Around the Island are the Pottery at Gorey where lunches are served, the chilly German Military Underground Hospital tunnelled into the rock during World War Two by slave labour, the Gerald Durrell Zoo, and the Battle of Flowers Museum displaying animals of the world made from dried grasses. Jersey's Battle of Flowers parade is in August, Guernsey's in September.

Pubs and Restaurants and Hotels in Jersey
Moulin de Lecq Inn (Greve de Lecq)

The Moulin de Lecq Inn was once a watermill. The French language is conspicuous in Jersey. Waitresses wear Breton costumes, but the Jersey Sealed Knot society re-enacts battles between King Charles I and Cromwell. The pub is floodlit at night. *Moulin de Lecq Inn, Greve de Lecq, Jersey, Channel Islands, tel: 0534 82818.*

Windmill Inn (St Peter)

See the granite Windmill Inn where churns are used as stools. This place is also floodlit at night. *Windmill Inn, St Peter, Jersey, CI, tel: 0534 81510.*

Old Court House Inn (St Aubin's Harbour)
The seventeenth century Old Court House inn on the harbour has bars with beams, parts of a galleon, and a well which supplied water to ships. Seafood is served in the sunny courtyard in summer. *Old Court House Inn, St Aubin's Harbour, Jersey, CI, tel: 41156.*

Hotel Revère (St Helier)
In the main town Hotel Revère features a small swimming pool, portcullis bar, woodcarvings, stone arches and beams.
Hotel Revère, Kensington Place, St Helier, Jersey, CI, tel: 0534 38773.

L'Horizon (St Brelade's Bay)
If you prefer to be on the beach modern l'Horizon is expensive but exquisite. Phone boxes have fresh flowers. A pianist or other entertainer plays live music in the restaurant.
L'Horizon, St Brelade's Bay, Jersey, CI, tel: 0534 43101.

The flight to Jersey from Heathrow takes about one hour. Sealink ferries go from Portsmouth.

More information
Jersey Tourist Board Information Bureau, Weighbridge, St Hellier, Jersey. Accommodation tel: 0534 31958; information tel: 0534 24779.

GUERNSEY
Guernsey, whose name means Green Isle in Norman French, is the home of Guernsey tomatoes which grow in greenhouses at the Tomato Museum, and Strawberry Farm offering strawberry trees. Along the leafy lanes houses sell potted plants and palms from boxes by the garden gate.

In the capital, St Peter Port, yachts crowd the harbour, overlooked by the house of the French novelist Victor Hugo. The exiled author of 'The Hunchback of Notre Dame' fashioned an eccentric house. He installed candelabras built from cotton reels, turned doors into tables, constructed a four-poster from chair legs, and suspended plates on racks across the pantry ceiling. His rooftop studio had a tip-up bed in case he was tired. His studio with skylights overlooked the harbour and he could wave to his mistress who lived a short distance away.

From St Peter Port harbour below, boat trips go to the smaller islands. By the harbour, shops sell souvenir Guernsey sweaters which were originally made for fishermen and are said to last a lifetime. Many are machine-made nowadays. The more expensive ones are still hand-knitted. Other bargains in VAT-free souvenirs include perfume, camera cases, and leather goods.

Climb up cobbled Mill Street to lunch in Scandinavian Ulla's kitchen, serving gravad lax (pickled salmon), live lobsters from a tank, and Auslese wine by the glass. The decor is South Seas batiks. *Ulla's Kitchen, Mill Street, St Peter Port, Guernsey, CI, tel: 0481 23730.*

GUERNSEY HOTELS

St Pierre Park Hotel (St Peter Port)
Plush St Pierre Park Hotel is built next to its own small lake, and ducks wander into the dining room. Overlooking the lake are bedroom suites whose en suite bathrooms are provided with a ceramic swan containing heart-shaped soap. The hotel has just about every active entertainment, golf, a children's playground and an indoor swimming pool.

In the health centre you can lie on your back being massaged, watching a gently swirling mobile. A soothing beauty treatment programme reduces stress, so long as your wallet bulges as much as your waistline and you are happy to be persuaded to buy creams and cosmetics.
St Pierre Park Hotel, Rohais, St Peter Port, Guerney, CI, tel: 0481 28282.

Old Government House Hotel (St Peter Port)
Seafront Old Government House has an outdoor swimming pool and caters for families in summer and the retired in winter. But there is an excellent romantic bedroom suite with a huge bed in a spacious room with a magnificent harbour view.

Old Government House Hotel, St Ann's Place, St Peter Port, Guernsey, CI, tel: 0481 24921.

Le Fregate Hotel (St Peter Port)
Uphill there's the elegant Le Fregate where you dine overlooking the harbour lights. One very attractive bedroom has beams.
Le Fregate (hotel and restaurant), Les Cotils, St Peter Port, Guernsey, CI, tel: 0481 24624.

Havelet Court Hotel (St Peter Port)
The small Havelet Court Hotel has an exotic Bali bar and oriental bedrooms along a terrace.
Havelet Court Hotel, Havelet, St Peter Port, Guernsey, CI, tel: 0481 26410.

Duke of Richmond Hotel (St Peter Port)
Uphill from the port The Duke of Richmond Hotel incorporates a pub decorated like a ship.
Duke of Richmond Hotel, Cambridge Park, St Peter Port, Guernsey, CI, tel: 0481 26221.

Le Chalet (Fermain Bay)
Edward VII's love-nest with Lillie Langtry, Jersey Lillie, is now the midprice Le Chalet Hotel. It is half way up the cliff, enjoying a spectacular view between trees either side of the V-shape valley to the blue sea in the bay.
Le Chalet Hotel, Fermain Bay, Guernsey, CI, tel: 0481 35716.

Guernsey holiday packages are available for botany and sports. You can also learn to fly at the flying school which takes a few weeks to cover the number of flying hours required for qualifying as a pilot. They say that the absence of VAT makes the cost of the course and longstay accommodation cheaper here than on the mainland.

A colour book containing photo advertisement of hotels, their spa baths and four-poster beds is available from:
Guernsey Tourist Board, P O Box 23, St Peter Port, Guernsey, Channel Islands, tel: 0481 23552 or 24 hr answerphone 0481 23557.

ALDERNEY, SARK, AND HERM
Alderney

Up to 1,500 people a day visit Alderney during August, which is almost as many people as the resident population. They go either out of curiosity or to get away from it all. You'll find very little to do on Alderney except walk around the clifftops, sit on the seashore or hire a bicycle. The island has no traffic lights, and the speed limit is 35 m.p.h. There is one police car, number 999.

The pace is slow. You rarely see a car and never hoot anyone, unless you're hurrying to catch a plane. A local resident explained this while we waited behind a vehicle blocking our road. We sat incredulously watching a man unloading a small four-drawer bedside cabinet, one drawer at a time.

The most exciting part is the flight. I loved that.

From Southampton, or Jersey or Guerney, you can fly on one of the small Aurigny airline planes to Alderney island and back in a day.

The planes are so small that one of the passengers sits next to the pilot and his little joke is to tell you that you're wearing his seat belt! The little yellow planes are immortalised in a series of children's books about 'Joey' the plane. If you travel on Joey you can get a Joey Flight Certificate signed by the captain saying you have flown aboard Joey.

Aurigny Air Services, The Airport, Alderney, Channel Islands, tel: 048182 2886.

Sark

Sark is also traffic free. A horse drawn buggy takes tourists along to the dramatic clifftop causeway leading to the other half of the island. The home of the Dame of Sark, who defied the Nazis when they occupied the Channel Islands, opens on certain days. A play about her is performed in summer months on the larger islands of Jersey and Guernsey.

Herm

The smallest Channel Island is charming Herm which has one hotel, and a harbour where ferries arrive with day-trippers. A breezy walk along a sandy, dappled path leads across the grass to a shell beach with tiny shells.

ISLE OF WIGHT

The Isle of Wight off the south coast of Britain is only a short ferry ride away from the mainland and as you would expect holds Britain's best holiday resort sunshine record, apart from the British Channel Islands.

The 26 mile wide Isle of Wight can be driven around in a day, although excursions and museum visits, or simply watching the colourful boats at Cowes with binoculars, could keep you busy for a week.

Queen Victoria loved the Isle of Wight, and the seaview house that Prince Albert and she built there, named Osborne House, became her favourite residence and was where she chose to die. The Empress of India received her Indian empire visitors in an Indian style room in the house, which is open to visitors in summer. *Osborne House, Whippingham, East Cowes, Isle of Wight, tel: 0983 200022.*

In winter you can visit Carisbrooke Castle where Charles I was imprisoned. Another all-year attraction is Haseley Manor, where visitors can try making a mouse in the pottery. After a snack lunch, walk around Haseley Manor, now a museum. A medieval tableau depicts the island's governor dying of plague in a four-poster bedroom. Photographs show how the entrepreneurial present owners Mr and Mrs Young have rebuilt the derelict house they bought in the 1970s. *Haseley Manor, Arreton, Isle of Wight, tel: 0983 865420.*

Yacht racing regattas take place every summer weekend at Cowes. During Cowes week in August there is a free fireworks display. Illuminated processions are held in Cowes, Ventnor, Newport and Ryde on different dates in August.

Summertime attractions include Blackgang Chine Fantasy Theme Park, the Museum of Clocks, a Museum of Smuggling History, Cranmore Vineyard, Calbourne Water Mill, Bembridge Windmill, a dairy farm, a butterfly farm, a zoo, Roman villas, a museum of dolls and toys, and a model railway.

Alum Bay chair lift rises up the cliff giving you a view of the white Needles rocks in the sea. The lift never stops and if you hesitate to board the attendant quickly shoves you into the seat and you take off! By the rainbow-coloured cliffs is a glassmakers and a shop sells souvenir paperweights, glass lighthouses and miniature bottles all containing striped sands.

The Island Vouchers 'Where To Go on the Isle of Wight' booklet, sold to passengers queuing for the Sealink car ferry to the Isle of Wight, gives discounts to attractions.

Shanklin on the west of the island is a pretty picturesque village of thatched cottages, tearooms and museums. The delightful seafront, illuminated in season, has a pier. Shanklin has also been the British annual sunshine record holder more times than any other resort. Nearby Godshill also has thatched tearooms, giftshops, potteries and museums.

ISLE OF WIGHT HOTELS
Glenbrook Hotel (Shanklin)
The thatched Glenbrook Hotel and Henry VIII restaurant in the main street at Shanklin is worth a photograph.
Glenbrook Ye Olde Village Hotel and Henry VIII Lodge Restaurant, Old Village, Shanklin Road, Shanklin, Isle of Wight PO37 6NU, tel: 0983 863119.

I stayed at two seaview hotels selected from the Minotels brochure. Minotels are three star hotels, family-run and therefore each has a different character.

Bourne Hall Hotel (Shanklin)
Mr and Mrs Douglas of modern Bourne Hall Hotel welcomed us in a newly decorated bar featuring ship pictures. Unlike many hotels which have no cocktail menu, they keep a book of cocktail recipes.

Both hotels can provide vegetarian food. Mrs Douglas makes carrot puree pancake au gratin from a recipe left by a vegetarian guest who sent her own recipe book before arriving. Mrs Douglas says, 'Just tell us what you wouldn't eat – or would like to eat. I couldn't do this for large numbers of people in high season, but I can in the autumn.'

Mr Douglas installed a spa bath in the indoor swimming pool and sauna complex, which he built himself. The pear-shaped outdoor pool, overhung by a willow tree, is illuminated at night. The use of sauna and spa bath costs under £1 for half an hour. By day you can play tennis, putting, or croquet.

A four-poster bedroom with sea view is available.

Bourne Hall Hotel, Luccombe Road, Shanklin, Isle of Wight, tel: 0983 862820.

Wellington Lodge Hotel (Ryde)
On the East coast the Wellington Lodge Hotel with little vases shaped like boots offers sea views from the dining room, which is candle-lit at night. Mr Joliffe refuses to repaint the old dining room ceiling, preferring to keep the fading pattern as it was originally painted in the 19th century. He can tell tales about the house's history.

Their hotel won the three bluebirds award, one of the top three awards, in the 1986 Peadouce Guide to family holidays. It is an old-fashioned family hotel, with a big children's playroom filled with books and old toys, and an in-house video on all bedroom televisions so you can tune in watching the outdoor pool and bar areas, detecting your children, or your missing spouse. Holidaymakers can also borrow a metal detector to hunt for treasure by the beach, or tune the TV to the satellite station.

Bedrooms include a four-poster room and a large family room with a bay seating area overlooking the sea.
Wellington Lodge Hotel, Augusta Road, Ryde, Isle of Wight, PO33 3AT, tel: 0983 68844.

Biskra House Hotel & Restaurant (Ryde)
A good place to eat in Ryde is Biskra House, a small hotel in a terrace backing onto the beach. You must book a table at weekends in the jolly basement restaurant. The ground floor restaurant is more formal. They serve an excellent dinner with fresh vegetables. Bijou bedrooms have a tin of home-made biscuits by the bed. Room prices from about £30 per night, dinner about £10.
Biskra House Beach Hotel, 17 St Thomas's Street, Ryde, Isle of Wight, tel: 0983 67913.

Bonchurch Manor (Ventnor)
Bonchurch Manor, a country house hotel with Adam fireplaces, log fires, and a heated indoor pool, offers winter breaks. A five course dinner includes local seafood.
Bonchurch Manor, near Ventnor, Isle of Wight, PO38 1NU, tel: 0983 852868.

Winterbourne Hotel (Ventnor)
Winterbourne Hotel, a country house with sea views was the home of Charles Dickens in 1849. Spring and autumn breaks are available.
Winterbourne Hotel, Ventnor, Isle of Wight, tel: 0983 852535.

George Hotel (Yarmouth)
The George Hotel in Yarmouth has the room where Charles II slept at the top of the staircase, with a plaque over the door. The bedrooms are unexciting, but the hotel's harbour view is pretty, and the pine bar with cartoons has distinctive character – a good place for a drink.
George Hotel, Quay Street, Yarmouth, Isle of Wight, tel: 0983 760331.

Calverts Pub & Hotel (Newport)
Another amusing pub is in Newport. Stop to see the picturesque pedestrian alley called Quay Street running off the High Street. An overhead walkway crossing the alley links hotel bedroom corridors on either side. Downstairs is the hotel's public bar.
Calverts Hotel, Quay Street, Newport, Isle of Wight, tel: 0983 525281.

Getting There
A return Sealink crossing for 2 passengers with car from Portsmouth–Ryde/Fishborne (45 minutes) or Lymington–Yarmouth (30 minutes) costs from about £40 according to season. *Sealink Portsmouth Harbour, tel: 0705 827744 or dail-a-brochure 0705 751751.*

Another ferry service operates from Southampton to West Cowes, and a passenger-only hydrofoil takes just 20 minutes. For details contact Southampton, *tel: 0703 333042.*

More information from:
Isle of Wight Tourist Board, 21 High Street, Newport, Isle of Wight, PO30 1JS, tel: 0983 524343.

PART VI

Bargain budget breaks and other tips

CHAPTER 24
City Breaks

Great English City Breaks, hotel breaks in English cities, are brought together in one brochure by the English Tourist Board and National Holidays, offering a choice of four hotels in each city.

At all these locations the standard hotel price is about £20 per night per person, assuming you travel in your own car. Packages for express coach or rail travel go from eight areas of England.

Spring and autumn coach breaks costing about £50 from London and the south-east include bed and breakfast, coach travel and two sightseeing tours.

Plymouth and the Pilgrim Fathers
The Americans' first choice has to be Plymouth, from where the Pilgrim fathers sailed in 1620 to the New World. Mothers went too, 101 people arrived, two born en route!

Harbour tours go past modern day ships and submarines, starting from the area where plaques tell you about the pilgrims. Some interesting boats arrive in Plymouth, and this was where Sir Francis Chichester was welcomed on his return from his solo circumnavigation.

See an Elizabethan House, a merchant's house, and the church associated with Drake. In the cobbled old town the olde world Black Friars distillery has a wine bar offering the famous gin-based Singapore Sling, a restaurant, and shows an audio visual presentation about gin. *Black Friars Distillery, Southside Street, Plymouth, Devon, tel: 0752 665292, restaurant 0752 224305.*

Opposite notice a huge mural by Jewish artist Robert Lenkiewicz, portraying nudes of local people. They posed clothed, and didn't know they were going to be naked until the mural was unveiled amid gasps of horror. The uproar and protests still continue. His earlier mural shows Drake and Elizabethan characters modelled by Plymouth residents.

Sir Francis Drake's house, Buckland Abbey, is owned by the National Trust and situated 12 miles from Plymouth. It displays Drake's huge drum, banners from Drake's ship the Golden Hind, letters bearing Elizabeth I's seal, tapestries, and maps showing where Drake reached America, returning in 1580. An ancient portrait of Drake's wife was recently identified by the rings on all her fingers. *Buckland Abbey, near Yelverton, Devon, tel: 082285 3607.*

Holiday Inn, not in the scheme but offering other weekend breaks, is very pleasant with a rooftop breakfast room overlooking Plymouth Hoe and Drake's statue, looking out to sea.

The Mayflower Post House (THF) which is in the brochure has a lovely breakfast room overlooking the harbour.

Read 'Plymouth England and its links with America'.

More details from: *Plymouth Marketing Bureau Ltd, St Andrew's Court, 12 St Andrew's Street, Plymouth, Devon, PL1 2AH, tel: 0752 261125.*

Stoke-on-Trent and the Potteries

Wedgwood's factory tour is the highlight of the weekend in Stoke. You see a slide show explaining how Josiah Wedgwood experimented, keeping meticulous notes, until he discovered how the Chinese blue on white used in the willow pattern was made. See the black pottery, imitating the style of the famous ancient Greek Portland vase. A museum shows fairyland lustre, the pottery of royalty, and Wedgwood's great invention – of pottery that everybody could afford, providing employment in Arnold Bennett's 'five towns' of the pottery area for centuries afterwards.

Josiah Wedgwood & Sons Ltd, Barlaston, Stoke-on-Trent, tel: 078139 3218.

At Gladstone Pottery huge bottle-shape brick ovens surround the courtyard. The pottery collection displays the history of sanitary ware showing toilets of all types, one called 'The Deluge', and a revolving lift-up inset washbasin, preceding the sort with drain outlets.

In summer you can dine in a restaurant on a horse-drawn barge, or visit Britain's first purpose built theatre in the round. The circular stage seems tiny and intimately close.

Excursions can be made to Chatsworth stately home, 'Palace of the Peak', with a grand frescoed entrance, or half-timbered Little Moreton Hall.

When motoring through this area I also bought seconds at other potteries such as the Denbyware factory.

Birmingham

In Birmingham the city break hotels offered include lakeside Penns Hall Hotel which is the current setting of the 'Crossroads' TV series, and the more central Grand Hotel and Albany. You could pick the August weekend when racing cars roar through the city centre. Guided excursions go to the Ironbridge Gorge.

If money is no object stay at Crest's plush Plough & Harrow. The interior has the most amazing decoration, crammed with exotic woodcarving and complicated lampshades. Other hotels near Birmingham are mentioned in Chapter 14 on wet weekends.

If you can't get accommodation in Birmingham when visiting the National Exhibition Centre, try the *Lansdowne Hotel, Clarendon Street, in Leamington Spa, Warwickshire, tel: 0926 21313.* They have an intriguing box of games, samples left by representatives at the gift fairs.

Coventry

Coventry is known for the modern Cathedral. Lady Godiva's statue stands in Broadgate and the nearby mechanical clock features Peeping Tom who couldn't resist watching as the naked lady rode past. One hotel in the scheme allows you to see Lady Godiva's statue and another has a jogging trail. Guided excursions go to Stratford and Warwick Castle.

Leicester

Leicester is 12 miles from Bosworth field where Henry Tudor won the last battle of the Wars of the Roses against Richard III. Trail boards bring the battle alive and the visitor centre has a medieval street. Belvoir Castle which holds mock battles was filmed in 'Little Lord Fauntleroy', while Rockingham Castle appeared in the BBC TV series 'By the Sword Divided'. Other local attractions are the Donington collection of racing cars, and the chimps who appeared in the tea party at Twycross Zoo.

Bradford and the Brontes

Bradford's 'big' attraction is the five storey cinema screen at the National Museum of Photography, Film and Television. Saturday excursions go to the 'Emmerdale Farm' TV series village, and Ilkley Moor, which every schoolchild will remember singing about 'On Ilkley Moor baht 'at' (Yorkshire for on Ilkley Moor without a hat). Do take your own hat, and boots, if you want to explore the windswept Wuthering Heights on the moors. Sunday excursions go to the Bronte village of Haworth.

At the Bronte Parsonage the miniature books the children wrote are displayed. You learn that their father banned curtains because of the numbers of local children who died in fires. Branwell drank himself to death at the local pub and got his dangerous drugs from the chemist in the high street, after an ill-fated love affair. He fell asleep setting fire to the bedclothes, an incident Charlotte used in her novel 'Jane Eyre'. The tragic family had only a few incidents of hope: their father's successful eye operation for cataract – one of the first, Charlotte's sudden fame, and her happy marriage in the last year of her life. *Bronte Parsonage Museum, Haworth, Keighley, West Yorkshire BD22 8DR, tel: 0535 42323.*

Industrial Leeds

Leeds has the largest fish and chip shop in the world with chandeliers, also Victorian shopping arcades, and an old music hall. A hotel holds Victorian evenings. One of the four City Break hotels offered is the Windmill Hotel, Stakis, built around an original windmill.

Outside town, not in the scheme, is the modern lakeside Chevin Lodge Hotel, offering split level apartments featuring wood cladding. *Chevin Lodge, Yorkgate, Otley, West Yorkshire LS21 3NU, tel: 0943 467818.*

'A Woman of Substance' tours in spring and autumn take you to places where the TV series based on Barbara Taylor Bradford's book was filmed. The rags to riches story includes Armley Mills Industrial Museum, showing the Jewish tailoring shops where heroine Emma Harte starts work, and Leeds market where Marks & Spencer's penny bazaar began. The tour cost is under £50 including two nights accommodation, breakfast, tour guide, entrance fees and a souvenir copy of one of the novels. Details from *Enterprise Travel, Clifton Villas, Bradford BD8 7BY, tel: 0274 488116.* Enterprise arranges packages for tour operators and can usually put you in touch with the nearest group.

Viking York

The City Breaks Saturday excursion goes to Herriot country, where scenes from the vet's best selling books such as 'All Creatures Great and Small' and the TV series were filmed. The other destination is York. See the medieval Shambles, where the upper storeys of medieval buildings lean across the narrow lane. The traditional attractions of walks around the city walls, and the castle museum containing a Victorian street, are now eclipsed by the even more exciting and unique Jorvik Centre.

The Vikings' tenth century city was discovered below York as builders dug foundations for a skyscraper. Archaeological finds are preserved underground in a museum alongside Tussaud's lifesize town with bustling market and busy wharf. You travel backwards on time cars listening to Magnus Magnusson's commentary, hearing animal noises and Viking voices talking Old Norse, smelling the smoking city and pigsties, and then you pass through the reconstructed archaeological dig. Allow about one hour. *Jorvik Viking Centre, Coppergate, York, tel: 0904 643211.*

York also has the National Railway Museum and the Friargate Wax Museum.

Other holiday/hotel packages to York are available from Crest, Anchor, Moat House, Labrokes, Post House, Saga, Golden Rail, etc.

Liverpool – Beatles and Americans' City

Liverpool's Beatle City museum is part of the Footsteps of the Beatles tour which takes place on Sunday, passing Strawberry Field, and the new Cavern Club.

On Saturday you can visit Chester, Port Sunlight Village and the Lady Leverhulme art gallery. Lord Leverhulme, the soap king, created the Port Sunlight garden city for his workers. The art gallery contains a wonderful collection of Pre-Raphaelite paintings, plus amusing letters to *The Times* expressing outrage that Lever Bros had debased a beautiful painting by using it in a soap advertisement. *Lady Lever Art Gallery, Port Sunlight Village, Bebington, Wirral, tel: 051 6453623.*

The Pilkington Glass Museum is another possible excursion. *Pilkington Glass Museum, Presco Road, St Helens, tel: 0744 28882 x 2499.*

Or see black and white Tudor Speke Hall which has priest holes, and was visited by Harriet Beecher Stowe, author of 'Uncle Tom's Cabin' (a National Trust property). *Speke Hall, The Walk, Liverpool, Merseyside, L24 1XD, tel: 051-427 7231.*

Down by the harbour Albert Dock village has a new 'Emigrants to the New World Gallery'. A book called 'The American Connection' by Ron Jones outlines a walking trail you can join at any point, passing such landmarks as the memorial to the Titanic which was built in Liverpool's shipyard.

'The Discovery of America was the maker of Liverpool' is the inscription on the statue of Christopher Columbus, who stands in Sefton Park, with his hand held to his forehead, sighting land. A wreath is laid on Columbus Day, October 12th.

If you have to change trains, e.g. on your way to Southport, Liverpool's two main railway stations are within walking distance of each other, but connected by a train link. Liverpool Museums and the Walker Art Gallery are next door to each other near the railway station. *Walker Art Gallery, William Brown Street, Liverpool, tel: 051 2275234.*

Also see the Catholic Cathedral, the Anglican Cathedral, and the Philharmonic Pub with its eagle gates, all in Hope Street (*Philharmonic Pub, 36 Hope Street, Liverpool, tel: 051 7091163*).

Manchester

Manchester Jewish Museum is in a former Spanish and

Portuguese synagogue, with exhibitions in the galleries. *Manchester Jewish Museum, 190 Cheetham Hill Road, Manchester, Greater Manchester, M8 8LW, tel: 061-834 9879.*

L. S. Lowry's paintings of 'matchstick men' described in the pop song can be seen at the *Gallery of Modern Art, Princess Street, Manchester M1 4HR, tel: 061 236 9422,* and the *Fletcher Moss Museum, the Old Parsonage, Stenner Lane, Didsbury, Manchester, tel: 061 236 9422.* The largest collection is in *Salford Museum and Art Gallery, The Crescent, Peel Park, Salford, Greater Manchester, M5 4WU, tel: 061 736 2649,* which also has a reconstructed street.

Wigan Pier
Your Saturday excursion could be to Wigan Pier. The "road to Wigan Pier" (a phrase made famous by George Orwell) may be dull, but the rebuilt pier is interesting. A multiple ticket enables you to take a barge ride along the canal, see the world's largest steam engine in the old ropemaking works and visit a museum containing a reconstructed schoolroom, complete with a schoolmaster brandishing a cane. *Wigan Pier, Wallgate, Wigan, Greater Manchester, WN3 4EU, tel: 0942 323666.*

Hotels in the City Break scheme include the Britannia which has an indoor swimming pool and health club.

Newcastle-upon-Tyne
The Tyne bridge is said to be the symbol of Newcastle, which seems to be a city full of bridges. Your city break includes an excursion to Holy Island – if the tide allows. A Polanski film started with two escaped criminals racing their car along the causeway to reach the castle before the tide. Bamburgh is associated with heroine Grace Darling, and the lifeboat in which she went to sea with her father. Craster is the kipper centre – also part of the tour. I visited Newcastle from Catherine Cookson country (chapter 18) and also when staying at Lumley Castle Hotel.

Durham
They suggest that from Newcastle you visit picturesque Durham, a small cathedral city on a mound encircled by a loop in the river, just like the Mantegna painting in London's National

Gallery. If you are not opting for the economical City Break you might stay at the Gosforth Park Thistle Hotel which has a swimming pool or visit Newcastle from Durham instead.

Cobbled streets surround Durham's magnificent cathedral, one of the best in Europe. It has a statue of Bede, and his tomb, frescoes of Abraham and Sarah and other early biblical stories, and a stained glass window donated by Marks & Spencers. Nearby cafes overlook the river.

An interesting hotel in Durham is the Royal County Hotel which has everything in the hall from an aquarium to a waxwork figure in military costume. It is also possible to stay in Durham Castle on breaks run by the university.

Other nearby attractions are Beamish Museum which has an outdoor street of small terraced houses where you see the dentist's surgery, and also a museum displaying more sanitary ware and a splendid tiled fish and chip shop counter.

Nottingham

The Royal Hotel with cafes and restaurants in the tropical tree-lined arcade, sunlit through a glass roof, is a must whether you stay in this prestigious hotel or elsewhere.

Your guided excursions include a city tour taking in The Castle, the Lace Centre, and a ride out to the Sherwood Forest Visitor Centre. See the huge oak tree where Robin Hood hid, and an excellent indoor waxworks with forest scenes. *Sherwood Forest Visitor Centre, Edwinstowe, near Mansfield, Nottinghamshire, NG21 9HN, tel: 0623 823202.*

The Nottingham Big Three weekend at the Stakis hotel is excellent. You begin with the medieval banquet (described in Chapter 9). Next day you visit Sherwood Forest. This is followed by poet Lord Byron's grand home, Newstead Abbey, where you learn about his damaged leg, and the four-poster which he took with him to university. *Newstead Abbey, Linby, Nottinghamshire, tel: 0623 793557.*

Then see D. H. Lawrence's tiny terraced house – how different. *D. H. Lawrence's Birthplace, 8a Victoria Street, Eastwood, Nottinghamshire, tel: 0773 763312.*

On Sunday outside the castle naturally you will photograph Robin Hood. If Robin Hood didn't exist when the forest was there, or the forest didn't exist when Robin was there, or the tree they've chosen wasn't the right tree, or the right age for the Robin Hood era, it doesn't really matter, does it?

Details from: *East Midlands Tourist Board, Exchequergate, Lincoln, Lincolnshire LN2 1PZ, tel: 0522 31521.*

Portsmouth

Portsmouth is the flagship of Maritime England. Here is HMS Victory, Lord Nelson's flagship, containing his cot and the chair Lady Hamilton gave him. See the deck where he died.

Near Henry VIII's salvaged warship Mary Rose, a museum displays sailors' possessions, bibles, sewing kits and games. In the D Day Museum *(tel: 0705 827261)* is the colourful 80 metre long Overlord Embroidery, depicting features of the Allied invasion of Normandy; it also houses military equipment and waxwork scenes (including Eisenhower) vivified with sound effects.

The Holiday Inn which is in the City Break scheme has a lovely swimming pool illuminated from underwater and a spa bath within Greek style pillars. The hotel also runs its own off-season weekend family breaks.

From Portsmouth day trips can be taken to the Isle of Wight, and to Winchester to view King Arthur's Round Table.

Portsmouth Tourist Information Centre, The Hard, Portsmouth, PO1 3QJ, tel: 0705 826722.

Southampton

The City Break excursions include sightseeing trips to Winchester, Bournemouth, and Beaulieu. Alternatively, Howards' Way weekends for a supplement of £17 begin with a welcome reception at which you meet the cast or crew of BBC TV's 'Howards' Way'. You then tour the locations, seen from a river cruise boat.

London

The London Tourist Board publishes a guide to inexpensive accommodation. The best deals are offered through numerous package breaks, such as those offered by THF, the Thistle Hotels' Highlife Breaks, and others.

Of the hundreds of interesting London Hotels my favourite is the Colonnade Hotel, a former home of Freud, as the blue plaque outside tells you. Couples might select the four-poster bed ordered for an American president. Or for the single, there's a pine bunk bedroom like a ship's cabin, with a porthole overlooking the staircase, a little claustrophobic, very Freudian.
Colonnade Hotel, 2 Warrington Crescent, London W9, tel: 01-286 1052.

New features of interest to visitors in London are inexhaustible. One-and-a-half miles from the Colonnade Hotel is the house that Freud lived in during the time up to his death. It has recently been opened to the public as a museum in his memory, and the famous couch on which his patients had lain down to be psychoanalysed rests for visitors to see in Freud's study.
The Freud Museum, 20 Maresfield Gardens, Hampstead, London NW3 5SX, tel: 01-435 2002.

CHAPTER 25
Bed & Breakfast, Caravanning, Farms, Friaries

Bed and breakfast in a guesthouse provides a home-cooked British breakfast and the chance to meet people all over Britain. An excellent way to enjoy the countryside is by staying at a farmhouse, in a self-catering cottage, caravanning at a farm, or camping. Finally, for something different, get thee to a nunnery, or friary.

BED AND BREAKFAST
Everybody knows that Britain has the best bed and breakfast in the world. Americans like British breakfast bacon which is really meaty, not streaky like they usually get at home.

The Best Bed and Breakfast in the World annual guidebook on sale in the UK and USA includes guesthouses all over Britain including several farmhouses. Each year the association publishing the book picks winning members who are presented with the Kellogg's award.

Top prize in 1986 went to Robin and Philippa Watson who offer fresh vegetables, and game in season. They serve dinner to everybody at one table with the family 'like a dinner party'. The Watsons stock peanut butter which American children ask for at breakfast. *Robin and Philippa Watson, Old Stowey Farm, Wheddon Cross, Minehead, Somerset, tel: 064384 268.*

North-east winner in 1986 was Mrs Bateson of Harrogate. She and her husband have a policy of keeping the house warm, so that it is welcoming when somebody knocks at the door. *Mrs Bateson, Alexa House, 26 Ripon Rd, Harrogate, North Yorks, tel: 0423 501988.*

The 1987 winner is a thatched farmhouse with four-posters including Lillie Langtry's bed. So if you're following a farm trail, or a Lillie Langry Trail, phone *Mrs Sylvia Citron, Horselake Farm, Cheriton Bishop, near Exeter, Devon, tel: 064724 220.*

Another home of a famous woman is the former home of Catherine Cookson, *Town Barns, Off Trinity Terrace, Corbridge NE45 5HP, tel: 043471 3345,* near Newcastle-upon-Tyne, Tyne & Wear, Northumbria.

You can use the book to do a grand tour staying in bed and breakfast accommodation all around Britain, taking in a guesthouse with a minstrel's gallery, or a working watermill.

The London hotels described in the book include one with a four-poster and they can only be booked centrally through the World Wide Bed and Breakfast Association booking service, which could be an advantage. You quote your credit card number for the deposit to confirm your booking. *Phone 01-370 7099, 24 hrs,* or contact *WWBBA, Suite One, PO Box 134, 15 Gledhow Gardens, London SW5 0TX, UK; USA Dept 634, Box C, 34069 Seattle, Washington 98124 1069.*

Guestaccom is another organisation dealing with guesthouse accommodation all over Britain. Send postage and they will supply one or more of their four brochures on Guestaccom Good Room Guide, Executive, Country, and Top accommodation. For details contact: *Claremont House, 2nd Avenue, Hove, East Sussex, BN3 2LL, tel: 0273 722833.*

When touring look out for the circular Les Routiers signs divided diagonally into blue and red. These will help you find good value eating and accommodation in Britain. Routiers began as a French organisation, Relais meaning stopping place, and routiers road users, in the days when France was the best country for superb food at budget prices. Now Britain has caught up. The Routiers *Good Value Guide* is useful for locating eating places in large towns, or when driving to distant areas and deciding where to stop.

Winner of the 1987 Relais Routiers award for accommodation is in the Herriot country of North Yorkshire and run by a jolly couple, Susan Jutsum and her bearded husband Brian. Breakfast consists of black pudding, liver, kidneys, mushrooms, sausages, fried bread, eggs and bacon, or anything else you ask for in advance, such as kedgeree. At 6 pm the dinner menu is delivered to guests in the bedrooms which include a beamed bridal suite, a four-poster from 1770, a half-tester from 1860, and a bed they had made specially for back sufferers. An extension built from part of a demolished church includes neo-gothic windows. A three-storey cantilevered stone spiral staircase is another feature.

Their four course dinner, bed and breakfast is from about £28 to £35 per person depending on the type of bedroom you choose. Dinner for non-residents is just over £11 per person. Winter breaks are available. Honeymooners paying an extra £12.50 or so each can have a package including a welcoming drink, champagne, breakfast in bed and a bouquet of flowers with a message from the husband to his new wife, or a wedding anniversary greeting. *Rookhurst Georgian Country House, Gayle, Hawes, North Yorkshire, D18 3RT, tel: 096 97 454.*

In addition to watching for guesthouses, hotels and restaurants bearing the Routiers signs, and using the guidebook, you can join the Club Routiers for a little under £20. This gives discounts on the Routiers guides to England and France, and discounts and concessions at selected Relais Routiers. Details from: *Routiers, Freepost, London SW10 9BR (from the UK only)*; from abroad contact: *Routiers Ltd, 354 Fulham Road, London SW10 9UH, tel: 01-351 3522.*

If you are staying in one area free leaflets on hotels, guesthouses and farm accommodation for each regional tourist board are available from the British Tourist Authority. In summer many tourist board kiosks in town centres and at motorway service stations offer a book a bed ahead scheme.

CAMPING AND CARAVANNING

British weather makes camping and caravanning best in summer, but there are intrepid souls who caravan in the cold at Christmas time. For the gregarious, regular rallies and weekends are organised by the Camping and Caravanning Club, which publishes details in its magazine. For example, one popular annual event is going to see the spring bulb show at Spalding. Details of membership from: *Camping and Caravanning Club, Freepost, 11 Lower Grosvenor Place, London SW1W OEY, tel: 01-828 1012.*

Advantages of caravans are that they are cheap for families. And they can offer home comforts too. Your clothes hang crease-free in the cupboard, no unpacking on arrival, or living out of a suitcase. Your supplies of real coffee or favourite food can travel with you. And you can take your dog or pet along.

The Caravan and Camping Holiday Show at Earls Court, London, in late autumn is a useful event to attend to find out what is new in caravans. You could hire – or buy.

To select a site with particular facilities use the book published by the English Tourist Board. If you prefer seclusion, many farms have small sites where you can park a caravan. No more than five caravans are allowed on the Caravan Club's little Certified locations, more than 4,000 secluded spots. Britain's Caravan Club is the world's largest caravanning organisation and reciprocal membership is arranged for holidaymakers who belong to caravan clubs in other countries. *The Caravan Club, East Grinstead House, East Grinstead, West Sussex, RH19 1UA, tel: 0342 26944.*

FARMHOUSE HOLIDAYS

You can milk a cow the old fashioned way, or simply meet the farmer and the farmer's wife, at farmhouses all over Britain. And learn how cheese is made, while living, walking, eating and sleeping in the peace of the countryside.

'How are you gonna keep 'em down on the farm, after they've seen Paris?' asked a song earlier this century. But nowadays farm holidays are increasingly popular. One attraction is the involvement in country life, seeing newborn lambs in springtime and calves in autumn. It is delightful for mothers and fathers, and full of surprises for city children, who love holding lambs. After watching impressive modern milking machinery, enjoy the challenge of trying to milk the cow yourself, without getting kicked!

Farm holidays also offer fresh food. And a farmhouse tea of freshly-baked scones is delicious, particularly when served with clotted cream in Devon and Cornwall. *Huxtable Farm at West Buckland, Barnstaple, North Devon, EX32 0SR, tel: 05986 254* features local produce such as clotted cream, and homemade wine. Somerset farms serve farmhouse cider.

Grange Lodge Farm in Northants serves clotted cream from a Jersey cow named Clover. There's a no smoking guesthouse and

log fires. Bed and breakfast costs from around £10 with dinner at under £5. Private fishing is available. The Grange Lodge Mini Farm Park is open to day visitors March to October and winter weekends except January and February. For a small charge visitors can see farm animals and rare breeds of poultry, picnic by the adventure playground, pat a pig or stroke a goat and try the home grown and home-made produce in the Country Food Cafe.
Grange Lodge Mini Farm Park, Naseby Road, Welford, Northants, tel: 0858 81 625.

For more details contact: *East Midlands Tourist Board, Exchequergate, Lincoln LN2 1PZ, tel: 0522 31521.*

Farms in Wales
For those on a budget most farm holidays are delightfully informal, offering both a friendly welcome and remarkably low prices. The Wales Farm Holidays brochure includes farmhouses on working farms. Some farms welcome vegetarians, children, or let you bring your own pets.

Unusual farms include a 400-year-old converted mill whose owner, Pat Skidmore, specialises in goat farming. This farm produces beef, pork, lamb, bacon, milk and eggs, as well as serving home-baked granary bread. The cheesemaking was featured on Radio 4's 'Breakaway' holiday programme. Prices for bed and breakfast are a bargain, around £10 per person per night. *Ffarm Plas Cyrnant, Waunfawr, nr Caernarfon, Wales,* is a good base for touring North Wales.

Another Tudor farmhouse, *Lower Gwestydd Farm, at Llanwchaiarn, near Newtown* in Powys, Mid Wales, is on a 200 acre farm. It supplies home-produced chicken, fruit and vegetables. Bed and breakfast again costs about £10. Book through travel agents or directly through the central booking office at *Machynlleth, Mid Wales, tel: 0654 2727.*

Farm Outings
Don't think that you have to miss out on visiting a farm if your main holiday is a package tour, staying in a luxury hotel, or visiting relatives. You can take a short weekend break on a farm, or simply visit one for an afternoon out.

Numerous farm museums and working farms are open to

visitors. Some organise guided tours and therefore accept only large pre-booked groups. Others prefer individuals and small groups to wander around on their own. The national and local tourist boards supply lists of farms open to visitors, including fish, livestock and dairy farms.

Cogges Farm Museum, near Witney, Oxfordshire, is a medieval farmhouse with animals. In July and August there are demonstrations including butter-making, sheep-sheering, honey extracting, and bread-making. It is open May to October. For more details *tel: 0993 72602.*

I also went to see Cheshire cheese being made at Overton Farm, near Chester, and bought a big Cheshire cheese.

To find a cheese-maker or farm which is accepting visitors, contact: *North West Tourist Board, Last Drop Village, Bromley Cross, Bolton, BL7 9PZ, tel: 0204 591511,* or call the *Chester Visitor Centre, Chester, Cheshire, tel: 0244 318916.*

Cheddar cheese makers and also honey farms welcome tourists. You can learn how delicious Acacia honey and stem ginger ice cream is made with fresh Jersey double cream, and how apricot sorbet and other ices are produced at Loseley Park Farm (AD 1562) near Guildford from June to September on Wednesday to Saturday afternoons. *Loseley Park Farms, Guildford, Surrey, visitors information tel: 0483 505501.*

A new attraction in Northumberland is the Redesdale Dairy and Apiary which has a continuous video about the cheese farm and bee keeping. The tea-room serves scones, cheesecakes, and farmhouse cheese lunches. Redesdale is a wheel-shape cheese, and their Wensleydale cheese is made from a mixture of cows' and sheep's milk. You'll see the cows and sheep being milked, there are pigs and maybe lambs, and bees buzzing about busily behind the perspex glass. Honey and beeswax candles are sold. There's a small nature trail and quiz for children on trees. They are open in summer. For hours contact: *The Redesdale Dairy & Apiary, The Soppitt, Otterburn, Northumberland NE19 1AF, tel: 0830 20276.*

Details of other cheese farms can be obtained from the *Milk Marketing Board, Thames Ditton, Surrey KT7 0EL, tel: 01-398 4101.*

Farm Holiday Agencies
Farmhouse holidays in the Lake District and North Yorkshire can be booked through Upcountry Holidays. In one of the houses offered you can stay where Arthur Ransome's series of children's books 'Swallows and Amazons' were written and filmed. Jersey cream from the farm's cows is provided and other farm fare. A booklet describing farms and including a location map is sent out. Exact addresses are given when booking is made. Contact: *Upcountry Holidays, Alston, Cumbria CA9 3LG, tel: 0498 81563, until 9 pm.*

Farm & Country Holidays, Jordans, First Raleigh, Bideford, Devon, EX39 3NJ, tel: 02372 79698. Colour brochure of holiday accommodation in Devon, Somerset and Cornwall.

Farm Holiday Bureau, National Agricultural Centre, Stoneleigh, Kenilworth, Warwickshire, tel: 0203 555100.

RELIGIOUS HOSTS
Not only Roman Catholics but people of all religions are welcome to stay at a Carmelite Friary in Kent. Most weekends they are fully booked with their programme of seminars, but there is a fair chance of getting in midweek. The subsidised cost is merely £15 per day for a single room, including meals which are served at set times.

If you want to join in services you may do so. You are asked to respect the religious nature of the establishment, but people of all ages, including children, are admitted. The conference centre can be booked by groups. The year's events and courses have included a scouts and guides pilgrimage, co-workers of Mother Teresa pilgrimage for peace, a Jewish/Christian study weekend with humorous media personality Rabbi Blue, and preparing for Christmas with Delia Smith, better known for her TV cookery programmes.

Retreat weekends cost about £35 in a single room. A conference including meals from Friday supper to Sunday tea costs about £120. You can make a day outing to the friary cloisters, shop and tea-room – quite a bustling place. Contact:

The Carmelite Friary, Aylesford, Maidstone, Kent ME20 7BX, tel: 0622 77272.

Alternatively, get thee to a nunnery, where nuns grow their own food. Full board in the guest house is about £9 a day. The Benedictine nuns live in the Abbey which was founded in the year 670 and they welcome visitors to a contemplative summer break.
Contact: *Mother Superior, Sister Concordia, Minster Abbey, Isle of Thanet, Kent, tel: 0843 821254.*

SELF-CATERING
In a monastery
If you'd rather be alone, go self-catering in an ancient red sandstone 14th century monastery. You will be staying on the banks of the river Wye looking towards the wooded gorge of Symonds Yat and hilltop Goodrich Castle. Three miles away is the cliffside town of Ross-on-Wye in the Wye Valley, Herefordshire, England, on the border with Wales. Flanesford Priory is a grade I listed building converted into self-catering cottages for families or couples – with draped four-poster beds. The average price is £120 per unit including electricity, linen and a welcome food basket. Three night winter weekend breaks and four night midweek breaks are about £40 or £50 for two person accommodation. Contact:
Oak Tree Cottages Ltd, 6 King Street, Richmond, Surrey, TW9 1ND, tel: 01-940 1398, or 24 hour brochure ansaphone 01-948 8500.

In Thatched Cottage and other real English buildings
Self-catering cottages including thatched cottages in the Norfolk Broads, and a thatched barn, are available from Blakes Holidays. Their other typically British buildings are oast houses in Kent with picturesque white-tipped conical chimneys formerly used for drying hops.

Blakes' blue chip properties include cottages in the grounds of Bowden House, Devon, one mile from Totnes where shopkeepers wear Elizabethan dress on summer Tuesdays; a manor in Cornwall with columns, jacuzzi and sauna; and a mansion with daily maid service and a cook.

There is a surprising range of accommodation including some with bidets, one with an invalid bath, and A-frame wooden lodges in Scotland. The most unusual buildings are a converted chapel with a solid wood roof in Suffolk within five minutes of the sea, and two circular brick windmills in Norfolk, one having a bedroom reached through a trapdoor.

Prices vary considerably according to the season chosen. Three day minibreaks are available off-season. Details from: *Blakes Country & Seaside Holidays, Wroxham, Norwich, NR12 8DH, tel: 06053 2917*. In the USA, *Blakes Bare Boats, 4939 Dempster Street, Skokie, Illinois 60077, USA, tel: 312 677 0040*.

Guidebooks
The Automobile Association's annual *Guesthouses, Farmhouses and Inns in Britain* gives regional awards and contains vouchers for discounts on accommodation.

The Farm Holiday Guide England and the Channel Islands; the Farm Holiday Guide Scotland; and also separate Farm Holiday guides to Wales and to Ireland, are all published by Farm Holiday Guides Ltd, Abbey Mill Centre, Seedhill, Paisley, PA1 1JN.

Farm Holidays in Britain covers England, Wales and Northern Ireland, published by the Farm Holiday Bureau in association with the English Tourist Board.

The Routiers *Good Value Guide* is published by Macdonald Orbis.

CHAPTER 26
How to read a hotel brochure and test the service

Many of the hotels in this book are top hotels where nobody could be dissatisfied with anything except the price of the bill. Some of the hotels I have chosen because they have just one exceptional feature, such as a spiral staircase leading to the bedroom; others were really excellent within their price range. I trust that you will check all prices and if possible obtain brochures together with the Tariff before committing yourself to a weekend or longer holiday.

BROCHURE LANGUAGE
'A Good Base for touring'
Read brochures carefully and be suspicious. A hotel brochure which says 'this is a good base for touring' is ambiguous – it could mean you can't wait to leave.

One evening we checked into a hotel which had different colour schemes for every item in the bedroom, yellow curtains, brown carpet, and a dark green candlewick bedspread whose fringes kept tripping me up. The bathroom had pink tiles, cream paint, blue towels and multicolour linoleum.

The hotel dining room which had been quite smart several decades previously now had peeling paint. Lukewarm food was being served by an apologetic elderly waitress hobbling around long after she deserved to retire. I said, 'She'll tell you that she's been here forty years and nobody has ever complained before. The other waitress is new. She started this morning, doesn't know, and can't ask the manager because he's away'.

The diners were a coach party of pensioners, five of whom had walking sticks and needed hip replacements and cheering up. So did we.

Sneaking out, we drove round the small provincial town on an off-season Sunday night, looking for an alternative dinner venue. Initially we rejected a dreadful ethnic restaurant with a stained menu half discernable through steamed-up filthy windows. But after circling the one way system and finding nothing else open, we started panicking because the ethnic restaurant had vanished and we asked ourselves, 'What's happened to that lovely little restaurant?'

Its menu offered a choice of chop suey – which was off that night, curry, or omelette, which we ordered, accompanied by a bottle of rosé vinegar. The cloakroom had toilet paper unwrapped sitting on the windowsill in the dust.

Despite this, the nearby hotel is popular because it runs a most amusing weekend at budget prices, and it is 'a good touring base'. A map printed on the hotel brochure, with a list of places to visit and distances given, is a good sign.

Secluded Location

'Secluded' conjures up visions of country cottages nestling amid woods displaying a rainbow of autumn colours, and cosy evenings reading beside log fires. Secluded might merely mean there is nothing to do for miles around. When you finally locate your cold, windswept hotel or guesthouse it is too late to go off elsewhere in the dark.

Secluded often means a map is essential. The destination is impossible to find. The signposts say Little Wottlehampton to the left, and Little Wottlehampton to the right. No distances are given and you spend an hour passing deserted farms.

At one crossroads the left hand option ends up in the middle of a field. The other road narrows, then becomes rutted and virtually impassable. You finally meet a tractor and a herd of sheep blocking the road. The farmer says, 'Ee, you've com wrong way. Go back t'soin t' Li'l Wo'l'ampton. You can't miss it'.

Ravenously hungry, you ruin your new shoes in the gravel or mud, and reach the hotel which stopped serving food at 9 pm when the chef left. Your chocolate bar and nightclothes, bedtime book, and several other essentials are in the boot of the car two hundred yards down the road in total darkness in a howling gale. Don't even bother to ask if they have a porter.

Secluded locations are not ideal for those without cars, unless you like walking or are honeymooning with somebody exceptionally handsome and able to provide fourteen days worth of non-stop amusing conversation. A hotel in a pleasant location just outside a town is a good compromise.

Service Included
What does this mean? 'Free' I was taught at college, 'means that you pay for it whether you get it or not'. This applies to service charges. The latest trick is to charge twice for service. You pay a normal service charge for getting any kind of service at all. Then business executives pay a second service charge for fast service called 'express check-out'. This means service at a reasonable speed instead of a go-slow.

BALANCING CONS AND PROS
Good beds and bathrooms
The four-poster with the new wide mattress is better than the bedroom with the sagging twin hammocks. If you have a bad back and like spotless bathrooms the Holiday Inn is probably better for you than the olde worlde place with olde worlde mattresses and cobwebs.

Food Versus Decor
Every brochure claims that the hotel provides good food. If the food is truly unusual they will send sample menus or mention particular dishes. Small hotel restaurants may serve wonderful food and yet have boring bedrooms upstairs with peeling wallpaper, and carpets that need cleaning. But a luxury gourmet hotel will not suit you if it is so expensive that you eat elsewhere. Similarly, the beautifully decorated hotel does not necessarily have good food. Is the hotel recommended for its food, its decor, its location, its price, or all four? What do you want?

Non-Smoking Rooms
Most hotel chains now have a section of non-smoking rooms. If they forget to enquire whether you want one, you must remember to ask for it. At an English hotel we had two rooms, one for a child. 'Our room's dreadful', I said, 'But he's got such a lovely room'.

I went from one bedroom to the other trying to identify the

differences. Apart from the fact that they were on opposite sides of the corridor, so that they were mirror images of each other, the furnishings were identical. The only difference was the smell. His room was freshly scented. Ours was stale with smoke.

During the night I woke, thinking the hotel was on fire. It was just the smoky smell of the bedding. So if you're a non-smoker, remember to ask for a non-smoker's room. It could increase your comfort, and your good opinion of the hotel.

Town Hotel Noise
In the centre of town old High Street inns may be subject to traffic noise. Enquire if there is double glazing or ask for a quiet room. Back rooms are often quieter, providing they are not above car parks and kitchens, or adjacent to a lift shaft. People in the street outside or staying in adjacent rooms can be noisy too, which is why countryside self-catering cottages are preferred by families who hate noise, or like to create it!

Oddly enough the modern purpose-built airport hotel with its double or triple glazing designed to keep out the sound of aircraft is sometimes better protected against noise.

Recommendations
You may have noticed that sometimes other people unaccountably adore the places you find abysmal, and vice versa. One reason is that family-owned hotels have bedrooms of different standards. They invest their money in decorating the honeymoon suite and the new annexe, then the top floor.

On bank holidays when they are fully booked you might get the small back room which is normally given free to the courier or coach driver. That explains why the receptionist sometimes says they are full, but when you insist that there must be a free room they reluctantly discover one.

Varying Decoration and outlooks
Other large hotel groups refurbish a section of 'executive' rooms for which they charge higher prices. These rooms are occasionally given to VIPs, regular business customers belonging to a scheme including upgrading, or honeymoon couples. Whether you get a seaview room or one with the noise, kitchen smells and dustbin view can affect your attitude to the hotel.

TESTING SERVICE
Pubs and hotel bars clear away used glasses by carrying four at a time with a finger in each. Glasses and jugs should never be presented with the waiter's fingers inside. But what about the restaurant?

Restaurant service: the Glass of Water Test
One test of good service is how long it takes to supply a glass of water. The top restaurants bring iced water immediately and enough glasses for everybody. The restaurant which tries hard but fails has a jug of lukewarm water on the table, full of bubbles. The most memorable failure was the restaurant where I asked three separate waiters and never got a glass of water.

Brown Sugar and Orange Juice
Hotels should be able to provide brown sugar for coffee and porridge, and fresh orange juice for your breakfast or the cocktail hour vodka and orange.

Old-fashioned Service
Modern hotels have dispensed with the old-fashioned soup and cereal plates which had handles or a wide lip. Instead you get a deep bowl. The staff should present the bowl to you on an underplate, not with their thumb inside the bowl!

Those old-fashioned doileys and thick tablecloths and napkins in smart hotels have a purpose, too. At an otherwise delightful hotel, the rickety circular breakfast table had no cloth but displayed the polished wood. I misplaced my coffee cup on the edge and scalded myself with hot coffee. This could have been prevented by a large saucer and an absorbent doiley, plus a thick tablecloth and table napkin on my lap. I reflected on this while waiting for a waitress who was busy somewhere else.

Eventually I managed to summon her from the kitchen to bring me an ice cube. The waiter should wait, not the customer. Top hotels have a waiter literally waiting, watching from a distance so that when you look up to catch his eye he comes over straight away. Perfect service is included.

Receptionist Service: Special Requests
Staff shouldn't say, 'We've never been asked before', or 'nobody

ever complains'. The reason why nobody ever complains is that they meet these responses.

Recently I found myself in a bedroom with no bath, just a shower and I didn't have a shower cap. I phoned reception and was told that they had no shower caps. A few minutes later I decided I needed an Elastoplast. They didn't have that either. I heard the receptionist saying to someone at her end, 'It's the same woman who wanted the shower cap!'

Surely the items a guest will request are quite predictable? One good hotel receptionist said they had Elastoplast, 'Don't come down, we'll send the porter up to you with it'. Another kept a first aid box like a miniature hospital, and wouldn't let me look after myself but bandaged my arm after using antiseptic to clean the wound.

How To Avoid a Letdown
If you want expensive soaps, perfect food and superb service, you need a five star luxury hotel which charges appropriate prices. If you are on a budget a good compromise is to choose a hotel with the leisure facilities you require. In winter you need indoor activities at your hotel or nearby. Choose a town or location where excellent restaurants are available. Find two restaurants, in case one is closed or full, and book a table at your first choice.

FINDING PERFECTION
I took a course run by a consumers' association on grading hotels. In the five star 'de luxe' hotel all materials are 'the real thing'. The chairs are not plastic but leather; the fireplaces and tables are not woodchip but top quality solid wood.

Good hotels often do one thing really well, and many restaurants serve several interesting main courses, though their other hors d'oeuvres or desserts are disappointing. But when hotels and restaurants get everything right, visiting them is such a pleasure that you remember them for the rest of your life.

CHAPTER 27
Useful Information

(i) Booklist

Hotels and Restaurants
The Good Hotel Guide (Consumers' Association).
The Good Food Guide (Consumers' Association).
The Good Pub Guide (Consumers' Association).
Egon Ronay's Cellnet Guide.
Just A Bite by Egon Ronay (Mitchell Beazley).
Derek Johansen's Recommended Hotels in Great Britain.
Ashley Courtenay Guide (Purnell).
The Historic Country Hotels of England by Wendy Arnold (Thames & Hudson).
The Historic Hotels of London by Wendy Arnold (Thames & Hudson).

Budget Accommodation
London Hotels and Inexpensive Accommodation (London Tourist Board).
The Good Value Guide (Les Routiers).
The Best Bed and Breakfast In The World by Sigourney Welles, Jill Darbey, Joanna Mortimer (UKHM London/East Woods Press, Charlotte, North Carolina).
Staying off the Beaten Track by Elizabeth Gundrey (Hamlyn Paperbacks).
Activity & Hobby Holidays England (English Tourist Board).

Romance
The Lovers' Guide to Britain by Mr & Mrs Smith (Corgi).
The Romantic Weekend Book by Richard Nissen (Futura).
The Dirty Weekend Book by Charlotte du Cann and others (Quartet Books).

Children
Kid's Britain by Betty Jerman (Pan).
The Peaudouce Guide by Wendy Steavenson.
Discovering London for Children by Margaret Pearson (Shire Publications).
A Capital Guide for the Kids by Vanessa Miles (Allison & Busby/Schocken Books Inc).
Children's London (London Tourist Board).

Americans
The American Connection (Liverpool's Links with America) by Ron Jones.

Jewish
Jewish Travel Guide (Jewish Chronicle Publications).
World Guide for the Jewish Traveller by Warren Freedman (E. P. Dutton Inc New York).
Jewish London by Linda Zeff (Piatkus).

Museums & Gardens
Museums & Galleries in Great Britain and Ireland (British Leisure Publications).
Historic Houses, Castles & Gardens (British Leisure Publications).
Britain For Free (Automobile Association).
The National Trust Guide (Jonathan Cape).
Gardens of England and Wales Open to the Public (National Gardens Scheme).

Touring Britain
AA Illustrated Guide to Britain (Automobile Association).
Great Britain and Ireland (Michelin).

London
Exploring Central London (London Tourist Board).
A Guide to Royal London by Christopher Hibbert (Macmillan).
Blue Plaque Guide to London by Caroline Dakers.
London Statues by Arthur Byron (Constable).

The London Tourist Board has books and leaflets on every aspect of London such as London on Sunday or inexpensive accommodation, and it has a bookshop on the forecourt of Victoria Station.

London's public libraries have books on London's attractions, history, buildings, etc., and leaflets on what to see in the local area.

The Automobile Association, Royal Automobile Club, and Michelin publish numerous guides to hotels, farm holidays, guesthouses, regions and touring routes.

(ii) Some Highlights of the British Calendar

Following are some of the more prominent regular events through the British year.

January

London International Boat Show.
Earls Court Exhibition Centre, London SW5.
Mid January, for two weeks.
Information: tel: Weybridge (0932) 54511.

February

Crufts Dog Show.
Earls Court Exhibition Centre, London SW5.
Mid February, four days.
Information: The Kennel Club, 1 Clarges St, London W1 8AB., tel: 01-493 6651.

March

Oxford v Cambridge University Boat Race.
Putney to Mortlake, River Thames, London.
Late March or early April.
Information: from Tourist Board offices (see following section).

April

Grand National Meeting.

Highlights of the Calendar

Aintree Racecourse, Merseyside.
The world's greatest steeplechase, held in early April. Three day meeting.
Information: Aintree Racecourse, Aintree, Liverpool L9 5AS, tel: 051-523 2600.

Badminton Horse Trials.
Badminton, Avon.
International trials of showjumping, cross country and dressage which take place at the home of the Duke of Beaufort.
Mid April, four days.
Information: Box Office, Badminton Horse Trials, Badminton, Avon GL9 1DF, tel: Badminton (045 421) 272.

May

Royal Windsor Horse Show.
Home Park, Windsor, Berkshire.
Four day showjumping event, mid May.
Information: Shows Box Office, 54 Brooksby Walk, London E9 6DA, tel: 01-533 3332.

Chelsea Flower Show.
Royal Hospital, Chelsea, London SW3.
Late May, four days.
Information: Royal Horticultural Society, Vincent Square, London SW1P 2PE, tel: 01-834 4333.

Glyndebourne Festival Opera Season.
Glyndebourne, near Lewes, Sussex.
Four month opera season from late May to late August. (Tickets for the general public are very difficult to obtain and the best chance is to try very early postal bookings, enclosing s.a.e.)
Box Office, Glyndebourne Festival Opera, Lewes, East Sussex BN8 5UU, tel: Brighton (0273) 54111.

June

Derby Day.
Epsom Racecourse, Surrey.

Early June. The Derby is held on the first day of a four day meeting which includes the Coronation Cup and the Oaks.
Information: Racecourse Paddock, Epsom, Surrey KT18 5NJ, tel: Epsom (037 27) 26311.

Trooping the Colour.
Horse Guards Parade, Whitehall, London.
This is the official birthday parade of HM The Queen.
Tickets by ballot; apply in writing between January and end February to The Brigade Major, HQ Household Division, Horse Guards, Whitehall SW1A 2AX (overseas applicants should include international reply coupon).

Royal Ascot.
Ascot Racecourse, Ascot, Berkshire.
Mid June, four days.
Information: The Secretary, Ascot Racecourse, Ascot, Berkshire SL5 7JN, tel: Ascot (0990) 22211.

Wimbledon Lawn Tennis Championships.
Late June to July, two weeks.
Information: All England Lawn Tennis Club, Church Road, Wimbledon, London SW19 5AE, tel: 01-946 2244.

July

Henley Royal Regatta.
First week in July, five days.
Information: The Secretary, Henley Royal Regatta, Regatta House, Henley-on-Thames, Oxfordshire RG9 2LY, tel: Henley-on-Thames (0491) 572153.

Llangollen International Musical Eisteddod.
Eisteddfod Field, Llangollen, Clwyd, Wales.
For one week in early July this small Welsh town is host to folk dancing and folk music from countries around the world.
Information: Llangollen International Musical Eisteddfod Office, Llangollen, Clwyd LL20 8NG, tel: Llangollen (0978) 860236.

Motor Racing: British Grand Prix.
Silverstone Circuit, Towcester, Northamptonshire NN12 8TN.
Information: above address, tel: Towcester (0327) 857271.

Royal Tournament.
Earls Court Exhibition Centre, Warwick Road, London SW5.
Military spectacular with displays by members of the Royal Navy, the Royal Marines, the Army and the Royal Air Force. Continues from two to three weeks.
Information: Royal Tournament Office, Horse Guards, Whitehall, London SW1A 2AX, tel: 01-930 4288.

Golf: Open Championship.
Played in mid July over four days on one of the championship courses in England and Scotland.
Information: The Royal and Ancient Golf Club, St Andrews, Fife KY16 9JD, tel: St Andrews (0334) 72112.

Goodwood Races – Glorious Goodwood.
Goodwood Racecourse, Chichester, Sussex.
Late July, five days.
Information: Goodwood Racecourse, Chichester, West Sussex, PO18 0TX, tel: Chichester (0243) 774107.

August

Cowes Weeks: Sailing.
Cowes, Isle of Wight.
Yachting festival covering all classes of yacht racing. Nine days at beginning of August.
Information: Cowes Week Organisers, 18–19 Bath Road, Cowes, Isle of Wight, tel: Cowes (0983) 295744.

Edinburgh International Festival.
Mid August to early September. Three weeks.
Information: Edinburgh Festival Society, 21 Market Street, Edinburgh EH1 1BW, tel: 031-226 4001.

Edinburgh Military Tattoo.
Mid August to early September. Three weeks.

Information and tickets: Tattoo Office, 22 Market Street, Edinburgh EH1 1QB, tel: 031-225 1188.

September

Braemar Royal Highland Gathering.
Princess Royal and Duke of Fife Memorial Park, Braemar, Grampian.
Held first Saturday in September, the most prestigious Highland Games meeting.
Information: Mr W A Meston, Balcriech, Ballater, Aberdeenshire, tel: Ballater (0338) 55377.

Farnborough International Aerospace Exhibition and Flying Display.
Royal Aircraft Establishment Airfield, Farnborough, Hampshire.
Early August, five days trade only followed by three days public.
Information: Society of British Aerospace Companies, 29 King Street, London SW1Y 6RD, tel: 01-839 3231.

Burghley Horse Trials.
Burghley House, Stamford, Lincolnshire.
Three-day eventing in the grounds of England's largest Elizabethan house. Mid September.
Information: Burghley Horse Trials Office, Stamford, Lincolnshire PE9 2LH, tel: Stamford (0780) 52131.

October

Horse of the Year Show.
Wembley Arena, Wembley, London.
Early October, six days. The world's top showjumpers over tough courses in this indoor arena.
Information: Francis Crawley, Shows Box Office, 14 Brooksby Walk, London E9 6DA, tel: 01-533 3332.

November

London to Brighton Veteran Car Run.

Hyde Park in London to Brighton, Sussex, on first Sunday of November.
Information: RAC Motor Sports Division, 31 Belgrave Square, London SW1X 8QH, tel: 01-235 8601.

Lord Mayor's Procession and Show.
The City, London. Procession from Guildhall to the Royal Courts of Justice.
Information: Public Relations Office, Guildhall, London EC2P 2EJ, tel: 01-606 3030.

December

Olympia International Showjumping Championships.
Olympia, Hammersmith Road, London W14.
Mid December, four days.
Information: Earls Court Exhibition Centre, Warwick Road, London SW5 9TA, tel: 01-385 1200.

(iii) Addresses of Hotel Groups, Package Breaks and Tourist Boards

HOTEL GROUPS, TOUR OPERATORS AND ACCOMMODATION PACKAGE BREAKS

Anchor Hotels: see address for Trusthouse Forte.
Best Western Hotels, Vine House, 143 London Road, Kingston upon Thames, Surrey KT2 6NA, tel: 01-541 0033; 90 Mitchell Street, Glasgow G1 3NQ, tel: 041-204 1794.
Capital Breaks London Mini-Holidays, 11 Thurloe Place, London SW7 2RS, tel: 01-581 1414.
Consort Hotels, Ryedale Building, Piccadilly, York, YO1 1PN, tel: 0904 643151.
Crest Hotels Ltd, Bridge Street, Banbury, Oxfordshire, OX16 8RQ. tel: 0295 67722/01-902 8877.
De Vere Hotels, De Vere House, Chester Road, Daresbury, Warrington, WA4 4BN, tel: 0925 65050.

Embassy Hushaway Breaks with Embassy Hotels, Embassy Reservation Centre, PO Box 671, London SW7 5JQ, tel: Link Line (0345) 581811.
Getaway Breaks, Best Western Hotels: see Best Western above.
Golden Rail Holidays, PO Box 12, York, YO11 1YX, tel: 0904 28992/38973.
Great English City Breaks, National Holidays Ltd, George House, George Street, Wakefield, W. Yorks, WF1 1LY, tel: 0924 387387.
Greatstay Holidays, Norfolk Capital Hotels, 8 Cromwell Place, London SW7 2JN, tel: 10-589 7000.
Highlife Breaks with Thistle Hotels, PO Box 1RA, Newcastle, NE99 1RA, tel: 01-889 9336/091-232 1073/061-228 1654.
Scenechanger Weekends, Kingsmead Hotels Ltd, The Old Brewery, High Street, Theale, Berks RG7 5AH, tel: 0734 302925.
Ladbroke Hotels, PO Box 137, Watford, Herts, WD1 1DN, tel: 0923 38877.
Leisure Breaks: see Trusthouse Forte Hotels, and De Vere Hotels.
National Express Ltd, Bargain Breakaways, 1 Vernon Road, Edgbaston, Birmingham B16 9SJ, tel: 021 455 9333.
Keith Prowse Londoners, 1 Melcombe Street, London NW1 6AE, tel: 01-935 6666/061-431 9000.
Quality International Hotels, Piccadilly House, 33 Regent Street, London SW1Y 4NB, tel: 01-439 2811, tollfree 0 800 44 44 44.
Rainbow Mini Holidays, Ryedale Building, Piccadilly, York, YO1 1PN, tel: 0904 643355.
Saga Holidays for the over 60s, PO Box 64, Folkestone, Kent, CT20 3SG, tel: 0303 30030.
Stakis Holidays, 244 Buchanan Street, Glasgow G1 2NB, tel: 041 332 4343.
Stardust and Camelot Holidays Ltd, Kiln House, 210 New King's Road, London SW6 4NZ, tel: 01-736 5700.
Town & Country Classics, Queens Moat Houses PLC, Moat House, 111-115, North Street, Romford, Essex RM1 1ES, tel: 0708 25814.
Trusthouse Forte Hotels, 24-30 New Street, Aylesbury, Buckinghamshire, HP20 2NW, tel: 01-567 3444. Prestel page 512.

CAR TOUR PACKAGES

AA Travel Services Ltd, Fanum House, Basing View, Basingstoke, Hampshire, RG21 2EA, tel: 0256 492269.
Inter Hotels, 35 Hogarth Road, London SW5 0QH, tel: 01-373 3241.
See also: Consort, and Ladbroke, above.

TOURIST BOARDS AND INFORMATION CENTRES

British Travel Centre, 12 Regent Street, Piccadilly Circus, London SW1 4PQ. Tel: 01-730 3400.
This offers the most comprehensive information and booking service available under one roof (will book travel, tours, tickets, accommodation).
Open Monday to Saturday 9.00 to 18.30, Sunday 10.00 to 16.00, to personal callers only.

English Tourist Board, Thames Tower, Black's Road, Hammersmith, London W6 9EL. Tel: 846 9000.
London Tourist Board, 26 Grosvenor Gardens, London SW1W 0DU. Tel: 01-730 3450.
London Tourist Board Information Centre, Victoria Station Forecourt, London SW1 (open daily 09.00–20.30; reduced hours in winter). Tel: 01-730 3488.
Scottish Tourist Board, 23 Ravelston Terrace, Edinburgh EH4 3EU. Tel: 031-332 2433.
Scottish Tourist Board London Office, 19 Cockspur Street, London SW1Y 5BL. Tel: 01-930 8661.
Wales Tourist Board, PO Box 1, Cardiff CF1 2XN. Tel: 0222 27281.
Wales Centre (London office of Wales Tourist Board), 34 Piccadilly, London W1. Tel: 01-409 0969.
Northern Ireland Tourist Board, River House, 48 High Street, Belfast BT1 2DS. Tel: 0232 246609.
Northern Ireland Tourist Board London Office, 11 Berkeley Street, London W1X 6BU. Tel: 01-493 0601.
Irish Tourist Board, Ireland House, 150 New Bond Street, London W1Y 0AQ. Tel: 01-493 3201.

British Tourist Authority, Thames Tower, Black's Road, Hammersmith, London W6 9EL. (Written enquiries only.)

There are also Tourist Boards for the Isle of Man and for the Channel Islands – for the States of Jersey and for the States of Guernsey. The addresses of these are given in Chapter 25 on islands.

There are 12 regional tourist boards in England: information about these can be obtained from the English Tourist Board. There are 34 Area Tourist Boards in Scotland and 3 Regional Tourist Councils in Wales: for information about these local tourist boards contact the national Tourist Boards listed above. In addition, there is a network of more than 700 Tourist Information Centres throughout Britain. Use these to make the most of your visit to whichever part of Britain you go to.

Many towns and some counties which have a significant holiday trade also have their own tourist organisation to promote tourism and provide information to visitors.

British Tourist Authority (BTA) Offices in USA
The British Tourist Authority, 3rd floor, 40 West 57th Street, New York, N.Y. 10019, tel: 010-1-212-581 4700.
The British Tourist Authority, John Hancock Center Suite 3320, 875 North Michigan Avenue, Chicago, Illinois 60611, USA, tel: 010-1-312-787 0490.
The British Tourist Authority, Cedar Maple Plaza, Suite 210, 2305 Cedar Springs Road, Dallas, Texas, 75201, USA, tel: 010-1-214-720 4040.
The British Tourist Authority, World Trade Center Suite 450, 350 South Figueroa Street, Los Angeles, California 90017, USA, tel: 010-1-213 623 8196.

Some other BTA Overseas Offices
Canada: British Tourist Authority, 94 Cumberland Street, Suite 600, Toronto, Ontario M5R 3N3. Tel: (416) 925 6326.
Australia: British Tourist Authority, Associated Midland House, 171 Clarence Street, Sydney, N.S.W. 2000. Tel: (02) 29 8627.
New Zealand: British Tourist Authority, 8th Floor, Norwich Union Building, Cnr Queen and Durham Street, Auckland. Tel: (09) 31446.

INDEX OF PLACES
(principle towns and counties)

Aberdeen   52, 123, 144
Aberdeenshire   91
Alderney   198
Anglesey   57
Arundel   92-96
Ascot   41, 72, 106, 111
Avon   19, 105, 111, 126
Ayrshire   109, 123, 145, 146

Badminton   111
Bath   19
Bedfordshire   31, 130
Berkshire   22, 40, 41, 44, 49, 92, 100, 102, 112, 121, 130
Birmingham   110, 120, 205
Blanchland   68-69
Bournemouth   32, 99-100
Bradford   73, 206
Brighton   131, 174-179
Bristol   105

Cambridge   172-173
Canterbury   90
Cardiff   75, 123, 135
Carlisle   35, 82
Channel Islands   193-198
Cheshire   87, 88, 121, 122
Chester   87
Chichester   39, 92-94
Clwyd   74, 155, 156
Cornwall   65, 132, 133, 180-187, 219
Cotswolds   113
Coventry   77, 205
Cowes   199
Crieff   145
Cumbria   23, 35, 40, 63, 82, 121, 122, 161-166, 219

Derbyshire   121
Devon   13-17, 33, 57, 213, 216, 219, 220
Dorset   32, 99
Dublin   36
Durham   35, 209
Durham, County   35, 68-69, 76

Edinburgh   77, 123

Eire   36

Fort William   142

Gatwick   22
Gloucester   111
Gloucestershire   50, 130
Glasgow   123, 140-142
Goodwood   96
Guernsey   195-197
Guildford   218
Gwent   76, 82, 151
Gwynedd   24, 34, 153, 154, 156

Hampshire   21, 73, 98, 100, 115, 130
Herefordshire   220
Hertfordshire   25, 49, 78, 108
Huddersfield   122

Jersey   194-195

Kent   17-19, 32, 52, 90, 91, 136, 219, 220

Inverness-shire   143
Isle of Man   113, 188-193
Isle of Wight   199-202

Lake District   23, 46, 63, 161-166, 219
Lancashire   121, 122
Lancaster   121
Leeds   206
Leicester   206
Lincolnshire   91
Liverpool   208
London   20, 21, 28-31, 44, 45, 47, 48, 50, 51, 79, 80, 97, 98, 113, 119, 120, 125, 128, 134, 211, 212, 214
Lothian   108
Ludlow   85

Maidenhead   23, 76, 208
Maidstone   17-19, 79
Man, Isle of   113, 188-193
Manchester   23, 76, 208

Newcastle-upon-Tyne   209, 214

239

Norfolk 221
Northamptonshire 217
Northumberland 159, 160, 165–166, 218
Nottingham 78, 210

Oxford 39, 49, 171
Oxfordshire 218

Peebles 104, 123
Perth 36
Perthshire 109
Peterborough 72
Plymouth 13–17, 66, 67, 203–204
Portsmouth 211
Powys 33, 52, 89, 151, 152, 154, 217

Reading 120
Ruthin 74, 156

St Andrews 108
Salisbury 89
Scarborough 58–60, 122
Scotland 36, 41–43, 52, 91, 102, 104, 105, 108, 109, 123, 138–146
Sheffield 25
Shrewsbury 86, 133
Shropshire 85, 86, 87, 133
Somerset 67, 79, 126, 213, 219
Southampton 73, 211
Southport 54, 122
South Shields 62, 63, 157, 158
Staffordshire 129
Stoke-on-Trent 204

Stratford-upon-Avon 43, 44, 113, 120, 167–171
Suffolk 63, 221
Surrey 22, 32, 72, 83–85, 96, 105, 129, 218
Sussex 92–94, 99, 131
Swansea 74, 126, 148

Thames, River 64, 69, 102
Tyne and Wear 62, 63, 69–72, 157–160

Wales 147–156. Also see following entries.
Wales, Mid 24, 33, 52, 89, 151–155, 217, 220
Wales, North 34, 57, 74, 126, 135, 155–156, 217
Wales, South 74, 75, 81, 123, 126, 135, 147–150
Warwick 79, 102, 171
Warwickshire 43, 44, 72, 77, 79, 101, 102, 113, 120, 167–171, 205
Welshpool 33
Wigan 209
Wight, Isle of 199–202
Wiltshire 89, 130
Windermere 23, 46, 162, 163
Windsor 22, 40, 44, 49, 100, 130
Worcester 44

York 61, 207
Yorkshire 25, 61, 102, 213, 214–215, 219